# The Sacred in Music

*Dedicated to the
choir, congregation,
clergy, and staff at
St. James Episcopal Church,
Greenville, South Carolina*

# The Sacred in Music

Albert L. Blackwell

Westminster John Knox Press
Louisville, Kentucky

© 1999 Albert Blackwell

This edition published by arrangement with The Lutterworth Press

Published in the United States in 1999 by
WESTMINSTER JOHN KNOX PRESS
Louisville, Kentucky

99 00 01 02 03 04 05 06 07 08 — 10 9 8 7 6 5 4 3 2 1

A catalog card for this book may be obtained from the Library of Congress.

ISBN 0-664-22171-8

# Contents

# Acknowledgements

Thanks first of all to my family, Marian, Christopher, and Jody, for their steady encouragement, and to my brother- and sister-in-law, Jonathan and Karen Slater, for their hospitality and support throughout my academic career. Likewise for the kind hospitality of Dottie and Donald Gonson. Special thanks to Dr. Frank Burch Brown and to Dr. Joyce Irwin for reading a preliminary draft and offering most valuable criticisms and suggestions, and to my subsequent readers, Dr. Doug Anderson and Ms. Karen Esterl, for their intelligent insights. That I have failed to follow all their advice should free them from any repercussions. Thanks also to Ms. Lilli Ann Hall for her skilled assistance in inter-library loans, and to Furman University for a sabbatical year of research.

# The Sacred in Music

We know the most perfect way of seeking God, and the most suitable order, is not for us to attempt with bold curiosity to penetrate to the investigation of God's essence, which we ought more to adore than meticulously to search out, but for us to contemplate God in his works whereby he renders himself near and familiar to us, and in some manner communicates himself. The apostle was referring to this when he said that we need not seek God far away, seeing that he dwells by his very present power in each of us. For this reason, David, having first confessed God's unspeakable greatness, afterward proceeds to mention God's works and professes that he will declare God's greatness. It is also fitting, therefore, for us to pursue this particular search for God, which may so hold our mental powers suspended in wonderment as at the same time to stir us deeply. And as Augustine teaches elsewhere, because, disheartened by God's greatness, we cannot grasp God, we ought to gaze upon God's works, that we may be restored by his goodness.

John Calvin, *Institutes of the Christian Religion*, 1.5.9

# Introduction

*Nichts weset ohne Stimm: Gott höret überall*
*In allen Kreaturn sein Lob und Widerhall.*[1]

Naught exists without voice: God hears always
In all created things his echo and his praise.

A number of years ago a national meeting of the American Academy of Religion and the Society of Biblical Literature in Washington D.C. had as its highlight a Saturday evening performance by the Maryland Gospel Choir. For an hour the choir's celebration transformed a bland hotel ballroom into sacred space and time. The audience responded with an ovation.

More than seven thousand scholars attended the meeting. We gathered in over seven hundred different sessions for seminars, workshops, and lectures on almost every imaginable subject relating to the academic study of religion. Of those seven hundred sessions, however, only three bore any relation to music. Two of the three treated music as a sociological indicator of cultural conditions. Only one session, a presentation by Bernice Johnson Reagon from her work *We'll Understand It Better By and By: Pioneering African American Gospel Composers*,[2] gave direct attention to music and religion as rich and interrelated experiences. The discrepancy, so conspicuous to me at my professional meeting, between the centrality of music in religious experience and the peripheral attention given to music in the academic study of religion strengthened my resolve to undertake this study of the sacred significance of music.

A further experience at the meeting confirmed my decision to write of music in theological terms. On Sunday morning some of us left the conference warren of our hotel for a hike up Wisconsin Avenue to the spacious Washington National Cathedral. There, in the company of visiting and residential choirs, organ and clergy, a parish congregation swelled with tourists, and cathedral carillon and bells, we participated in a religious service that was announced, prefaced, inaugurated, expressed, punctuated, heightened, concluded, dismissed, and succeeded by music. I left the service convinced anew that music serves and manifests the sacred in ways that can be specified and articulated.

Others besides myself have noted the relative neglect of music in the

---

1. The epigrams at chapter headings are by the 17th-century Christian mystical poet Johannes Scheffler, known as Angelus Silesius, from *Angelus Silesius: Sämtliche Poetische Werke*, ed. Hans Ludwig Held, 3 vols. (München: Carl Hanser, 1949).
2. Washington: Smithsonian Institution Press, 1992.

study of religion. Robin Maconie speaks of "the profoundly erroneous abandonment of musical philosophy by the centres of religion."[3] Joyce Irwin observes that "phenomenological evidence from the world's religions demonstrates that the association of music and religion is nearly universal. . . . But its theoretical grounding has often been omitted or slighted in theological systems."[4] Scholarly neglect is not confined to my tradition of Christian scholarship. Writing of Jewish studies, Lawrence A. Hoffman notes that "the role of music in contemporary worship is practically unresearched and undiscussed." Hoffman observes from Jewish religious history what has also been the case in the scholarly study of religion more generally, that "the written text was deserving of study, whereas the musical means by which it was presented was not." Hoffman concludes: "In part, we are victims of an unfortunate logocentrism going back at least to the founders of the *Wissenschaft* tradition."[5] In his study of the theological implications of black spirituals, on the other hand, James Cone diagnoses a converse problem. The music and poetry of black spirituals, he writes, have received ample attention, but the theology of the spirituals has traditionally been neglected, as if black people "cannot think."[6] My hope in this study is to balance attention to music and theology.

We may wonder why scholarship has so generally tended to neglect the interdependent realms of religious experience and musical experience. One reason is surely the complexity of each domain. Join the two domains and the complexity increases exponentially. Ter Ellingson opens his article "Music and Religion" in *The Encyclopedia of Religion* with an admirable paragraph on this theme:

> Music and religion are closely linked in relationships as complex, diverse, and difficult to define as either term in itself. Religious believers have heard music as the voices of gods and the cacophony of devils, praised it as the purest form of spirituality, and condemned it as the ultimate in sensual depravity; with equal enthusiasm they have promoted its use in worship and sought to eradicate it from both religious and secular life. Seldom a neutral phenomenon, music

3. *The Concept of Music* (New York: Oxford University Press, 1990), 59.
4. *Neither Voice nor Heart Alone: German Lutheran Theology of Music in the Age of the Baroque* (New York: Peter Lang, 1993), ix. Irwin goes on to list the "few short books" in English that have been published "on music and religion in the last forty years."
5. "Musical Traditions and Tensions in the American Synagogue," in Mary Collins, David Power, and Mellonee Burnim, *Music and the Experience of God* (Edinburgh: T. & T. Clark, 1989), 31-2.
6. "Black Spirituals: A Theological Interpretation," in Collins, *Music and the Experience of God*, 41. For a constructive exploration of the concern Cone expresses, see Jon Michael Spencer, *Sing a New Song: Liberating Black Hymnody* (Minneapolis: Fortress, 1995).

    has a high positive or negative value that reflects its near-universal
    importance in the religious sphere.

Even as he emphasises music's importance for religion, Ellingson fore-
warns the author who would attempt to unite these two realms.

    I believe that one way of passage into the complex and interrelating
realms of musical and religious experience is by speaking of music's
sacramental potential. Let us admit that such an approach may not satisfy
everyone. On the one side, many may find sacramental talk alien, even
objectionable. Cultured despisers of religion as well as religious readers
from non-liturgical traditions have legitimate grounds for hesitation or
resistance. Yet I have noticed that many who are suspicious of theological
talk about sacramental experience none the less speak of music as echoing
transcendent beauty, even of musical experience as communicating divine
blessing, not realising that in speaking this way they approach traditional
uses of sacramental language. For this reason, I am hopeful that nonreligious and non-liturgical readers who are willing to give my presentation a hearing may come to agree that "sacramental" is an adjective that
may describe familiar experiences we either know by other names or
scarcely know how to name at all. At the other extreme, some readers with
proprietary interests in the doctrine of sacrament may resist any application of "sacramental" beyond accustomed ecclesial rubrics. I share their
conviction that traditional usages deserve honour. Ironically, however,
traditionalists are sometimes short on memory, forgetting that sacramental
experience has a history much older and much broader than post-
Augustinian church history. In relation to music in particular, Erik Routley
reminds us "that the human race was born singing but was not born
Christian."[7] I am hopeful that these readers will consider the possibility
that a broader, more experiential application of the adjective "sacramental"
may describe and disclose deeper dimensions of religion.

### *Basic Modalities and Methods*

This is a work of theological interpretation in a musical mode. Its basic structure is theological. Chapter 1 explains the concept of sacramental experience and delineates two great sacramental traditions of Christian tradition, which I have chosen to call the Pythagorean and the
Incarnational. Chapters 2 and 3 explore those two traditions in order to
appreciate how they regard music as a gift of God, transcending historical contingency and manifesting divine transcendence to human minds
and hearts. Chapter 4 relates to fallen humankind, noting the Church's
ambiguous attitudes towards music, exploring music's resources for
expressing life's cacophony and dissonance, and presenting music as a

7. *The Church and Music* (London: Gerald Duckworth, 1950), 9.

companion in our pilgrimage through the struggles and sufferings of history. Chapter 5 addresses the theme of salvation, exploring music's role in our search for healing and harmony – individual, communal, and cosmic. Chapter 6 considers the eschatological theme of final bliss, relating music to experiences of mystical ecstasy and spiritual fulfilment.

The method of this work of theological interpretation in a musical mode is what I would like to call a hermeneutics of appreciation. "Hermeneutics" is study of the art of interpreting, after Hermes, classical god of the message. My conviction is that appreciation of music can help us interpret theological traditions with heightened sensitivity to their perennial insights and contemporary meanings. Or more simply, I believe that religion and music are complementary resources for interpreting our lives.

As with the realms of musical and religious experience, appreciation is itself a richer realm than we often pause to consider. The word conveys at least five distinct meanings, all of which I hope to honour in this study. First, to appreciate may mean simply to register or attend to: "The brain's occipital lobe appreciates the influence of light upon the retina." Second, to appreciate means to understand: "Napoleon, appreciating the magnitude of the danger, reigned his horse about." To appreciate may mean simply to be grateful for – "I appreciate your kindness" – or to evaluate – "I appreciate the sacrifice your kindness has cost you." Finally, to appreciate may mean to enhance, the opposite of depreciate: "In the international metals market today the price of gold appreciated."

Most hermeneutical methods heighten our capacities for attending and for understanding. Some interpretation also sharpens our ability to evaluate. An art of interpreting that widely pervades our age, however – the hermeneutics of suspicion, in its varied forms – seems to me deficient in the appreciative qualities of gratitude and enhancement. In particular I am thinking of the deconstructionist hermeneutics of certain literary critics and of the musical application of that hermeneutics in the writings of certain music analysts, whom I shall address at several points.

The first challenge in a hermeneutic of appreciation is to develop musical and theological appreciations that do not slight the critical obligations of attending, understanding, and evaluating – lest our tonal systems join many of our theological systems in reinforcing provincial and exclusivist attitudes so inexcusable in our age of invigorating pluralism. The further challenge, however, is to move musical and theological interpretation beyond critical description and explanation – beyond reduction and suspicion – to a kind of appreciation mature enough to express gratitude for traditions, and creative enough to enhance traditional meanings by rediscovering, reinforming, and representing them in modes that resonate with our age. With Patrick Sherry, I believe that the time is ripe for hermeneutics to move beyond Antony Flew's "death by a thousand qualifications" to Ian

Ramsey's "life by a thousand enrichments."[8]

Our method of appreciation will first involve rediscovering and documenting the rich western tradition, both classical and Christian, that has revered music as a potentially sacramental experience. With this aim of recovering a largely neglected tradition, this book devotes considerable space to presenting relevant texts. Our method will also involve presenting and interrelating various complex phenomena of musical and religious experience, such as fundaments of musical acoustics and types of religious mysticism. Finally, our method will involve considering what an appreciation of music as potentially sacramental may mean in our lives, particularly in relation to our culture's predominating emphasis upon verbal language and post-modernist tendencies to relativise our experiences.

## *Basic Presuppositions and Predilections*

Believing that other traditions have much to teach and that my own has much to learn as well as much to offer, I have given as much attention as I am able to musical and religious experiences of places and times and perspectives other than my own. Finally, of course, I am situated in my own place and time and limited to my own perspective. The modalities of my experience are of necessity particular and by definition not all inclusive. For this reason, then, a few introductory words may be appropriate about the point of view for my work as an author.

**Musical Predilections**. In Christian tradition since Augustine, most discussions of music as a potentially sacramental experience assume that the music in question accompanies a religious text and contributes directly to the liturgy of worship. The 1963 document *Sacrosanctum Concilium* ("Constitution on the Sacred Liturgy") of the Second Vatican Council, for example, extols music in the following terms:

> The musical tradition of the universal Church is a treasure of inestimable value, greater even than that of any other art. The main reason for this pre-eminence is that, as sacred melody united to words, it forms a necessary or integral part of the solemn liturgy. . . . Therefore sacred music increases in holiness to the degree that it is intimately linked with liturgical action, winningly expresses prayerfulness, promotes solidarity, and enriches sacred rites with heightened solemnity.[9]

As the director of a small church choir, I feel considerable sympathy with this liturgical point of view. However, I believe there is more to say

---

8. *Spirit and Beauty: An Introduction to Theological Aesthetics* (Oxford: Clarendon Press, 1992), 154.

9. "Constitution on the Sacred Liturgy," *The Documents of Vatican II*, ed. Walter M. Abbot, tr. Joseph Gallagher (New York: Herder and Herder, 1966), 171.

on behalf of the sacramental potential of music without words and apart from liturgical uses. In a commentary on Psalm 33 (Psalm 32 in the *Vulgate*) Augustine writes of the spiritual value of what he calls the *jubilus*, a spontaneous, wordless, musical outpouring of the heart's joy before God:

> Sing *in jubilation*: singing well to God means, in fact just this: singing in jubilation. What does singing in jubilation signify? It is to realise that words cannot communicate the song of the heart. Just so singers in the harvest, or the vineyard, or at some other arduous toil express their rapture to begin with in songs set to words; then as if bursting with a joy so full that they cannot give vent to it in set syllables, they drop actual words and break into the free melody of pure jubilation. The *jubilus* is a melody which conveys that the heart is in travail over something it cannot bring forth in words. And to whom does that jubilation rightly ascend, if not to God the ineffable? Truly is He ineffable whom you cannot tell forth in speech; and if you cannot tell Him forth in speech, yet ought not to remain silent, what else can you do but jubilate? In this way the heart rejoices without words and the boundless expanse of rapture is not circumscribed by syllables. *Sing well unto Him in jubilation*.[10]

Thus Augustine praises the spiritual value of music without words. Echoing Augustine, John Calvin also extends the spiritual value of singing beyond the sphere of church texts and liturgy: "For even in our homes and in the fields it should be an incentive, and as it were an organ for praising God and lifting up our hearts to Him, to console us by meditating upon His virtue, goodness, wisdom, and justice, a thing more necessary than one can say."[11] I would extend the spiritual value of music further still. I believe that music associated not with words, nor with sacred liturgy, nor the human voice, music from any source, music as sheer "moulded sound,"[12] has potential to bear sacramental meaning. The sacramental potential of music is to be our theme, not only the sacramental potential of textual, liturgical, or vocal music. I am at this point less near to Calvin than to Martin Luther, who calls music "a noble, wholesome, and cheerful creation of God" and wishes that his reader "may by this creation accustom yourself to recognise and praise the Creator."[13] Luther's abundant praise for music as God's creation and gift to humankind leads Oskar Söhngen to conclude that "for Luther all music is 'spiritual,' i.e., theologically relevant. There is for him

---

10. *St. Augustine on the Psalms*, tr. Dame Scholastica Hebgin and Dame Felicitas Corrigan, 2 vols. (New York: Newman Press, 1961), 2:111-12.
11. "Foreword" to *Geneva Psalter*, in Oliver Strunk, *Source Readings in Music History* (New York: W. W. Norton, 1950), 346-7.
12. Ernst Bloch, *Essays on the Philosophy of Music*, tr. Peter Palmer (Cambridge: Cambridge University Press, 1985), 138.
13. "Preface to Georg Rhau's *Symphoniae jucundae* 1538," tr. Ulrich S. Leupold, *Luther's Works*, ed. Jaraslov Pelikan (Philadelphia: Fortress, 1965), 53:324.

no secular music in the strict sense, only degenerate music."[14]

Luther's evaluative principle suggests what we might call the two-kinds school of music criticism: that there is good music and bad music in all genres. I embrace this idea with enthusiasm, provided only that I am allowed my opinion that some genres have lots of bad music and others lots of good. Many genres offer examples of what I would call "perfect" works of art, precisely defined by Aristotle as works we would neither add to nor take from: "hence the common remark about a perfect work of art, that you could not take from it nor add to it – meaning that excess and deficiency destroy perfection."[15] I think of certain Mazurkas of Chopin as perfect in Aristotle's sense, or of "Rock of Ages" by the popular singer Gillian Welch in her alternative bluegrass or American Primitive Style.[16] These are works in which I would not wish to change a single detail. Enjoying music of such perfection, I sometimes think of the exclamation of Simone Weil: "Music – time that one wants neither to arrest nor hasten."[17]

Many genres of music also offer what I would call "classics": works that reward repeated exposure with new disclosure. I treasure the first two albums issued by the popular singer Joni Mitchell[18] as classics in this sense, for example, and certainly the four symphonies of Johannes Brahms. Hearing and rehearing such music, I not only take pleasure in its perfection but also discover things I had not noticed before. In this musical experience I sense parallels with Weil's religious observation that the value of sacramental experiences consists "in their infinite capacity to furnish truths that may be grasped by anyone who contemplates them for a long time with a religious attention."[19]

Neither "perfect" nor "classic" is an exclusive category. Great works of art are enhanced, not diminished, by others in their class. What is more, not all perfect works are classics, and some classics are not perfect works. We must acknowledge that flawed works and works of transient interest also have genuine value. We enjoy music for innumerable reasons, each with its own sort of validity. Depending upon its kind and its time and manner of presentation, music offers us novelty and nostalgia; stimulation and stupefaction; textures and colours; thrills of virtuosity and spectacles of production; associations with celebrity and participation in cults of

14. "Music and Theology: A Systematic Approach," in *Sacred Sound: Music in Religious Thought and Practice,* ed. Joyce Irwin (Chico, CA: Scholars Press, 1983), 13. See Irwin's discussion of Söhngen's view of Luther in *Neither Voice nor Heart Alone,* 2-7.

15. *Nichomachean Ethics* 2.6.9, tr. H. Rackham (London: William Heinemann, 1956), 9.

16. *Hell among the Yearlings,* Almo Sounds. AMSD-80021, 1998.

17. *The Notebooks of Simone Weil,* tr. Arthur Wills, 2 vols. (London: Routledge and Kegan Paul, 1956), 1:39.

18. *Joni Mitchell,* Reprise Records, 6293, 1968; *Clouds,* Reprise Records, 6341, 1969.

19. *Notebooks,* 2:344.

personality; outcries of alienation and contexts of belonging; affirmations of our occupations, social ranks, and geographical regions; social enjoyment amidst a world of individual competition; individual abandon amidst social restraints; harmony amidst cultural cacophony; escape from life's utilitarian expectations; companionship in our loneliness and longings. Who would wish to limit the list of music's functions and values? But since life is short, I tend to spend more time among the perfect and classic works I have discovered, basing my evaluations upon the richness and variety of intrinsic musical qualities such as melody, harmony, rhythm, timbre, and compositional structure. For me rich and various musical works that reward attention and sustain reflection usually offer fuller satisfaction and deeper disclosure than less substantial music, whatever its setting or functions. In the chapters that follow I shall attempt to articulate some of the religious fullness and depth I find in music of classical perfection. Still my theology leads me to believe that music of many kinds can assume religious value, depending upon our context and state of mind as we experience it, whether as listeners, performers, or composers. To make musical judgements and give reasons for musical preferences, as I shall do, is not the same as to dismiss other kinds of music, which would require other kinds of reasons, and which I have no interest in doing.

**Religious Predilections**. Like most people who think about their religion, I have come to my theology through a deliberate process of selecting from influences that have formed me. I am a Christian, a person whose fundamental convictions are most profoundly shaped by the biblical values of justice, mercy and humility, faith, hope and love, repentance, forgiveness, and amendment of life, and a person whom the figure of Christ confronts and beckons and haunts. I am a protestant, in the fundamental sense that Paul Tillich has insisted upon (within which Tillich includes self-critical Roman Catholics and Orthodox Christians as well), one who believes that religion must keep self-criticism vital if it is not to become smug and idolatrous.[20] I am in my fashion a trinitarian, believing that whatever we mean by God, the concepts we apply must be dynamic, whole, and commodious, relational, mutual, and stable, such as triangularity is well suited to symbolise.

Foremost among my theological mentors in this study of theology and music is Augustine, particularly early Augustine as represented in the *Confessions* and other works of the late 4th century, whose spiritual dwelling place is a synthesis of the classical and Christian traditions and whose spiritual life was steeped in music. Foremost among my 20th-century companions is Weil, who continues both Augustine's classical-Christian synthesis and his passion for music, but in embodiments unique to herself

---

20. *The Protestant Era*, abridged edition, tr. James Luther Adams, (Chicago: The University of Chicago Press, 1957), 163.

and in forms appropriate to our age. In between these figures I especially honour the Augustinian theologians Calvin, his Colonial American heir Jonathan Edwards, and his heir in the periods of Enlightenment and Romanticism, Friedrich Schleiermacher.[21] All of these theologians love biblical scripture as a casebook of religious experience, not a sourcebook of proof texts, as we see in Calvin's wonderful characterisation of the Psalms as "An Anatomy of all the Parts of the Soul."[22] Together with Tillich, these theologians recognise a religious impulse to worship as intrinsic to our humanity, yet requiring salvation – that is, healing, making whole – lest that impulse turn demonic and devour us. What is more, all of them recognise deep relations between aesthetic sensibility and religious sensibility.[23]

From Baptist roots I draw a tendency to value biblical scripture and earliest church practice as normative for Christian life, along with a nonconformist tendency toward independent spiritual judgement. For Baptists, reciting creeds with mental reservation is not a sin but a requirement of conscience. Also, Baptists are born singing. Yet my chosen denomination is Episcopal. From that heritage I draw a love for theologians of the early Christian church, if not exactly as normative, certainly as formative, challenging Christians not to give up in the quest for responsible norms, and not to neglect tradition in the process. I prefer reciting the church's creeds in their "we believe" rather than their "I believe" forms. Some things in the various creeds of Christendom I have never accepted. Some things I no longer accept. Some things I do not yet accept. And some things I embrace wholeheartedly. I am a willing participant in the church's dynamic process of transmitting the creeds so that others may enjoy the same opportunity of selecting. Most of all in Episcopal tradition I value the sacred liturgy, concentrated and burnished across the ages like an ancient, holy ballad. And of all the liturgy's components, I most love the Episcopal treasury of "perfect" hymns and "classic" anthems.

For an erstwhile Baptist, I make a moderately high Episcopalian. I am in fact a not-so-secret admirer of the even higher sacramental traditions – Roman Catholic, and also Orthodox (if only my explorations into that tradition were further advanced) – for their liturgical wealth, though not for some of their ecclesiastical and social polity. In these higher liturgical traditions, manifestation of the divine is more central than proclamation

21. Corresponding perspectives on music's "sacramental overtones" (72) in Lutheranism, sometimes developed in a context of theological "rivalries" with Calvinism (43) are the subject of Irwin's valuable survey *Neither Voice nor Heart Alone*.

22. John Calvin, *Commentary on the Book of Psalms*, tr. James Anderson, 6 vols. (Grand Rapids: Baker Book House, n.d.), 1:xxxvii.

23. See the reflections on art and religion in Earle J. Coleman, *Creativity and Spirituality: Bonds between Art and Religion* (Albany: State University of New York Press, 1998), especially chapter 8, "The Aesthetic versus the Spiritual."

of the divine, and worship tends to be more symbolic than verbal.[24] In his survey of Catholicism, Richard P. McBrien articulates certain differences between Protestantism and Catholicism in relation to life and art in a way that describes my own experiences and conclusions: "But given the historic emphases on justification-as-transformation in Catholicism and on justification-as-declaration in Protestantism, the otherness of God tends to be more strongly stressed in Protestantism than in Catholicism, while the sacramental availability of God in our ordinary everyday lives tends to be more strongly stressed in Catholicism than in Protestantism."[25] McBrien is not being judgmental, I believe, but simply accurate when he further observes that "Protestantism, as a religion of the word, has had a 'mixed' record when it comes to the arts."[26] Sadly, since Vatican II in the 1960s, Catholicism's own aesthetic record has also been mixed, especially in the realm of liturgical music, where traditions of music that I regard as perfect and classic, in the senses I have explained, have been largely eclipsed by music that I, with many others, find transient and trite.[27]

**Culture and Language**. Having confessed something of my own point of view, I shall attempt in the chapters that follow to come to terms with certain alternative perspectives. First, I shall diverge from contemporaries such as literary critic Richard Rorty and music critic Susan McClary who would limit the significance of human experiences, including our experiences of religion and art, to the contingencies of time and culture, thereby rejecting any transcendent dimension of meaning and value. Vasilii Kandinsky, in his 1910 essay "On the Spiritual in Art," which George Steiner has rightly called "a profound religious manifesto,"[28] expressed his concern for the human spirit, which he found threatened by the materialistic culture surrounding him:

> Our soul, which only now is awakening from a long period of materialism, conceals within itself the seeds of despair, of faithlessness, or purposelessness. The nightmare of materialist ideals has still not passed, and these are ideals which have made an evil, pointless joke out of the universe. The awakening soul is still very much under the influence of this nightmare.[29]

24. See David Tracy's fine discussion of these two classical forms of religious expression – manifestation and proclamation – in *The Analogical Imagination: Christian Theology and the Culture of Pluralism* (New York: Crossroad, 1981), 202-15.
25. *Catholicism*, 2 vols. (Minneapolis: Winston Press, 1980), 1:317.
26. *Catholicism*, 2:1182.
27. See Thomas Day's feisty critique, *Why Catholics Can't Sing: The Culture of Catholicism and the Triumph of Bad Taste* (New York: Crossroad, 1990).
28. *Real Presences* (Chicago: University of Chicago Press, 1989), 222.

Kandinsky believed that the soul's awakening from the nightmare of materialism depended upon artists who would turn inward, resisting outward
determination and domination, discovering their own worlds of intrinsic
aesthetic values. Kandinsky's principal interest was visual art, but he was
an amateur pianist and cellist, and he turned to music, "the most non-
material of all the arts," as a source of inspiration and guidance in his
search for spiritual values:

> In this respect, music is the most instructive art. With some excep-
> tions and deviations, music is an art which never uses its media to
> make a deceptive reproduction of natural phenomena. On the cont-
> rary, music always uses its own media to express the artist's
> emotional life and, out of these media, creates an original life of
> musical tones. The artist who sees no point even in depicting nature
> artistically and, as a creator, seeks to effuse his *inner world* into
> the outer envies music – the most non-material of all the arts – in
> its facility to attain this aim.[30]

The spiritual challenge we face in our day, I believe, is somewhat different from the materialism that Kandinsky describes, and the sort of rem-
edy we must seek is different also, but I agree with Kandinsky that music
has a significant role to play. I do not wish to imply that materialism is less
a spiritual threat in our time than in Kandinsky's. In the arts and letters of
our day, however, I believe that another spiritual threat, akin to materialism, is more immediate. We might call it temporalism: the assumption that
spiritual values and indeed the human spirit itself are contingent to their
time, wholly reducible to influences of the culture in which they appear.
In Chapter 3 we shall consider critic McClary's application of this
temporalist assumption to her analysis of the music of Mozart.

My conviction is that the temporalist assumption is a half-truth. I have
included some autobiography in this Introduction because I acknowledge the
temporalist assumption that time and culture are immeasurably important in
the formation of our ideas and the shaping of our values. I shall devote part of
this study, however, to recovering something of what I believe is truth's neglected other half: that our human spirit and spiritual values have transcendent
anchorage in what is given and endures. In our post-modern spiritual quest
Kandinsky's help is not exactly of the kind we need. In resisting materialism,
I believe, Kandinsky's creative idealism asserts too much: "in art there is no
place for 'should' for art is eternally free. . . . There is nothing absolute."[31] In
contrast, I believe that musical art is partly free in Kandinsky's sense, and
partly dependent upon the given and enduring – in particular, partly de-

29. *The Life of Vasilii Kandinsky in Russian Art: A Study of "On the Spiritual in Art"*,
    tr. John E. Bowlt (Newtonville, MA: Oriental Research Partners, 1980), 64.
30. "On the Spiritual in Art," 71. Kandinsky's emphasis.
31. "On the Spiritual in Art," 79.

pendent upon laws of acoustics and principles of consonance. The musical octave, for example, is absolute in ways that we can clearly, if not comprehensively, articulate. And I believe that from such observations relating to musical experience we may, with circumspection, draw certain broader implications for our spiritual lives.

A second perspective from which my viewpoint diverges is that of my contemporaries who would restrict significant articulation of human experiences to the limits of verbal language. Against such logocentrism, Kandinsky's manifesto, with its assertions that artistic languages complement, supplement, and transcend verbal language, can help us:

> Art is a *language whereby we speak to the soul (in a form accessible and peculiar only to this language) of things which are the soul's daily bread and which it can acquire only in this form.*[32]

"Music possesses a grammar," Kandinsky asserts in this connection, "although this does change with each historical era."[33] Contemporary ethnomusicologists are helping us make Kandinsky's assertion more precise. Music's vocabularies change with each historical era and vary across each cultural boundary, yet I shall maintain that those vocabularies seem to arise from a fundamental grammar, or what ethnomusicologist Bruno Nettl calls a "deep structure," given and enduring, that "identifies the phenomenon of music."[34] Again I hope to show that such observations relating to deep structures of musical experience may yield certain broader implications for our spiritual lives.

**Analysis and Practice**. We might ask, Why speak of music at all? Why not let music speak for itself, with its own grammar and in its own vocabularies? My answer is that we speak of music precisely because verbal language is so inestimably important in articulating and interpreting our experiences. My point is by no means that verbal language is unimportant, but rather that verbal language is not all important. We verbalise our musical experiences in the interest of fuller appreciation, aware at the same time that "no theory can profess to give more than the osteology of an art."[35] And so also, I believe, with our attempts to verbalise our spiritual experiences.

In both realms of experience, musical and spiritual, and in their significant regions of overlap, interpretation is invaluable but practice is fundamental. In the realm of musical practice, German has a marvellous word without a satisfactory English counterpart: the verb *musizieren*. "To

---

32. "On the Spiritual in Art," 99. Kandinsky's emphasis.
33. "On the Spiritual in Art," 91.
34. "Ethnomusicology: Definitions, Directions, and Problems," in Elizabeth May, ed., *Musics of Many Cultures* (Berkeley: University of California Press, 1980), 3.
35. "Music," *The Oxford Classical Dictionary*, ed. N. G. L. Hammond and H. H. Scullard, 2d ed. (Oxford: Clarendon, 1970), 708.

make music" is too mechanical. "To perform" is too outer directed. We have to coin an English equivalent: "to musicise." *Musizieren* far transcends musical analysis and criticism. It embraces a truth that Kandinsky puts quite simply: "A creative work is born from the artist in a very mysterious, enigmatic and mystical manner."[36] *Musizieren* is to commune with music, with other persons through the medium of music, and – in contexts where music's sacramental potential is realised – with the transcendent source of music's deep structures and complex manifold. This communing is a matter of immediate experiences involving intuition and feeling, to which no verbal description or explanation is sufficient and for which no verbal possibility offers an adequate substitute. In specifically religious contexts the word corresponding to *musizieren* might be "communion." To worship is in part to commune with the transcendent source of the given and the enduring, and with other persons through that experience. In religious experience as in musical, no verbal exercise can substitute. In this connection the deuterocanonical book of Ecclesiasticus, or Sirach, offers advice as wise as it is amusing:

Speak, you who are older, for it is your right,
　　but with accurate knowledge,
　　and do not interrupt the music.[37]

As for interrelations of musical and religious experience, I am convinced that *musizieren* and worship are intimately related, that worship is wonderfully served by music, and that music often realises its sacramental potential most fully in contexts of religious worship. We must avoid the mistake of thinking of music as merely sacramental, however, or even as primarily sacramental. I find Immanuel Kant suggestive when he speaks of art as having at its basis "a merely formal purposiveness, i.e. a purposiveness without purpose."[38] We must be careful to honour music's integrity in its many genres. Enlisting music into utilitarian purposes, even if they be purposes of serving religious worship, can risk damaging music's sacramental value by compromising its quality. If music is sacramental, then we may relax in our deliberate efforts to make it sacramental. If we let our attempts to enlist music into religious causes become too insistent, we risk disrupting the "mysterious, enigmatic and mystical manner" in which artistic creativity is born. The result is more likely to be stillborn ideology than living art and viable religion. If we are to enjoy music's fullest sacramental potential, we must compose, play, sing, and listen for reasons of musical value, as we must assemble, pray, praise, and live virtuously for reasons of religious value.

36. "On the Spiritual in Art," 98.
37. Sir 32.3. For this reference I am indebted to Ivor H. Jones, *Music: A Joy for Ever* (London: Epworth, 1989), 29. All biblical quotations and abbreviations are from the New Revised Standard Version.
38. *Critique of Judgment*, Sec. 15, tr. J. H. Bernard (New York: Hafner, 1951), 62.

In summary, music and religion are realms of experience veiled in mystery, where verbal descriptions and cultural analyses are desirable and valuable but are finally inadequate and cannot substitute for the primary experiences manifested most fully in intuition and immediate feeling. William Ernest Hocking well describes the balance between analysis and primary experience to which this study aspires:

> Analysis is not solution: it offers truth, but something short of *the* truth. Its function is, not to replace intuitive persuasions . . . , but to cure the vagrancy of a feeling-driven imagination, ready to substitute itself for truth. The deeper the hold of feeling on any issue, the sterner must be the resolve that feeling be disciplined by analysis, and not only for the sake of truth, but for the sake of feeling. For feeling has its own truth and falsity; and the *truthfulness of feeling*, quite as much as of thought, is an issue of life and death which a self-indulgent civilisation has not yet begun to fathom. Without truth, feeling is corrupt: but conversely, without feeling, truth is barren. A true analysis must still seek its full truth in its organic unity with feeling.[39]

39. *The Meaning of Immortality in Human Experience*, rev. ed. (Westport, CN: Greenwood Press, 1957), 245. Hocking's emphases.

# I. Sacramental Traditions

*O süße Gasterei! Gott selber wird der Wein,*
*Die Speise, Tisch, Musik und der Bediener sein.*

O sweet the feast! God's self becomes the wine,
Meat, table, music, and the server when I dine.

## *Sacramental Encounter*

In the passage that serves as this book's epigraph, Calvin exhorts his reader "to contemplate God in his works whereby he renders himself near and familiar to us, and in some manner communicates himself."[1] The particular work of God that shall be our theme is music, and I shall refer to music's role in the contemplation and self-communication of the divine as "sacramental." Let me therefore try to be clear about the meaning of that term as I shall use it.

*Musterion*, "mystery," is the Greek word that engendered the Latin *sacramentum* from which our "sacrament" and "sacramental" derive. *Musterion* applied to the mystery or salvation cults of Hellenism, whose initiates were pledged to keep their cultic rites secret. This ancient usage is behind Schleiermacher's allusion to the "muse of harmony, whose intimate relation to religion still belongs to the mysteries."[2] In New Testament usage *musterion* refers to disclosures of God's intention, particularly the ultimate or eschatological intention, often but not always in association with revelation in Christ.[3] The early Latin translation *sacramentum* harkened back to meanings associated with initiation. The Roman empire employed *sacramentum* "as a technical term for a military oath, the vow of a soldier."[4] This initiatory application helps explain later Christian adoption of the term to designate initiation rites of baptism, confirmation, ordination, and marriage. That *sacramentum* was an adopted term also helps account for the fact that its applications in the early Christian church were not precise, as Schleiermacher notes: "It is natural enough that a term taken over from a realm wholly foreign to theology should have no exact delimitation."[5]

---

1. *Institutes of the Christian Religion* 1.5.9, tr. Ford Lewis Battles (Philadelphia: Westminster, 1960), 1:62.
2. *On Religion: Speeches to Its Cultured Despisers*, tr. Richard Crouter (Cambridge: Cambridge University Press, 1988), 166.
3. See Gerhard Kittel, ed., *Theological Dictionary of the New Testament*, tr. Geoffrey W. Bromiley (Grand Rapids: Eerdmans, 1967), 4:817-24.
4. Theodore W. Jennings, *The Encyclopedia of Religion*, s.v."Sacrament," 501.
5. *The Christian Faith* 143.1, tr. H. R. Mackintosh and J. S. Stewart (Edinburgh: T. & T. Clark, 1928), 657-8.

For the first three centuries of the church Christian uses of the terms *musterion* and *sacramentum* were flexible and commodious. Philip Sherrard writes that in early Christian language *sacramentum* applied "to any action or object which as mirror or vehicle or form of the Divine was regarded as revealing the Divine,"[6] a usage that echoes in McBrien's assertion that "every contact with God is mysterious, or sacramental."[7]

Among modern theological usages of "sacramental" to which this study is particularly indebted, the Episcopal *Catechism* is explicit in broadening its understanding of God's self-communication beyond the sacraments of baptism and eucharist and the "sacramental rites," such as "confirmation, ordination, holy matrimony, reconciliation of a penitent, and unction":

Q. Is God's activity limited to these rites?

A. God does not limit himself to these rites; they are patterns of countless ways by which God uses material things to reach out to us.[8]

This Episcopal tradition of created things as potentially sacramental embraces quite naturally the rich tradition of church music.

Tillich defines "sacramental" with similar breadth: "Objects which are vehicles of the divine Spirit become sacramental materials and elements in a sacramental act."[9] Tillich's discussion enlarges "the question of the media of the divine Spirit so that it will include all personal and historical events in which the Spiritual Presence is effective":

The term "sacramental," in this larger sense, needs to be freed from its narrower connotations. The Christian churches, in their controversies over the meaning and number of the particular sacraments, have disregarded the fact that the concept "sacramental" embraces more than the seven, five, or two sacraments that may be accepted as such by a Christian church. The largest sense of the term denotes everything in which the Spiritual Presence has been experienced; in a narrower sense, it denotes particular objects and acts in which a Spiritual community experiences the Spiritual Presence; and in the narrowest sense, it merely refers to some "great" sacraments in the performance of which the Spiritual Community actualises itself. If the meaning of "sacramental" in the largest sense is disregarded, sacramental activities in the narrower sense (sacramentalia) lose their religious significance – as happened in the Reformation – and the great sacraments become insignificant – as happened in several Protestant denominations.[10]

6. *The Sacred in Life and Art* (Ipswich: Golgonooza Press, 1990), 1. My appreciation for Sherrard is echoed in my book's imitation of his title.

7. *Catholicism*, 1:232.

8. *The Book of Common Prayer* (New York: The Church Hymnal Corporation, 1977), 861.

9. *Systematic Theology*, 3 vols. (Chicago: University of Chicago Press, 1951-63), 3:120.

10. p.121. See also Tillich's discussion of sacramental religion in *Dynamics of Faith* (New York: Harper Torchbooks, 1957), 58-9.

Tillich appeals to the traditions of Orthodoxy, with their sense of "the multidimensional unity of life and the consequences it has for the sacramental manifestation of the holy":

> Strongly sacramental churches, such as the Greek Orthodox, have a profound understanding for the participation of life under all dimensions in the ultimate aim of history. The sacramental consecration of elements of all of life shows the presence of the ultimately sublime in everything and points to the unity of everything in its creative ground and its final fulfilment. It is one of the shortcomings of the churches of the "word" . . . that they exclude, along with the sacramental element, the universe outside man from consecration and fulfilment. But the Kingdom of God is not only a social symbol; it is a symbol which comprises the whole of reality. And if the churches claim to represent it, they must not reduce its meaning to one element alone.[11]

Writing from a Greek Orthodox perspective in his beautiful study *The Sacred in Life and Art*, Sherrard elaborates on the multidimensional, sacramental unity of life to which Tillich alludes:

> Each of the elements of the partnership – God and man, the Divine and nature – is, or represents, not simply the same reality, but that reality in its fullness. Each is, or represents, both the whole and the same whole. And it is their vital conjunction, their dynamic interpenetration, which gives birth to the sacred and makes the whole visible universe theological, the matter of a sacrament.[12]

Like Tillich, Sherrard views the more general and the more particular meanings of "sacramental" as complementary, and as united in the primordial concept of *mysterium*:

> From the historical point of view, it was only later that Christians began to reckon as the main mysteries of the Church the seven sacraments which nowadays people have in mind when they speak of the sacraments. But from a strictly doctrinal point of view, the number of sacraments cannot be fixed either at two or seven or indeed at any number at all, for the simple reason that . . . the sacrament is not, and cannot be a part of, or included in, any quantity or quantitative reckoning: everything is capable of serving as the object of the sacrament, for everything is intrinsically consecrated and divine – is, in fact, intrinsically a *mysterium*.[13]

The universal and the particular senses of sacramental consciousness "do not contradict but, rather, complement one another," Sherrard concludes: "A failure to connect the universal with the individual point of view, as

11. p.377.
12. p.10.
13. pp.22-3.

must be done if relative distinctions of this kind are to be synthesised and not taken as absolute, is always a sign that the full sacramental consciousness is being obscured by a too shallow approach to things."[14]

McBrien summarises the basic viewpoint of our study in describing what he calls "sacramental encounter":

> Catholicism has never hesitated to affirm the "mysterious" dimension of all reality: the cosmos, nature, history, events, persons, objects, rituals, words. Everything is, in principle, capable of embodying and communicating the divine. God is at once everywhere and all-powerful. There is no finite instrument that God cannot put to use. On the other hand, we humans have nothing else apart from finite instruments to express our own response to God's self-communication. Just as the divine reaches us through the finite, so we reach the divine through the finite. The point at which this "divine commerce" occurs is the point of *sacramental encounter*.[15]

Sacramental encounter as "divine commerce," or as "a path of human and divine meeting,"[16] is a particularly useful foundation for our study of music's sacramental potential. Marius Schneider has written, for example, that the "fundamental idea" of Gregorian chant is "creation of the good path to God."[17]

McBrien then provides a definition of "sacramental" as we shall apply that term to music: "The word *sacramental* is being used here in its *widest sense* of course. It applies to *any finite reality through which the divine is perceived to be disclosed and communicated, and through which our human response to the divine assumes some measure of shape, form, and structure*."[18] Our thesis is not that all music is sacramental in these terms, nor that any particular music is necessarily sacramental. Our thesis is rather that the phenomenon of music, in all its great variety, is potentially sacramental, and not only in explicitly religious contexts.[19] Dwelling at music's heart is a sacramental potency, awaiting only appropriate times and places for its actualisation, for manifesting the holy and for expressing our experiences of the holy.

John W. Dixon has warned against extending theological terms such as

---

14. p.23.
15. *Catholicism*, 2:731. McBrien's emphasis.
16. Collins, *Music and the Experience of God*, 3.
17. "On Gregorian Chant and the Human Voice," *The World of Music/Le Monde de la Musique/Die Welt der Musik: Journal of the International Institute for Comparative Music Studies and Documentation (Berlin) in association with the International Music Council (UNESCO)*, 24:3 (1982), 10.
18. *Catholicism*, 2:732. McBrien's emphases.
19. For a recent study of music's explicitly liturgical roles see Steven Plank, *"The Way to Heavens Doore": An Introduction to Liturgical Process and Musical Style* (Metuchen, NJ: Scarecrow Press, 1994).

"sacrament" and "incarnation" beyond their ecclesial sphere of application: "These are theological terms with a specific reference. To extend the
reference of these terms, even analogically, is to tread on dangerous ground.
To extend the reference deliberately and literally could be theologically
catastrophic, idolatrous, and blasphemous."[20] It is true that we could choose
terms other than "sacramental" to designate music as a path of human and
divine meeting. Some have suggested that we speak of music's "diaconal"
or serving role in religion, so that music "does not overwhelm the message
of salvation thought to be better carried by the Word."[21] We might call
music "emblematic" of the transcendent, as Edward Rothstein does (following William Wordsworth) in his book on music and mathematics, *Emblems
of Mind*.[22] Or we might call music a variety of charismatic or grace-filled
experience, or simply a gift of God. These are all valid possibilities. In the
end, however, I believe that music offers divine epiphany, real presence,
and for this reason I prefer the adjective "sacramental."

Among my encouragements in this preference is Steiner's essay *Real
Presences*, where he characterises as "sacramental" his conviction that
"music puts our being as men and women in touch with that which transcends the sayable, which outstrips the analysable."[23] A still bolder coll-
eague in the enterprise of theological reflection in a musical mode is Weil,
whose writings exude a sense of divine presence in beauty. Steiner rightly
urges Weil's "acolytes" to acknowledge her philosophical and personal
eccentricity, even "madness."[24] Yet even as he cautions against hagiography,
Steiner writes: "Simone Weil's is an utterly fascinating presence. There
are sentences, even whole pages, in her writings which make one's blood
stop. . . ."[25] Steiner describes my own response to Weil, especially to her
discussions of music's sacramental significance.

Weil defines sacrament as "contact with God,"[26] and with characteristic
freedom she applies the term beyond traditional Christian limits: "Greek
statues," she exclaims to her notebook: "Actual presence of God in a Greek
statue. The contemplation of such presence is a sacrament."[27] Weil speaks

20. *Nature and Grace in Art* (Chapel Hill: University of North Carolina Press,
    1964), 16.
21. Mary Collins, David Power, and Mellonee Burnim, *Music and the Experience
    of God*, 8. See also Harold M. Best, *Music through the Eyes of Faith* (San
    Francisco: HarperCollins, 1993), 194.
22. *Emblems of Mind: The Inner Life of Music and Mathematics* (New York:
    Times Books, 1995).
23. p.218.
24. *No Passion Spent: Essays 1978-1995* (New Haven: Yale University Press,
    1996), 171.
25. p.173.
26. *Waiting for God*, tr. Emma Craufurd (New York: Putnam, 1951), 214.
27. *Notebooks*, 2:440.

repeatedly of beauty as "the real presence of God in matter" and of contact
with beauty as "a sacrament in the full sense of the word."[28] She speaks of
the artist's sacramental experience with beauty: "Every true artist has had
real, direct, and immediate contact with the beauty of the world, contact
that is of the nature of a sacrament."[29] Finally, Weil speaks explicitly and
frequently of her sense of God's presence in music:

> In everything which gives us the pure authentic feeling of beauty
> there really is the presence of God. There is as it were an incarna-
> tion of God in the world and it is indicated by beauty. The beautiful
> is the experimental proof that the incarnation is possible. Hence
> all art of the highest order is religious in essence. (That is what
> people have forgotten today.) A Gregorian melody is as powerful
> a witness as the death of a martyr.[30]

## Divine Eminence and Divine Immanence

To appreciate Weil's sense of divine presence in music we need to share
something of her sense for the mystical theologies of classical Greek and
Christian tradition. She loves intensely both of these traditions. Christian
theology that either ignores the traditions of classical Greece or lacks
appreciation for its own traditions of mysticism is likely to share little of
Weil's particular sense of God's presence in music.

Mystical theology begins when we use the name of God to designate
the mysterious source of the world's being and order, or to designate the
world's mysterious being and order *per se*, or when we use both of these
designations in conjunction, as is the case with Weil. An influential figure
shaping the tradition of mystical theology from which Weil draws is the
Christian monk of the 5th or 6th century, Dionysius – called Dionysius the
Pseudo-Areopagite, or sometimes Pseudo-Dionysius, since his early
followers attempted to pass off his writings as those of the first-century
Dionysius the Areopagite, converted by the Apostle Paul.[31] Dionysius
speaks of God as the incomprehensible "Cause and Origin and Being and
Life of all creation," which we must think of as "nigh both everywhere
and nowhere."[32] In Dionysius's paradoxical language we encounter two
theological traditions. The one conceives of God as cause and origin of
the world, that is, as a transcendent source of all being and order, nowhere
nigh to us. This tradition we know as a form of theism. The other tradition
sees God as creation's Being and Life themselves, everywhere nigh to us.

28. *Gravity and Grace*, tr. Emma Craufurd (London: Ark Paperbacks, 1987), 138.
29. *Waiting for God*, 169.
30. *Gravity and Grace*, 137.
31. See Acts 17.34.
32. Dionysius the Areopagite, *The Divine Names and The Mystical Theology*, tr.
    C. E. Rolt (London: SPCK, 1940), 1.3, 3.2, 55, 83.

This tradition we call pantheism. A brief review of these two theological traditions will show their close relation to the idea of sacramental encounter we have considered and will help orient our subsequent explorations of music's sacramental potential.

Theism has constituted the Christian mainstream, and theists have often opposed pantheism. One of the earliest of Christian apologists, Athenagoras of Athens (2nd century), insists that we should speak of God as the musical artist to whom we attribute the harmony of the cosmos, but not as the harmonious cosmos itself, since the cosmos is but an instrument of the transcendent God:

> Now if the cosmos is an harmonious instrument set in rhythmic motion, I worship him who tuned it, who strikes its notes and sings its concordant melody, not the instrument. Nor do the judges at the contests pass over the cithara players and crown their citharas.[33]

In the next generation of Christian theologians, Origen likewise invokes musical imagery to make the theistic point that Christians should join the whole creation in singing praise to God, the cause and origin of the cosmos, but should not sing praise to elements of the cosmos itself. He writes against Celsus, a philosophical critic of Christianity:

> For Celsus says that we would seem to honour the great god better if we would sing hymns to the sun and Athena. We, however, know it to be the opposite. For we sing hymns to the one God who is over all and his only begotten Word, who is God also. So we sing to God and his only begotten as do the sun, the moon, the stars and the entire heavenly host. For all these form a sacred chorus and sing hymns to the God of all.[34]

In insisting upon God "who is over all" Christian theists have sometimes tended to suggest a divorce between God as creation's cause and origin on the one hand, and the being and life of creation on the other. Karl Barth, for instance, presupposes that "the Gospel proclaims a God utterly distinct from men," that God dwells in "another plane that is unknown."[35] This radical variety of theism, which Barth first presented in 1918, has exerted immense influence upon Protestant theology for the remainder of the 20th century. I believe, however, that this tendency to divorce God the creator from the created world is a cause of alienation for many in our day who marvel at the cosmos, revere its mystical origin and sacred integrity, and might do so within established religious traditions if only those traditions would give them greater opportunity. This alienation engendered by radical theism is as unnecessary as it is unfortunate, I believe.

---

33. *Supplication for the Christians*, 16. In James McKinnon, *Music in Early Christian Literature* (Cambridge: Cambridge University Press, 1987), 22.
34. *Against Celsus*, 8.67, in McKinnon, *Music in Early Christian Literature*, 38.
35. *The Epistle to the Romans*, 6th ed., tr. Edwyn C. Hoskyns (London: Oxford University Press, 1933), 28, 29.

I think this both for the reason that theists need not divorce God the creator from the created world, as we may see from the Christian theisms of Calvin and Edwards, for example, with their beautiful appreciations of God's created order, and also for the reason that Christian tradition offers other options.

True, one must search the corners of Christian theological tradition for outright statements of pantheism. More than one theologian has suffered the experience of Schleiermacher, who stepped beyond the boundaries of theistic tradition and praised the pantheistic piety of Benedict Spinoza, only to be rebuked by church superiors.[36] Securely within channels of both Judaism and Christianity, however, the biblical Wisdom tradition offers a complement to radical theism. The Wisdom tradition is a rich resource, not for pantheism, according to which Creator and creation are identical, but for an enlarged theism in which the Creator's transcendent and eternal Wisdom and Word are also immanent and vital in the being and life of creation. In particular relation to our theme, the Creator's Wisdom and Word are immanent and active in music. Thus the Wisdom tradition provides room for music's sacramental potential.

The biblical book of Proverbs offers a kind of prelude to this enlarged theism when God's Wisdom speaks of her intimate companionship with God the Creator, her activity and joy in the created world, and her delight in the human race:

When he established the heavens, I was there,
    when he drew a circle on the face of the deep,
when he made firm the skies above,
    when he established the fountains of the deep,
when he assigned to the sea its limit,
    so that the waters might not transgress his command,
when he marked out the foundations of the earth,
    then I was beside him, like a master worker,
and I was daily his delight,
    rejoicing before him always,
rejoicing in his inhabited world
    and delighting in the human race. (Prov 8.27-31)

The theme of the immanence of God's Wisdom in the world comes to a climax in the deuterocanonical book The Wisdom of Solomon. There God's

36. See my article "The Antagonistic Correspondence of 1801 between Chaplain Sack and his Protégé Schleiermacher," *Harvard Theological Review* 74:1 (1981). See also Hans Urs von Balthasar's discussion of 13th-century theologians of the Chartres school who "arrive at a true pantheism, against which . . . proceedings are instigated with ecclesiastical censures": *The Glory of the Lord: A Theological Aesthetics*, vol. 4, *The Realm of Metaphysics in Antiquity* (San Francisco: Ignatius, 1989), 365-6.

Wisdom is portrayed as a radiant presence, permeating and animating the world, available to all who seek her:

Wisdom is radiant and unfading,
> and she is easily discerned by those who love her,
> and is found by those who seek her.

She hastens to make herself known
> to those who desire her. . . .

She goes about seeking those worthy of her,
> and she graciously appears to them in their paths,
> and meets them in every thought. (Wis 6.12-13, 16)

Such joy and delight, so all pervading and so ready, are a measure of Wisdom's holy purity:

For wisdom is more mobile than any motion;
> because of her pureness
> she pervades and penetrates all things. (Wis 7.24)

Paradoxically, in light of his radical theology of divine transcendence, Barth echoes the spirit of this Wisdom tradition when he writes of the joy and delight, the transcendent purity of heart, that he hears in the music of Mozart:

> Why is it possible to hold that Mozart has a place in theology, especially in the doctrine of creation and also in eschatology, although he was not a father of the Church, does not seem to have been a particularly active Christian, and was a Roman Catholic, apparently leading what might appear to us a rather frivolous existence when not occupied in his work? It is possible to give him this position because he knew something about creation in its total goodness that neither the real fathers of the Church nor our Reformers, neither the orthodox nor the Liberals, neither the exponents of natural theology nor those heavily armed with the "Word of God," and certainly not the Existentialists, nor indeed any other great musicians before and after him, either know or can express and maintain as he did. In this respect he was pure in heart, far transcending both optimists and pessimists.[37]

Barth, theologian *par excellence* of the eminent creator God, hears in Mozart's music the immanence of divine goodness in creation.

The Wisdom tradition intimately associates God's three traditional attributes of wisdom (*sophia*), word (*logos*), and spirit (*pneuma*), and in doing so implies an immanence for them all. We see this intimate association suggested in the synonymous parallelism or thought-rhyme so characteristic of Hebrew poetry, echoed in the Greek translation, the Septuagint, which has transmitted these texts to us. God's word is paralleled with God's wisdom:

37. *Church Dogmatics*, 3.3, *The Doctrine of Creation*, ed. G. W. Bromiley and T. F. Torrance (Edinburgh: T. & T. Clark, 1960), 298.

O God of my ancestors and Lord of mercy,
>    who have made all things by your word (*logos*),
>    and by your wisdom (*sophia*) have formed humankind. (Wis 9.1-2)

Similarly, God's wisdom is paralleled with God's holy spirit:
>    Who has learned your counsel,
>    unless you have given wisdom (*sophia*)
>    and sent your holy spirit (*to hagion sou pneuma*) from on high?
>    Wis 9.17)

The theological imagery of these texts – three parallel divine attributions, wisdom, word, and spirit – informs the later Christian doctrine of God as Trinity, three in one.

It sometimes surprises Christians to learn of these pre-Christian intimations of Trinity and surprises even more to consider the suggestion that God's Holy Trinity is immanent in all creation. Most surprising of all, perhaps, is the fact that this ancient tradition calls Wisdom the "only-begotten" (*monogenes*, "unique") of God (Wis 7.22). This is unsettling for Christians accustomed to relating the phrase "only-begotten" exclusively to Jesus Christ – as is suggested in that most beloved verse for much of Christianity, John 3.16: "For God so loved the world that he gave his only (*monogene*) Son, so that everyone who believes in him may not perish but may have eternal life." The same may be true for Christians who assume that God's "Word" relates exclusively to Jesus Christ, whereas we have seen that the Wisdom tradition associates God's word with God's wisdom and God's spirit, all immanent throughout creation.

These tensions between widespread Christian convictions and the biblical Wisdom tradition can be resolved by a relatively simple principle, namely, that uniqueness and exclusiveness are by no means identical qualities. To say that God's wisdom is "only begotten" or "unique" is to say that God's wisdom has no rivals, that all truth is ultimately one. That is by no means identical, however, to saying that God's wisdom appears entirely and exclusively in one person, one place, or one mode. Quite the opposite. It is to make a most inclusive assertion: that wherever any person, place, or mode of wisdom is to be found, God's wisdom is manifest. Thus the profundity of Augustine's insistence that "wherever we taste the truth, God is there,"[38] of his exclamation to God that "there is no other teacher of the truth besides yourself, no matter how or where it comes to light,"[39] of his assertion that "every good and true Christian should understand that wherever he may find truth, it is his Lord's."[40] Calvin applies Augustine's principle of divine inclusivity explicitly to "the arts, both lib-

---

38. *Confessions* 4.12, tr. R. S. Pine-Coffin (Harmondsworth: Penguin, 1961), 82.
39. *Confessions* 5.6, 97.
40. *On Christian Doctrine* 2.18.28, tr. D. W. Robertson, Jr. (Indianapolis: Bobbs-Merrill, 1958), 54.

eral and manual," asserting that all truth – secular truth included – is from "the sole fountain of truth," God's spirit:

> Whenever we come upon these matters in secular writers, let that admirable light of truth shining in them teach us that the mind of man, though fallen and perverted from its wholeness, is nevertheless clothed and ornamented with God's excellent gifts. If we regard the Spirit of God as the sole fountain of truth, we shall neither reject the truth itself, nor despise it wherever it shall appear, unless we wish to dishonour the Spirit of God.[41]

In the New Testament, Christ himself appears not to confine God's wisdom to any one manifestation in his saying that "Wisdom is vindicated by all her children" (Lk 7.35). Similarly, both the New Testament and the Nicene Creed affirm that God's Holy Spirit has spoken through the Israelite prophets,[42] in contrast to any claim that God's Spirit is manifested exclusively in Jesus Christ.

This Wisdom tradition of the eminent God's all-pervasive immanence is close to what the modern age has chosen to call panentheism, as distinguished from pantheism. The word means everything-in-God (*pan-en-theos*). *The Oxford Dictionary of the Christian Church* explains panentheism, distinguishing it from pantheism:

> The belief that the Being of God includes and penetrates the whole universe, so that every part of it exists in Him, but (as against Pantheism) that His Being is more than, and is not exhausted by, the universe.

In panentheism, someone has said, the world minus God equals zero, God minus the world equals infinity. By way of illustration, Augustine speaks of God as "the Author and Founder of the universe . . . who is everywhere present."[43] Similarly the Episcopal liturgy adopts the tone of panentheism in its invocation of God as "eternal ground of all that is, beyond space and time yet within them, transcending all things yet pervading them,"[44] or in its hymn:

> To all life thou givest, to both great and small;
> In all life thou livest, the true life of all. . . .[45]

This Christian tradition, with its combined sense of divine eminence and divine immanence, sometimes makes appearances in surprising places. America's Puritan theologian Edwards, for example, defines God as "the

41. *Institutes* 2.2.14-15, 273.
42. Hebrews 1.1. John H. Leith, *Creeds of the Churches* (Garden City, NY: Anchor, 1963), 33.
43. *On Christian Doctrine* 1.10.10, p.13.
44. *The Book of Occasional Services* (New York: The Church Hymnal Corporation, 1979), 134.
45. "Immortal, invisible, God only wise," *The Hymnal 1982* (The Church Hymnal Corporation, 1985), #423.

sum of all being"[46] and characterises God in distinctly panentheistic language: "The infiniteness of God consists in his perfect comprehension of all things and the extendedness of his operation equally to all places."[47] Let us grant that Edwards is a complex figure who was capable of speaking in a tone quite different from this suggestion of panentheism. Edwards often pictured God's world as sharply divided between the redeemed and the damned. The same is true for Augustine and Calvin. That their reputations are widely coloured by their divisive tone alone, however, to the complete neglect of their visions of creation's holy unity, is by no means accurate or fair to these great theologians, as we shall have ample opportunity to appreciate.

Among contemporary theologians, Sherrard's theology is particularly imbued with a sense of panentheism, which he carefully distinguishes from pantheism:

> In all this there is no question of pantheism – pantheism always tends to involve idolatry and to demean . . . God, man and nature as a whole. What there is, on the other hand, is a panentheism – an immanence which we may experience and express as God being present in creation but which is really that of creation being present in God, as the unborn child is present in the mother.[48]

"If, then, divine transcendence is one presupposition of the sacred, so equally is immanence in God," Sherrard continues. "Transcendence and immanence are thus correlative, not contradictory terms":[49]

> Sacramental consciousness requires the simultaneous recognition of both the total transcendence *and* the total immanence of the Divine, the affirmation of the one at the expense of the other being the negation of this consciousness and a major doctrinal error.[50]

Let us now return to Weil. Panentheistic tradition permeates her sense of God's presence in music. Weil discovered the tradition both in Christian theology and in the philosophy of classical Greece. She gives a sympathetic account of Plato's idea of the Soul of the World, for example: "Plato describes the Soul of the World thus: outside the all and within the all."[51] Weil explicitly relates Christian tradition to Plato's panentheism – which she, like Sherrard and *The Oxford Dictionary of the Christian Church*, is careful to distinguish from pantheism. In another passage on the Soul of the World, for example, she likens Plato's phrase "only-begotten" to the

46. Miscellany #1077, in *The Philosophy of Jonathan Edwards from His Private Notebooks*, ed. Harvey G. Townsend (Eugene, OR: University of Oregon Press, 1955), 184.
47. Miscellany #194, *The "Miscellanies (Entry Nos. a-z, aa-zz, 1-500),"* ed. Thomas A. Schafer (New Haven: Yale University Press, 1994), 334-5.
48. *The Sacred in Life and Art*, 8.
49. pp.8, 9.
50. p.27. Sherrard's emphasis.
51. *Notebooks*, 2:372.

description of Christ as the unique Son of God in the Gospel according to John (1.14), and her phrase for Plato's Soul of the World, "begotten before the visible world," echoes both the opening of John (1.1-3) and the Nicene Creed's description of Jesus Christ as "eternally begotten of the Father":

> Plato, when he speaks of the world, or heaven, means essentially the Soul of the World. . . . This being which Plato calls the Soul of the World is the unique Son of God; Plato says *monogenes*, like St. John. The visible world is his body. That does not imply pantheism; he is not in the visible world just as our soul is not in our body. Plato says this explicitly elsewhere. The Soul of the World is infinitely more vast than matter, contains matter and envelops it from all parts. It was begotten before the visible world, before time, consequently from all eternity.[52]

In summary, Christian theology's panentheistic current continues the mystical tradition of Dionysius, using the name of God to designate both the transcendent "Cause and Origin" and the immanent "Being and Life" of all creation. The immanent God is eminent mystery, and the eminent God is immanent mystery. God is nigh both everywhere and nowhere. The importance of this theological tradition for our study of music's sacramental potential consists in the ease with which it speaks of manifestations of God in our experiences of the world, including our experiences of music, and yet preserves a sense of God's unfathomable transcendence. "God created the world for the shining forth of his excellency and for the flowing forth of his happiness," Edwards writes, and the harmony of earthly music "fits one for the contemplation of more exalted and spiritual excellencies and harmonies."[53] Edwards' panentheism, regarding the created world as a fabric of theophanies, readily embraces music as a medium of divine grace.

## Two Sacramental Traditions

When we speak of God as both eminent and immanent – as Cause and Origin as well as Being and Life of all creation – I believe we do well to think of theology as exploration of mystery, rather than as description of transcendental certainties. Hans Küng calls this doing theology "from below."[54] Calvin expresses this sense of theological modesty in our epigram: "We know the most perfect way of seeking God, and the most suitable order, is not for us to attempt with bold curiosity to penetrate to the investigation of his essence, which we ought more to adore than meticulously to search out, but for us to contemplate him in his works whereby he renders himself

---

52. *Intimations of Christianity among the Ancient Greeks.* tr. Elisabeth Chase Geissbuhler (London: Routledge and Kegan Paul, 1957), 92.
53. Miscellanies #332 and #95, *The "Miscellanies,"* 334-5, 263.
54. *On Being a Christian*, tr. Edward Quinn (Garden City, NY: Doubleday, 1984), 83.

near and familiar to us, and in some manner communicates himself."[55] In
a similar spirit Edwards opens some reflections on the Trinity with these
cautionary words: "We should be careful that we do not go upon uncertain
grounds, and fix uncertain determinations in things of so high a nature."[56]

In this spirit of theological modesty we can accept even Christianity's
formal creeds as occasions to contemplate the mysteries of divine dwelling
in our midst, rather than as dogmatic claims that finite human curiosity has
grasped the essence of the Infinite. The 4th-century Nicene Creed was the
first creed adopted as authoritative for the whole of Christendom. It is still
used widely in both eastern and western Christianity, and has been proposed
as a basis for modern Christian unity. The Creed begins: "We believe in
one God, the Father All Governing, creator of heaven and earth, of all things
visible and invisible. . . ."[57] The final task for this chapter is to prepare for our
next two by considering Christian tradition's appreciation of music both as a
thing visible (that is, perceptible) and as a thing invisible (that is, imperceptible).

The Nicene Creed's "visible and invisible" echoes the philosophy of
Plato, who clearly distinguishes the two kinds of reality. Plato gives strong
preference to the invisible as a source of human wisdom. His *Phaedo*
includes the following exchange, profoundly influential upon western
intellectual history, between Socrates and a Pythagorean named Cebes:

"Now," said he, "shall we assume two kinds of existence, one
visible, the other invisible?"

"Let us assume them," said Cebes.

"And that the invisible is always the same and the visible constantly changing?"

"Let us assume that also," said he.

"Well then," said Socrates, "are we not made up of two parts,
body and soul?"

"Yes," he replied.

"Now to which class should we say the body is more similar
and more closely akin?"

"To the visible," said he; "that is clear to everyone."

"And the soul? Is it visible or invisible?"

"Invisible, to man, at least, Socrates". . . .

"Then the soul is more like the invisible than the body is, and
the body more like the visible."

"Necessarily, Socrates."

"Now we have also been saying for a long time, have we not,

55. *Institutes* 1.5.9, 1:62.
56. "Observations concerning the Scripture Oeconomy of the Trinity, and Cov-
    enant of Redemption," *Treatise on Grace & Other Posthumous Writings in-
    cluding Observations on the Trinity*, ed. Paul Helm (Cambridge: James Clarke,
    1971), 77.
57. Leith, *Creeds of the Churches*, 33.

that when the soul makes use of the body for any inquiry, either through seeing or hearing or any of the other senses – for inquiry through the body means inquiry through the senses – then it is dragged by the body to things which never remain the same, and it wanders about and is confused and dizzy like a drunken man because it lays hold upon such things?"

"Certainly."

"But when the soul inquires alone by itself, it departs into the realm of the pure, the everlasting, the immortal and the changeless, and being akin to these it dwells always with them whenever it is by itself and is not hindered, and it has rest from its wanderings and remains always the same and unchanging with the changeless, since it is in communion therewith. And this state of the soul is called wisdom. Is it not so?"

"Socrates," said he, "what you say is perfectly right and true."[58]

For Plato, things invisible are nearer the divine. Things visible are impediments to human wisdom. This Platonic dichotomy echoes from various places in the New Testament as well, particularly from the writings of Paul: "For what can be seen is temporary, but what cannot be seen is eternal" (2 Cor 4.18).

What a striking contrast, then, when the Nicene Creed associates the creator God with things both visible and invisible. This departure from Platonism increases with the Creed's subsequent assertion that God's only-begotten (*monogenes*) – God's very Word and Wisdom, "Light from Light, true God from true God, begotten not created, of the same essence as the Father" – became "incarnate by the Holy Spirit and the Virgin Mary and became human."[59] Here the creed echoes the startlingly non-Platonic assertion of the Prologue to John's Gospel:

And the Word became flesh and lived among us, and we have seen his glory, the glory as of a father's only-begotten (*monogenes*). (Jn 1.14)

The Nicene Creed, then, inherits its categories of things visible and invisible from Plato, but in the spirit of the Wisdom tradition and John's Prologue, it grants the visible and the invisible a sacramental parity that is something radically new.

This parity of the visible and the invisible gives rise to two great traditions of Christian sacramental encounter, particularly as it pertains to music. The first is a tradition that I have chosen to call Incarnational theology, emphasising the perceptible – specifically, in our musical application, the audible – as a means of God's grace. The second is a tradition that I shall call Pythagorean theology, emphasising the imperceptible – or, in our

58. Plato, *Phaedo* 79a-c, tr. Harold North Fowler (London: Heinemann, 1943), 277.
59. Leith, 33.

**Figure 1. Frontispiece of Kircher's *Musurgia Universalis*.**

musical application, the inaudible. In the Incarnational tradition, God's
grace is sensed in the material world. Here the sounds of music – music's
resonances in our ears and hearts and bones and muscles – are potentially
sacramental. In the Pythagorean tradition, God's grace is perceived in our
minds. Here the logic of music – music's reflections in the appreciative,
analytical, and creative capacities of our intelligence – is potentially

sacramental. Steiner compasses these two traditions in his observation, "Music is at once cerebral in the highest degree . . . and it is at the same time somatic, carnal and a searching out of resonances in our bodies at levels deeper than will or consciousness. . . ."[60] Steiner calls our immediate experiences of music in these two traditions "sacramental":

> It is in and through music that we are most immediately in the presence of the logically, of the verbally inexpressible but wholly palpable energy in being that communicates to our senses and to our reflection what little we can grasp of the naked wonder of life.
>
> I take music to be the naming of the naming of life. This is, beyond any liturgical or theological specificity, a sacramental motion.[61]

What I am calling the Incarnational tradition is of course well known to Christian theology in relation to the figure of Jesus Christ,[62] but it is infrequently discussed in relation to music. What we are calling the Pythagorean tradition, on the other hand, is virtually defined by musical experience, but in contemporary Christian theology it receives little attention.[63] Let us begin our response to this general neglect with a brief introduction to each of these sacramental traditions, beginning with the Pythagorean.

**The Pythagorean Tradition.** It is easy to label almost anything "Pythagorean," since we know almost nothing about the historical figure of Pythagoras (6th century BCE).[64] We may introduce the particular tradition of Pythagoreanism that concerns us, however, by means of a fanciful representation in the frontispiece of a musical treatise of 1650, *Musurgia Universalis*, by Athanasius Kircher.

Kircher, famous throughout Europe as a mathematician, was also a music theorist and theologian. As this combination of talents might indicate, he

---

60. *Real Presences*, 217.

61. pp.216-17.

62. Classic theological treatments include the Prologue to *The Gospel according to John*, the Creed of Chalcedon (451), *On the Incarnation of the Word* by Athanasius (c.296-373), and *Why Did God Become Man?* by Anselm (c.1033-1109).

63. A welcome exception to this rule has appeared during my final preparations of this manuscript: Quentin Faulkner, *Wiser than Despair: The Evolution of Ideas in the Relationship of Music and the Christian Church* (Westport, CN: Greenwood, 1996). Faulkner includes an extensive historical survey of sources representing Christian Pythagoreanism. See also Westermeyer's sketch of Christian Pythagoreanism in his recent *Te Deum: The Church and Music* (Minneapolis: Fortress, 1998), 116-19.

64. For a good review of what we know see Charles H. Kahn, "Pythagorean Philosophy before Plato," in *The Pre-Socratics*, ed. Alexander P. D. Mourelatos (Garden City, NY: Anchor Books, 1974), 163-70. Also Walter Burkert, *Lore and Science in Ancient Pythagoreanism*, tr. Edwin L. Minar, Jr. (Cambridge: Harvard University Press, 1972).

was a Christian Pythagorean who discerned God's word and wisdom in the mathematics of music. He invokes a seminal theological text for Christian Pythagoreans, a verse from The Wisdom of Solomon:

> But you have arranged all things by measure and number and weight. (Wis 11.20)[65]

Kircher's musical treatise was immensely influential among composers of the European Baroque, including Bach. Its frontispiece is an allegorical engraving (Figure 1). At its top we see a triangular symbol of the Trinity, beaming rays of light and surrounded by a choir of seraphim singing the *Sanctus*: "Holy, Holy, Holy." In the centre we see the sphere of the universe, surmounted by a victorious classical figure holding lyre and pipes, labelled, not very modestly, as Kircher himself. The heavenly sphere bears a rhetorical question from the book of Job (38.37, Vulgate):

> *Quis concentum coeli dormire faciet?*
>
> Who will put to sleep the concert of heaven?

That is, who can cause the harmony of the heavens to cease? In the background of this cosmos, under the concert of heaven and the radiant streams of God's holiness, human figures dance on the shore and sport in the sea, in the company of a dolphin.

At the lower right of the engraving sits the allegorical figure of Music, surrounded by a clutter of musical instruments and pointing to the strings of her lute. At the lower left sits Pythagoras. With his right hand he points to a diagram of the Pythagorean Theorem: a right triangle with squares constructed on its legs of 3, 4, and 5 units. With his left hand he points to a representation of three blacksmiths pounding an anvil with their hammers. Various musical instruments lie under Pythagoras's feet, discarded.

Why blacksmiths, and why are the instruments discarded? The instruments are discarded because their sounds are no longer needed for understanding the harmonies of music and of the heavens. As Pythagoras has established the mathematical ratios relating the sides of a right triangle, so he has also applied mathematics to establish ratios among the weights of the blacksmiths' hammers, thus accounting for their different musical pitches when they strike the anvil. He has discovered that these same mathematical ratios govern the musical pitches of the lute's strings, to which Music's gesture directs our attention, and he has asserted that those ratios govern the harmonies of heaven as well.

The Pythagorean legend about blacksmith hammers lies behind lines from the partly-Shakespearean play *The Two Noble Kinsmen*:

> for, as they say, from iron
> Came music's origin. . . . [66]

65. *Musurgia Universalis*, ed. Ulf Scharlau (Hildesheim: Georg Olms, 1970), iv.
66. William Shakespeare and John Fletcher, *The Two Noble Kinsmen* 5.4.60-1, ed. Eugene M. Waith (Oxford: Clarendon, 1989), 210.

Of course it is not music but rather the science of music that had its origin in Pythagoras's acoustical discoveries. Those discoveries led to the philosophical conviction that as mathematics expresses cosmic order, so music echoes cosmic harmony. These convictions, in turn, gave rise to the complex philosophical and religious tradition that we call Pythagoreanism.

F. M. Cornford summarises the Pythagorean tradition in philosophy as follows:

> Viewing Pythagoreanism as a philosophical attitude or tendency in Western thought, one could give a general characterisation of it by listing seven doctrines. . . : (a) The fundamental realities of the world are structural and mathematical. (b) These structures necessarily articulate themselves into a single system. . . . (c) Structures in superficially dissimilar contexts can be isomorphic; indeed, there is a pervasive affinity or sympathy between the inanimate and the animate, between man's psyche and the whole cosmos. (d) This cosmic sympathy affords the possibility of moral improvement through a patterning of the individual psyche on the cosmos. (e) Beyond moral improvement, the cosmic sympathy affords the prospect of ascent to a trans-human level of existence, even to immortality, through a process of "purification". . . . (f) The process of knowing or understanding is inherently mystical and is consummated only by the elite. (g) The study of mathematics is the indispensable basis for all intellectual and spiritual progress.[67]

Cornford's account is not quite complete. To make it so, we must supplement his final point concerning the study of mathematics as the indispensable basis of Pythagoreanism by adding the study of music.

A complex philosophy, Pythagoreanism has undergone a complex history, as Cornford explains:

> Given the allusiveness of this complex of ideas, the influence of Pythagoreanism has often been felt on the side of numerology, superstition, occultism, and mindless formalism. But at crucial junctures and in important contexts, its influence has also been salutary and productive. In the words of a historian of science, "The founders of modern science were thoroughly imbued with the Pythagorean spirit. This is particularly true of Copernicus and Kepler, and almost as true of Galileo and Newton." Within the wider context of intellectual history, Pythagoreanism as a formative and creative force in the arts – especially music and architecture – can hardly be overestimated.[68]

67. "Mysticism and Science in the Pythagorean Tradition," in *The Pre-Socratics*, ed. Mourelatos, 8.
68. Cornford, 8. Cornford does not identify the historian of science whom he quotes here.

We might note that Cornford makes no mention here of Pythagoreanism as a formative and creative force in religion, particularly in Christian religion. His omission illustrates the characteristic neglect of Christian Pythagoreanism in recent intellectual history.

The most prominent representative of Christian Pythagoreanism is Augustine. In his commentary on the Genesis account of God's creation of the world he repeatedly cites the watchword text from The Wisdom of Solomon: "But you have arranged all things by measure and number and weight." In one passage he alludes to the text no fewer than eight times in four short pages.[69] Augustine inquires into the relation of measure, number, and weight to God. He concludes that the relation, properly conceived, is one of identity:

> God is identified with these three in a fundamental, true, and unique
> sense. He limits everything, forms everything, and orders everything.
> Hence, in so far as this matter can be grasped by the heart of man
> and expressed by his tongue, we must understand that the words,
> "Thou hast ordered all things in measure and number and weight,"
> mean nothing else than "Thou hast ordered all things in Thyself."[70]

In another treatise Augustine describes number and God's Wisdom as "somehow one and the same thing" and as "identical."[71] He marvels over number's eternity and universality: "Seven and three are ten, not only now, but forever. There has never been a time when seven and three were not ten, nor will there ever be a time when they are not ten. Therefore, I have said that the truth of number is incorruptible and common to all who think."[72] Augustine marvels likewise over the role that this "truth of number" plays in forming the entire world, from the heavens above us to the artistic creativity within us:

> Wherever you turn, wisdom speaks to you through the imprint it
> has stamped upon its works. . . . Look at the sky, the earth, and the
> sea, and at whatever in them shines from above or crawls, flies, or
> swims below. These have form because they have number. . . . Ask
> next what moves the limbs of the artist himself, and it will be
> number. . . . If you ask what is pleasant in dancing, number will
> answer you, "Behold, it is I."[73]

I suggest Edwards as another exemplar of this Pythagorean tradition, though so far as I have been able to discover he never invokes Pythagoras's name. Edwards envisions heaven itself as a surpassing state of "exquisite

69. *The Literal Meaning of Genesis* 4.4.8-12, tr. John Hammond Taylor, (New
    York: Newman, 1982), 108-11.
70. 4.3.7, p.108.
71. *On Free Choice of the Will* 2.11.123 and 127, tr. Anna S. Benjamin and L. H.
    Hackstaff (Indianapolis: Bobbs-Merrill, 1964), 64-5.
72. 2.8.83, p.54.
73. 2.16.163-6, 73-74.

spiritual proportions," "ratios," and "harmony":

> How ravishing are the proportions of the reflections of rays of
> light, and the proportions of the vibrations of the air! And without
> doubt, God can contrive matter so that there shall be other sort of
> proportions, that may be quite of a different kind, and may raise
> another sort of pleasure in the sense, and in a manner to us incon-
> ceivable, that shall be vastly more ravishing and exquisite. . . . Then,
> also, our capacities will be exceedingly enlarged, and we shall be
> able to apprehend, and to take in, more extended and compounded
> proportions. We see that the narrower the capacity, the more sim-
> ple must the beauty be to please. Thus in the proportion of sounds
> . . . little children are not able to perceive the sweetness of very
> complex tunes, where respect is to be had to the proportion of a
> great many notes together. . . . Then perhaps we shall be able fully
> and easily to apprehend the beauty, where respect is to be had to
> thousands of different ratios at once to make up the harmony.[74]

Surely we may assume that Edwards would relish Pythagorean analysis of
musical proportions, to which we shall turn in Chapter 2.

As a 20th-century exponent of this sacramental tradition, Weil invokes
the name of Pythagoras repeatedly. Calling Pythagorean tradition "the
mother of Greek tradition" she adds: "We do not know whether Plato was
the best of Greek spirituality; he is simply all that we have. Pythagoras
and his disciples were doubtless more marvellous."[75] Weil relates Pythagorean tradition to Christian tradition by joining their concepts of harmony
and incarnation: "The Incarnation of Christianity implies a harmonious
solution of the problem of the relations between the individual and the
collective. Harmony in the Pythagorean sense: the just balance of contraries."[76]

To conclude this introduction to Christian Pythagoreanism, Weil makes
the most important point. In the tradition of Christian Pythagoreanism,
contemplation, and in particular contemplation of music, is experienced
as a sacramental medium:

> When we listen to Bach or to a Gregorian melody, all the faculties
> of the soul become still and tense in order to apprehend this thing
> of perfect beauty – each in its own way – and among them the
> intelligence. The latter finds nothing in this thing it hears to affirm
> or to deny, but it feeds upon it. Should not faith be an adherence of
> this kind? The mysteries of faith are degraded if they are made a
> subject of affirmation and negation, when in reality they should be
> a subject of contemplation.[77]

74. Miscellany #182, *The "Miscellanies,"* 328-9.
75. *Intimations of Christianity*, 76-7.
76. *Waiting for God*, 77.
77. *Notebooks*, 1:245.

According to one traditional definition sacraments are "outward and visible signs of inward and spiritual grace."[78] Here, with Weil, we are deliberately harkening to a converse sacramental conception, namely, the Pythagorean sense that contemplation of music is an inward means of appreciating God's outward and palpable grace. This, Weil writes, "is what makes music sublime – an intellectual joy."[79]

**The Incarnational Tradition**. The second great sacramental tradition we are calling the Incarnational. This Incarnational tradition grows out of encounters with the divine in the material world perceived by our senses. Like the Pythagorean tradition, the Incarnational tradition takes a watch-word from The Wisdom of Solomon:

For from the greatness and beauty of created things

comes a corresponding perception of their Creator. (Wis 13.5)[80]

The Apostle Paul sometimes writes within this Incarnational tradition: "Ever since the creation of the world God's eternal power and divine nature, invisible though they are, have been understood and seen through the things he has made" (Rom 1.20).

Edwards represents the Incarnational tradition as well as the Pythagorean. He speaks of the material universe as a kind of incarnation of God. Remarkably for his time and place and position, Edwards cites the 17th-century pantheistic traditions of Benedict Spinoza and Charles Blount:

Reason did not hinder Spinoza, Blount, and many other modern philosophers from asserting that God may have a body, or rather that the universe, or the matter of the universe, is God. Many nations believed the incarnation of Jupiter himself. Reason, instead of being utterly averse to the notion of a divine incarnation, both easily enough admitted that notion and suffered it to pass almost without contradiction among the most philosophical nations of the world.[81]

How much less difficult, Edwards goes on to observe, is the Christian's acceptance of God's material incarnation in a spiritual person, the person of Christ.

Weil represents the 20th century's even greater capacity to accept our bodily senses as sacramental: "The beauty of the world is God's own Beauty, as the beauty of the body of a human being is the beauty which belongs to that being."[82] She speaks of our love of God implicit in various

---

78. *The Book of Common Prayer*, 857. This definition stems from Augustine, *De catechizandis rudibus* 26.50 (see McBrien, *Catholicism*, 2:734).

79. *Notebooks*, 2:602.

80. See for example Bonaventure, *The Soul's Journey into God; The Tree of Life; The life of St. Francis*, tr. Ewert Cousings (New York: Paulist Press, 1978), 64-5.

81. Miscellany #1233, in *The Philosophy of Jonathan Edwards*, 214.

82. *Intimations of Christianity*, 150.

sacramental forms within the visible world: "The implicit love of God can have only three immediate objects, the only three things here below in which God is really though secretly present. These are religious ceremonies, the beauty of the world, and our neighbour."[83]

Weil observes with regret that Plato had more sense of the indissoluble unity of religion and visible beauty, more sense of God's real presence incarnate in the material world, than most Christians do. She laments the Christian loss of incarnational sensibility: "We have lost this unity, we whose religion should be the most incarnate of any. We must rediscover it."[84]

> Today one might think that the white races had almost lost all feeling for the beauty of the world, and that they had taken upon them the task of making it disappear from all the continents where they have penetrated with their armies, their trade, and their religion. As Christ said to the Pharisees: "Woe to you, for ye have taken away the key of knowledge; ye entered not in yourselves and them that were entering in ye hindered." [Lk 11.52] And yet at the present time, in the countries of the white races, the beauty of the world is almost the only way by which we can allow God to penetrate us, for we are still farther removed from the other two [that is, from the other two forms of the implicit love of God: religious ritual and love of neighbor]. . . .The very idea of them has almost disappeared; the very meaning of the words has been debased.[85]

Despite her lamentation, Weil cherished the hope that Christians might yet rediscover and repurify a sacramental sense of incarnate beauty:

> On the other hand a sense of beauty, although mutilated, distorted, and soiled, remains rooted in the heart of man as a powerful incentive. It is present in all the preoccupations of secular life. If it were made true and pure, it would sweep all secular life in a body to the feet of God; it would make the total incarnation of the faith possible.[86]

In summary, Pythagorean tradition emphasises intellectual appreciation and finds God's grace revealed through our contemplating invisible objects of our understanding and subjects of our insight, in particular, through our contemplating the mathematics of music. Its counterpart, the Incarnational tradition, emphasises corporeal perception and finds God's grace embodied in the visible world, the world of matter, in objects of our senses and subjects of our desire, and in particular, in the sounds of music. The Pythagorean tradition touches our reason with God's logic. The Incarnational tradition touches our hearts with God's love. The confluence of these two traditions

83. *Waiting for God*, 137.
84. *Intimations of Christianity*, 115.
85. p.115.
86. *Waiting for God*, 162-3.

constitutes a broad stream of Christian theology, for as Edwards observes of biblical scripture: "I don't remember that any other attributes are said to be God, and God to be them, but *logos* and *agape*, or reason and love."[87]

These two traditions have sometimes had difficulty commingling. Turbulence has often marked their historical confluences, and the two great streams have tended to separate. I believe that the Nicene Creed's assertion that God is creator of all, visible and invisible, seen and unseen, suggests that we keep the two streams together. The two dimensions of music – the inaudible or cerebral, and the audible or aural – are distinguishable but not separable. Thus our sacramental appreciation of music may answer to Calvin's description when he speaks of "this particular search for God, which may so hold our mental powers suspended in wonderment as at the same time to stir us deeply."[88] I am convinced that a sacramental appreciation of music combining the mental powers of the Pythagorean tradition and the deep stirrings of the Incarnational tradition can help us with two important theological lessons: that we need not scorn body though we highly value spirit, and that we need not spurn time though we strongly yearn for eternity.

87. Miscellany #146, *The "Miscellanies,"* 299-300. See the same assertion in *Treatise on Grace*, 59, and again in *An Unpublished Essay of Edwards on the Trinity*, ed. George P. Fisher (New York: Charles Scribner's Sons, 1903), 113. Concerning God as *logos*, Edwards cites Jn 1.1; concerning God as *agape*, 1 Jn 4.8, 16.
88. *Institutes* 1.5.9, 1:62.

# II. Creation: Transcending Contingency

*Zwei Augen hat die Seel: eins schauet in die Zeit,*
*Das andre richtet sich hin in die Ewigkeit.*

Two eyes hath the soul: one seeth temporally,
The other looketh out into eternity.

## *The Pythagorean Tradition: Music's Sacramental Silence*

The West or Royal Portal of Chartres, dedicated to the majesty of God, conveys visitors into the nave of the great cathedral. Over the pilgrim's shoulder, carved on the right voussoir of the triple Portal's rightmost arch, sits Pythagoras at his desk. Around him are personifications and other human representatives of the liberal arts. Directly above Pythagoras, Music sits with harp and bells.

This placement of the liberal arts and their human representatives on the Royal Portal of Chartres is of course no accident. Christian theology of the 12th century valued the classical liberal arts – the quadrivium of arithmetic, geometry, astronomy, and music, and the trivium of grammar, rhetoric, and logic – as portals into God's glory. The proximity of Pythagoras and Music is no accident either. Through applications of arithmetic and geometry, Pythagoras founded the science of music, making music accessible to the mind's reflection as well as to the ear's audition. In this chapter we shall explore the tradition of Christian Pythagoreanism in which music is not so much perceived as conceived, not so much sensed as contemplated. In this contemplative tradition we may speak of Pythagorean science as music's sacramental silence.

The anonymous Christian document *Scholia enchiriadis* is "a commentary to a musical textbook by an anonymous Frankish clergyman of the 9th or 10th century."[1] The document embraces the quadrivium of the liberal arts as a means of coming to know God from God's works: "These four disciplines are not arts of human devising, but are investigations, such as they are, of divine works; and they lead noble minds, by wonderful arguments, to a better understanding of the work of creation. It is inexcusable to come by these means to know God and His eternal divinity, and then not to glorify Him or give thanks."[2] The *Scholia* gives protracted attention to Pythagorean appreciation of music as an expression of arithmetic, cast-

---

1. Weiss, *Music in the Western World*, 38.
2. Gerbert, *Scriptores ecclesiastici de musica* 1, tr. Lawrence Rosenwald. In Weiss, *Music in the Western World*, 39.

ing its discussion in the form of a dialogue between student and teacher:

> S: How, then, is Harmony born of its mother Arithmetic? And
> are Harmony and Music the same thing?
>
> T: Harmony is taken to mean the concordant mixture of differ-
> ent sounds. Music is the scheme of that concord. Music, like the
> other mathematical disciplines, is in all its aspects bound up with
> the system of numbers. And so it is by way of numbers that it must
> be understood. . . .
>
> S: . . . Arithmetic is unquestionably necessary to a knowledge
> of Music.
>
> T: Necessary indeed, for Music is entirely formed and fash-
> ioned after the image of numbers. And so it is number, by means
> of these fixed and established proportions of notes, that brings
> about whatever is pleasing to the ear in singing. Whatever pleas-
> ure rhythms yield, whether in song or in rhythmic movements of
> whatever sort, all is the work of number. Notes pass away quickly;
> numbers, however, though stained by the corporeal touch of pitches
> and motions, remain.[3]

The final sentence of this dialogue expresses the Pythagorean conception
of music's arithmetic as a portal into the transcendent.

A century or so before the *Scholia*, John the Scot speaks of music's
arithmetic as a portal into the eternal harmonies by which God orders the
entire cosmos. Known also as John Scotus ("the Irishman") or John Erigena
("born of Ireland") – thus as Joannes Scotus Erigena – John has been
called the most powerful intellect between Augustine and Anselm.[4] He
translated the mystical writings of Dionysius from Greek into Latin, thus
contributing to their profound influence on succeeding generations. John
the Scot relates the "reasoned principles of musical science" to the Creator's will by means of an extended simile:

> Just as a melody consists of notes of different character and pitch,
> which show considerable disagreement when they are heard indivi-
> dually and separately, but provide a certain natural charm when
> they are combined in one or another of the modes, in accordance
> with definite and reasoned principles of musical science; so the
> universe, in accordance with the uniform will of the Creator, is
> welded into one harmonious whole from the different subdivisions
> of nature, which disagree with each other when they are examined
> individually.[5]

John the Scot applies his concept of musical harmony to all things temporal

---

3. pp.38-40.
4. John the Scot, *Periphyseon: On the Division of Nature*, tr. Myra L. Uhlfelder,
   summaries by Jean A. Potter (Indianapolis: Bobbs-Merrill, 1976), ix.
5. Johannes Scotus Erigena, *De divisione naturae*, tr. Anselm Hughes, *The New
   Oxford History of Music*, (London: Oxford, 1954), 2:273.

and eternal: "Music is the discipline which, through natural ratios, discerns by the light of reason the harmony of all things endowed with being, whether they are in motion or in a knowable state of stability."[6] Then, in a teacher-student dialogue of his own, John praises Pythagoras, the discoverer of mathematics at the foundation of music as it is at the foundation of "all things visible and invisible":

> **T:** Is it [arithmetic], then, a natural art?
>
> **S:** Yes, and none is more so, since not only does it subsist as the immovable foundation and the primordial cause and beginning of the other three parts of mathematics which follow – namely Geometry, Music, and Astrology – but also the infinite host of all things visible and invisible receives its substance according to the rules of numbers which Arithmetic contemplates. Our first witness is the discoverer of the art, Pythagoras, a superlative philosopher who declares with sure reasoning that intelligible numbers are the substances of all things visible and invisible. Nor does sacred Scripture deny it, for it says that everything was made in measure, number, and weight.[7]

John's concluding sentence invokes yet again the watchword verse of Christian Pythagoreans, The Wisdom of Solomon 11.20. Likewise, John invokes Pythagoras in association with Job 38.37, the verse we encountered in Chapter 1 on the frontispiece of the 17th-century treatise by Kircher: "Pythagoras attempted to affirm by sure proofs that the structure of the whole world both rotates and is measured in accordance with musical propositions, which the divine Scripture does not deny either, for it says, 'Who will put to sleep the concert of heaven?'"[8]

The *Scholia* and John the Scot represent a Pythagorean tradition with widespread roots in Christian history. Early Christian literature preserves many endorsements of the liberal arts, and in particular of music as one of the liberal arts, and numerous honorific references to Pythagoras as founder of the science of music.[9] All of these early Christian figures share the basic Pythagorean conviction that number and proportion, manifest in the science of music, are at the foundation of reality, and that contemplation of music serves as a portal into sacramental experience of divine harmony and glory.

6. *Periphyseon* 1.27, 43.

7. *Periphyseon* 3.11, 163-64.

8. *Periphyseon (De Divisione Naturea)*, Book 3, ed. I. P. Sheldon-Williams (Dublin: The Dublin Institute for Advanced Studies, 1981), 261.

9. See Justin Martyr (2nd century), *Dialogue with Trypho* 106, and Hippolytus (3rd century), *The Refutation of All Heresies* 1.2, both in McKinnon, *Music in Early Christian Literature*, 21 and 46. Also Cassiodorus (6th century), *Explanation of the Psalms*, tr. P. G. Walsh, 3 vols. (New York: Paulist Press, 1990), 2:389.

Edwards echoes this Christian tradition in a later age. He raises the concepts of musical harmony and numerical pattern to the highest spiritual level, applying them to the harmony and pattern of being itself. In *The Nature of True Virtue* (1755), Edwards speaks of the universal harmony or "consent" of being as the highest of all beauty, which he calls "primary beauty": "That consent, agreement, or union of being to being . . . , viz. the union or propensity of minds to mental or spiritual existence, may be called the highest and primary beauty; being the proper and peculiar beauty of spiritual and moral beings."[10] Then Edwards speaks of a "secondary beauty," consisting in harmony, pattern, and proportion, wherever those qualities appear throughout all creation – as in geometric forms, both animate and inanimate, and in "the various notes of a melodious tune":

> Yet there is another, inferior, secondary beauty, which is some image of this [primary beauty], and which is not peculiar to spiritual beings, but is found even in inanimate things; which consists in a mutual consent and agreement of different things, in form, manner, quantity, and visible or end design; called by the various names of regularity, order, uniformity, symmetry, proportion, harmony, etc. Such is the mutual agreement of the various sides of a square, or equilateral triangle, or of a regular polygon. Such is, as it were, the mutual consent of the different parts of the periphery of a circle, or surface of a sphere, and of the corresponding parts of an ellipsis. Such is the agreement of the colours, figures, dimensions, and distances of the different spots on a chessboard. Such is the beauty of the figures on a piece of chintz or brocade. Such is the beautiful proportion of the various parts of a human body or countenance. And such is the sweet mutual consent and agreement of the various notes of a melodious tune.[11]

Edwards values these secondary manifestations of beauty both in themselves and as echoes of primary beauty, the spiritual harmony among moral beings. He values beauty, in all its forms, for what we are calling beauty's sacramental potential, namely, its capacity to awaken and assist our religious sensibilities, "to enliven in us a sense of spiritual beauty":

> It has pleased him [God] to establish a law of nature, by virtue of which the uniformity and mutual correspondence of a beautiful plant, and the respect which the various parts of a regular building seem to have one to another, and their agreement and union, and the consent or concord of the various notes of a melodious tune, should appear beautiful; because therein is some image of the consent of mind, of the different members of a society or system of intelligent beings,

10. *The Nature of True Virtue*, (Ann Arbor: The University of Michigan Press, 1960), 27.
11. pp.27-8.

sweetly united in a benevolent agreement of heart. And here by the way I would further observe, probably it is with regard to this image or resemblance which secondary beauty has of true spiritual beauty, that God has so constituted nature, that the presenting of this inferior beauty, especially in those kinds of it which have the greatest resemblance of the primary beauty, as the harmony of sounds and the beauties of nature, have a tendency to assist those whose hearts are under the influence of a truly virtuous temper to dispose them to the exercises of divine love, and enliven in them a sense of spiritual beauty.[12]

In summary, Edwards finds sacramental value in the world's patterns, proportions, and harmonies, including those of music: "the beauty of the world is a communication of God's beauty."[13]

## *Pythagorean Intervals*

In the spirit of Edwards' theology of beauty, recalling particularly his references the patterns and proportions of music, let us turn to some analysis of the concord of tunes and the harmony of sounds, in what we might call a sacramental exercise in music theory. Let it be said in advance that in this spiritual exercise we are steering for no proof of God's existence from design. Even in the midst of the 18th century, Edwards spoke of beauty's spiritual value in symbolic, not pseudo-scientific, terms. Still more in our day, I believe, we should shun apologetic exercises that attempt to wrestle faith from the realm of vital trust into the realm of sterile proof. Yet in the end our Pythagorean analysis will bring us to some claims that music is something considerably more significant than merely a source of pleasant theological metaphors, that music may contribute substantively to religious faith and life.

Let us begin our explorations with a definition of music as "patterned tone." We can accept the common assumptions that musical tone is composed of four constituents – pitch, timbre, loudness, and duration – and that musical pattern consists of five – melody, harmony, rhythm, tempo, and compositional structure. If we should wish to include performances on untuned percussion, as presented by the Japanese performance group Kodo, for example, we might relax our definition of music enough to do so. But to define music as "patterned sound" becomes too broad. Verbal speech is patterned sound, and music can be distinguished from most verbal speech. In places like western Ireland and certain islands of the Caribbean, of course, we hear verbal speech that is highly musical, but that is because its sounds approach tones and its patterns suggest melodies.

Pythagoras's great discovery was that number underlies musical pitch.

12. pp.30-1.
13. Miscellany #293, *The "Miscellanies,"* 384.

His discovery arises from some marvellous observations. According to the legend we have already encountered, Pythagoras co-ordinated the sounds of hammers on an anvil with the hammers' proportional weights to discover the principle that musical pitches are related by numerical ratios. Thus far his accomplishment represented epoch-making science. He also discovered that consonant musical pitches – that is, pitches that please our ears when they sound together – are related by simple numerical ratios of whole numbers. With this further discovery, Pythagorean accomplishment assumed momentous aesthetic, philosophical, and religious significance.

Commentators have found the blacksmith legend empirically implausible, but that need not distract us. To illustrate and explore their basic principles, the Pythagoreans made use of the monochord, a simple experimental instrument that any clever schoolchild can duplicate. Ernest G. McClain describes the monochord succinctly as "a string stretched over a resonator in such a way that one bridge can be moved without altering the tension, i.e., so that intervals can be defined as measures of string length."[14] The monochord demonstrates empirically the Pythagorean principle that consonant intervals are produced by string lengths related by whole number ratios. What is more, these whole number ratios form a regular series, with the smallest whole numbers producing the most consonant intervals.

The most consonant of all intervals, which we call the octave, is produced by string lengths related in the ratio of 2:1. That is, the string producing the ocave's lower tone is twice the length of the other. The next most consonant interval, which we call the 5th, is produced by string lengths related in the ratio of 3:2. If, as is often more convenient, we speak not of string length but rather of vibrational frequency, the tones of an octave are related in the ratio of 1:2 – that is, the octave's lower tone vibrates half as rapidly as the upper tone – and the tones of the 5th are related in the ratio of 2:3. According to the canons developed in western harmonic music, then, the seven most consonant intervals, together with their ratios, are these:

octave 1:2
perfect 5th 2:3
perfect 4th 3:4
major 3rd 4:5
minor 3rd 5:6
major whole tone 8:9
minor whole tone 9:10

**Figure 2. Basic Harmonic Intervals.**

14. *The Myth of Invariance: The Origin of the Gods, Mathematics and Music from the Rig Veda to Plato* (New York: Nicolas Hays, 1976), xviii.

We may notice that ratios involving 7 do not appear in this list of consonant intervals. This uncanny number generates intervals widely judged to be more dissonant than those listed in Figure 2. More about 7 – and 11 – later.

The Pythagoreans found their rudimentary list of consonant intervals and whole-number ratios mysterious, thrilling, and beguiling. From it, and from discoveries such as the Pythagorean theorem in geometry, they generalised to their motto: "all the things that are known have number."[15] Augustine states the Pythagorean motto theologically and in active voice: "Wisdom gave numbers to all objects . . . ; all objects, even the least ones, have their own numbers."[16] Elsewhere he speaks of "the beauty of ratio."[17]

If the beauty of these musical ratios moves us today less profoundly than it moved the ancient Pythagoreans, this may be for several reasons. First is widespread ignorance of the mathematical principles of musical acoustics. In my own college, for example, students who major in music performance are exempted from the mathematics courses required of all other students, and they are required to take only half as many courses in science. Can we therefore wonder that many of them are innocent of any Pythagorean appreciation of music? Second, we today are aware of historical and cross-cultural disagreements concerning the perceived consonance and dissonance of musical intervals, such as those produced by ratios involving the number 7, for example, so that ancient Pythagorean theories strike us as provincial and naive. Third, we are in a scientific position to understand the underlying cause of the series of consonant ratios, a cause that was unknown to the ancients. That cause is the "overtone series," first described at the beginning of the 18th century. Discovery of the overtone series offered much new insight into Pythagorean principles of consonance and dissonance, and it greatly extends our capacities for acoustical analysis, but in the process it also tends to demystify certain musical phenomena.

Before examining this elegant natural phenomenon, the overtone series, we might pause to ask whether scientific knowledge of the overtone series augments or diminishes the ancient Pythagorean's sense of religious wonder. A general form of this question is whether scientific understanding enriches or impoverishes religious wonder and sense of the sublime. The answer depends upon the kind of religion. For radical theists who see God as a cause and origin apart from creation – as a transcendent God whose plan for creation is arbitrary and whose creative design is inscrutable except by direct revelation – scientific understanding often poses a religious threat. The more we know by scientific means about creation's immanent principles,

15. G. S. Kirk, J. E. Raven, and M. Schofield, *The Presocratic Philosophers*, 2d ed. (Cambridge: Cambridge University Press, 1983), 326.

16. *Free Choice of the Will* 2.11.125, p.64.

17. *On Music* 6.11.33, tr. Robert C. Taliaferro, in *Fathers of the Church*, ed. Roy Joseph Deferrari (New York: Christian Heritage, 1947), 4:356.

the less remains attributable to the transcendent God's actions. For theists of broader perspective, however, and for pantheists and panentheists, with their sense of God's immanence, scientific knowledge can enrich religious wonder and sense of the sublime. Thrill may accompany every new discovery within God's realm of being and life, and a sense of mystery grows with the sense of endless possibilities for such discovery. During his student days at Yale, Edwards wrote in this spirit of scientific discovery and religious wonder: "For to find out the reasons of things, in Natural Philosophy, is only to find out the proportion of God's acting."[18]

## *The Overtone Series*

In their study of musical acoustics Siegmund Levarie and Ernst Levy call the overtone series a kind of Periodic Table, but of "musical tones instead of chemical elements." They also call it a spiritual "icon."[19] I take them to mean that the overtone series is an object of contemplation that discloses transcendent truth. In any case, their word "icon" suggests why analysis of the overtone series is an ingredient in our consideration of music as sacramental. The deuterocanonical book of Sirach asserts:

When the Lord created his works from the beginning,
    and, in making them, determined their boundaries,
he arranged his works in an eternal order. . . .
They do not crowd one another,
    and they never disobey his word. (Sir 16.26-8)

Like the periodic table of chemical elements, the overtone series is a part of creation's order – given, enduring, and constant. Its members do not "crowd one another" and never "disobey the Creator's word." Thus contemplation of the overtone series may be iconic or epiphanic, disclosing something of divine *sophia* and *logos*, something of what Edwards calls "the proportion of God's acting."

Graphic presentation of the overtone series is considerably simpler than that of the chemist's periodic table:

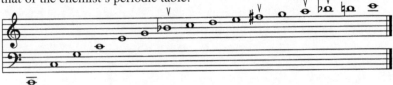

**Figure 3. The Overtone Series.**

18. *Notes on the Mind*, in *Jonathan Edwards: Representative Selections*, ed. Clarence H. Faust and Thomas H. Johnson, revised ed. (New York: Hill and Wang, 1962), 29.

19. *Tone: A Study in Musical Acoustics*, 2d ed. (Kent, OH: Kent State University Press, 1980), 38.

The tones of the overtone series are ingredient to all regular or "periodic" vibrations, such as vibrations of strings on musical instruments, including the Pythagoreans' monochord. For convenience I have chosen to illustrate the series arising from the tone of C, but any periodic tone, of any pitch, generates an exactly equivalent series. Let us note for future reference that the tones marked with an inverted caret, such as the seventh tone and the eleventh, are noticeably flat in comparison with the nearly corresponding tones used throughout western harmonic music – a discrepancy we shall consider in detail in Chapters 4 and 5.

The tones of the overtone series are called harmonic "partials," since they arise from a string's vibration in partial segments of its length as well as throughout its entire length. Non-periodic vibrating bodies, such as bells and other percussive instruments, give rise to partials as well, but they are non-regular, non-harmonic partials, often extremely complex. We shall see that music made with non-periodic instruments differs considerably from music made with periodic instruments. That the allegorical figure of Music on the Royal Portal of Chartres is portrayed with both a periodic lyre and non-periodic bells, therefore, is a sculptural touch symbolic of musical comprehensiveness.

For the moment let us restrict our attention to a periodic string secured at both ends, as on the monochord. The string's vibration along its entire length generates the lowest tone in the overtone series, called the fundamental tone. The string's vibration in two segments, with stationary nodes at its ends and its midpoint, generates the second partial in the series, also called the first overtone. Vibration of the string in three segments, with stationary nodes at its ends and at the one-third and two-thirds points, generates the third partial, also called the second overtone. And so on – in theory, at least – to infinity. The monochord's movable bridge allows an experimenter to adjust the string length to match the various nodal lengths of a vibrating string. Each nodal length can thus be made a fundamental length, and its tone thereby becomes clearly audible for means of comparison. Experimenters in the early 18th century discovered that any regular string set in motion and allowed to move without constraint vibrates in numerous of these partial segments simultaneously, thus generating a series. Small variations among actual strings, and large variations among the physical properties of the sounding boards that support them, cause variations in occurrence, intonation, and comparative loudness among the many partials, and these variations – together with details of each musical instrument's characteristic envelope of attack and decay – account in turn for the varying tonal quality or colour that we call "timbre."

From the overtone series we may see why its notes are related in the whole number ratios that so greatly impressed the ancient Pythagoreans. A string secured at both ends can vibrate as one whole segment, and as two segments, and as three segments, and so on, each mode of vibration generating its own harmonic partial in a never-ending sequence of integers: 1, 2, 3. . . . The ratio for the musical interval between any two partials or tones is simply comprised of the numbers of the two partials involved. In Figure 3, partial number 1 is a C, partial number 2 is a higher C, and the vibrational ratio between them is 1:2. Partial number 2 is a C, and partial number 3 is a G, and the ratio between them is 2:3. And so on, throughout the entire overtone series. Thus, all intervals between the tones of the overtone series represent ratios of whole numbers. We call the ratios of adjacent intervals of the overtone series, arranged in sequence (as in Figure 2), the "harmonic series."

As we have noted, the first interval of the overtone series, that between the fundamental tone and the second partial, we call the octave. Levarie and Levy write of this interval: "The two tones forming an octave achieve an identity that transcends their distinctness."[20] When people with different vocal ranges, such as sopranos and basses, join in singing a melody, for example, they instinctively sing in octaves, and consider themselves to be singing the same tune. Or to consider another example, most cultures that name the tones of their music give octave notes the same name: the name of "C," in the case of our graphic depiction of the overtone series in Figure 3, or the name of "do," in the case of the do-re-mi system of tonal naming we call solfeggio. Thus we speak of the "identity" or "equivalence" of octave notes.

Levarie and Levy assert that the octave is a universal fundament of music, "not only in Western tradition but in all civilisations of all times."[21] Yehudi Menuhin, on the other hand, observed that Thais "can tolerate octaves that seem out of tune to us."[22] Unable to observe "all civilisations of all times," particularly of future times, perhaps we should be a bit more exact than Levarie and Levy. Mathematically we may accept their assertion that the octave, as the interval defined by the first two partials of the overtone series, is "a cosmic absolute."[23] Experientially we may also say with Levarie and Levy that "all music systems are based" on the octave,[24] provided that we add a couple of qualifiers: so far as we know; and insofar as human ears, across epochs and cultures, seem to have tolerated only small departures from the octave's tuning of 1:2.

In his treatise *On the Trinity*, Augustine expresses wonderment over the natural, God-given identity of the octave, which he calls "the harmony between the single and the double":

20. *Tone*, 15.
21. p.15.
22. Yehudi Menuhin and Curtis W. Davis, *The Music of Man* (Toronto: Methuen, 1979), 50.
23. Levarie and Levy, *Tone*, 15.
24. p.15.

That which I mean by this coadaptation is what the Greeks call *harmonian*. But this is neither the time nor the place to show how important is the harmony between the single and the double . . . which has been naturally so implanted in us (by whom indeed, if not by Him who created us?), that not even the illiterate can remain unaware of it, whether they themselves are singing, or whether they are listening to others; for by means of it the treble and the bass voices blend together, and anyone who sounds a note that does not harmonise with it commits an offence not only against the musical art of which most people are ignorant, but against our very sense of hearing. It would require a long treatise, however, to prove this, but one familiar with the subject can demonstrate it to the ear itself on a properly adjusted monochord.[25]

With his reference to a "properly adjusted monochord," Augustine secures his place in our Christian gallery of Pythagorean experimenters and theorists: "We have the evidence of the world itself in all its ordered change and movement . . . which bears a kind of silent testimony to the fact of its creation, and proclaims that its maker could have been none other than God, the ineffably and invisibly great, the ineffably and invisibly beautiful."[26]

## *Division of the Diapason*

While the interval of 1:2 seems fundamental to all musical systems, the ways in which different cultures divide that basic unit into smaller intervals vary widely. Much depends upon two factors. The first is whether a culture's instruments produce mostly periodic vibrations, as with the keyboard, string, brass, and woodwind instruments of a symphony orchestra, or mostly non-periodic vibrations, as with bells, gongs, and the myriad of other percussive tonal instruments that we hear in much of the world's folk music. The second factor is whether a culture's music is predominately harmonic, consisting in sustained tones that sound simultaneously in chords, as is the case with most music deriving from post-medieval European culture, or predominately melodic, consisting in transient tones that sound successively, as is the case with many folk musics of the world.

Let us first consider the most common ways in which musical systems of the world divide the basic unit of 1:2, and then consider certain wider variations. I have been careful to refer to the basic interval of 1:2 as "the interval we call the octave," since the word "octave" prejudices discus-

25. *The Trinity* 4.2.4, tr. Stephen McKenna, in *The Fathers of the Church*, ed. Roy Joseph Deferrari (Washington: Catholic University of America Press, 1963), 45:134

26. *Concerning the City of God against the Pagans* 11.4, tr. Henry Bettenson (New York: Penguin Books, 1984), 432.

sion of the question we are now entering upon. Our question is how different musical systems divide that basic interval of 1:2. "Octave" derives from the Latin for "eight," however, and thus presupposes division into 8 steps (including the fundamental tone at the bottom of the interval and its equivalent at the top), thereby prejudicing, if not predetermining outright, the results of our inquiry. A neutral and therefore preferable term for the interval 1:2 is the Greek *diapason*, meaning "through all" – namely, through all the steps, of whatever number and size they may be, from a tone to its repetition at a frequency ratio of 2:1. Thus John Dryden uses the term in his *Song for St. Cecilia's Day, 1687*:

From Harmony, from heav'nly Harmony

    This universal Frame began:

    From Harmony to Harmony

Through all the compass of the Notes it ran,

The Diapason closing full in Man.[27]

Here I shall continue to use the more familiar word "octave" because it is convenient and virtually impossible to avoid, but we must be careful to guard against its prejudicial implication.

Among the musical systems of the world, by far the most common divisions of the octave are into five, seven, or twelve intervals.[28] Let us first consider division of the octave into seven intervals or steps. In our illustration of the overtone series in Figure 3 we may notice that each successive octave – C to C to C to C – includes all the same intervals as the octave just below, but with a new tone appearing within each interval. That is, the first octave consists of the empty interval C to C. The second octave consists of C to C, with G between. The third consists of C to G, with E between, plus G to C, with B-flat between. And so on. Thus successive octaves accumulate more and more tones in the universal pattern of a geometric series.

As we have seen, the second partial, relating to the first in the vibrational ratio of 2:1, creates the octave, the fundamental tone "in miniature."[29] The third partial, G, relates to the second partial, C, in ratio 3:2. We call the interval between these latter two tones, C to G, the 5th (again, let us note, in language that, unless we are careful, prejudges the question of diapasonal division). The 5th is an interval by which the Shofar summons the religious to Jewish festival. It was the first harmonic interval allowed in medieval Christian music. These primal uses of the 5th are not accidental.

27. *The Poems of John Dryden*, ed. James Kinsley (Oxford: Clarendon, 1958), 2:538.

28. See the cross-cultural surveys in Elizabeth May, ed., *Musics of Many Cultures* (Berkeley: University of California Press, 1980) and in William P. Malm, *Music Cultures of the Pacific, the Near East, and Asia*, 2d ed. (Englewood Cliffs, NJ: Prentice-Hall, 1977).

29. Bloch, *Essays*, 184.

The third partial, and therefore the interval of the 5th, is intrinsic in the overtone series generated by almost every periodic tone that sounds. If we listen for the 5th, sometimes we can hear it and sometimes not. Most often our awareness of the intrinsic 5th is subliminal. In rare circumstances, however, the 5th is as prominent as the tonic. Buddhist monks of Tibet provide an instance widely admired. Chanting in a remarkably low vocal range, some of the monks are able to sustain a tone and reinforce the partials in the vibrations of their vocal cords in such a way as to bring the 5th into clear audibility. For this effect to be impressive, the monks need a building with acoustics resonant enough to reinforce the 5th. The relatively dead spaces of most United States performance halls, I have noticed, give the monks a difficult time with their chordal chanting.

In this connection, the resonance of medieval stone chapels and churches must surely have played a role in the introduction of the 5th into Christian liturgical music. The 5th is always in the air around singers, requiring only a resonant building to render it audible. For other voices to sing the 5th as a new tone along with the original, as happened in the liturgical music of medieval Christianity known as *organum*, is thus a completely natural first step beyond singing in unison and octaves. Visitors to a truly vital acoustical space, of which the Crusader church of St. Anne in Jerusalem is the most astonishing I have ever encountered, may discover that with a bit of low humming with open lips, and some experimenting with the placement and curling of their tongues, they can produce a clearly audible 5th. (Homebound readers might experiment in a resonant bathroom, or in the bare stairwell of some nearby hospital or hotel.) I have also heard, in another acoustical space – the football stadium used for my college's commencement exercises – an echo that returns the complex of pitches that comprise spoken language as a distinct intonation on a single musical tone, and I am led to wonder whether this acoustical phenomenon might have influenced the origins of single-tone chanting or "cantillation" in certain religious traditions, including my own Episcopal tradition.

But let us return to our analysis. The fourth partial of the overtone series is another C. The ratio between this C and the fundamental C is 4:1. However, the ratio between this C and the third partial of the series, G, is 4:3. This interval within the overtone series we call the 4th. Amongst its first four partials, therefore, the overtone series has now provided a basic repertory of intervals: the octave, the 5th, and the 4th. The Pythagoreans marvelled at these most basic musical intervals, with their aural consonance and mathematical simplicity. As ratios of the four smallest whole numbers, their proportions are simplicity itself: 1:2, 2:3, and 3:4. Tradition credits Pythagoras with bringing from Babylon the discovery that by using low multiples of these whole numbers – namely, 6, 8, 9, and 12 – he could combine these basic proportions in a master musical proportion: 6 is to 8 as 9 is to 12 (6:8::9:12).[30] This master proportion encodes and reiterates the three fundamental intervals. The octave, 1:2, is equivalent to 6:12. The 5th, 2:3, is equivalent to 6:9 and 8:12. The 4th, 3:4, is equivalent to 6:8 and 9:12. Whoever wrote the classical dialogue *Epinomis*, questionably attributed to Plato, refers to this elegant musical proportion in a tone of religious wonder, calling it "a device of God's contriving which breeds amazement in those who fix their gaze upon it."[31] In Plato's authentic dialogue *Timaeus*, he invokes the master musical proportion in his account of the Creator's designing of the universe: "And whereas the insertion of these intervals formed fresh intervals in the former intervals, that is to say, intervals of 3:2 and 4:3 and 9:8, He went on to fill up the 4:3 intervals with 9:8 intervals."[32] In this account of the Creator's filling the diapason with intervals of ratio 9:8, which our Figure 2 identifies as major whole tones, Plato's underlying principle seems clear: contemplating the mathematics of music constitutes a silent disclosure of the Creator's cosmic order. This is what we mean by music's sacramental silence.

This most basic repertory of three intervals from the overtone series is sufficient to produce all the tones that are thought to have composed ancient Greek melodies. That is, a Greek flutist could generate all the notes needed for melody by stepping about the flute's limited range in various intervals of octave, 5th, and 4th. We can do the same to generate the seven tones that comprise our most common melodies today. C up a 5th gives us G. G down a 4th gives us D. D up a 5th gives us A. A down a 4th gives us E. E up a 5th gives us B. Finally, upper C down a 5th gives us F. And so, within the span of an octave, we have generated seven different tones that fill the diapason with the small intervals or steps of a scale: C D E F G A B C. The scale requires fine tuning – a challenge that fascinated the ancient Greeks and has perplexed musicians and music theorists ever since – but we shall save the immensely complicated issue of tunings and temperaments for our discussion of harmony in Chapter 5.

So far we have considered articulation of the diapason into seven steps. As for articulation into five and twelve steps, it will help us to realise we can analyse the world's various musics by two distinct methods, divisive and cyclical. Near Eastern and Indian tonal systems, as well as those of ancient Greece, are generally of the divisive kind, that is, they are "based on the divisions of a vibrating string."[33] In contrast, the tonal system characteristic of Chinese music is generally cyclical, "created from a cycle of tones generated by blowing across the tops of a set of tubes closed at

30. Ernest G. McClain, *The Pythagorean Plato: Prelude to the Song Itself* (Stony Brook, NY: Nicolas Hays, 1978), 8-9.
31. *Epinomis* 990e, quoted in McClain, *The Pythagorean Plato*, 8.
32. *Timaeus* 36a-b, tr. R. G. Bury (London: William Heinemann, 1942), 69.
33. Malm, *Music Cultures*, 146.

one end (like a bottle), whose lengths were arranged in a set mathematical proportion."[34] The harmonic system of European-derived music is also intimately related to cyclical generation of tones. In another artistic touch symbolic of musical comprehensiveness – like the Chartres personification of Music holding both periodic lyre and non-periodic bells – the central figure in the frontispiece of Kircher's *Musurgia Universalis* (Figure 1) holds both divisive strings and cyclical pipes.

We must go on to say that in the world's actual musics these two methods of tonal generation, divisive and cyclical, are by no means clearly distinguishable, still less separable or mutually exclusive, and are probably not a matter of conscious procedure among most practicing musicians. For purposes of analysis, however, distinguishing the two methods is useful. Both methods of tonal generation can account for articulation of the diapason into seven, five, and twelve steps. In our derivation of the seven-step division of the octave we have been using essentially divisive procedures. For convenience, let us turn to cyclic procedures to gain corresponding insight into the diapason's articulation into five and twelve steps.

Accordingly, let us switch our experimental instrument from the ancient monochord to the modern piano. For convenience let us begin at the keyboard's lowest F – an arbitrary choice, except that it will keep our exercise on the piano's white keys for as long as possible. Using the 5th, that most basic and most consonant Pythagorean interval after the octave, we may make successive steps up the keyboard. The first five notes we obtain by this stepwise procedure are F, C, G, D, A, and our hand will have traversed a bit more than two octaves. If we collect these five tones into the range of a single octave and arrange them in ascending order, we obtain F G A C D. The cycle of 5ths has generated a five-tone or "pentatonic" scale.

The world's earliest known reference to scale intervals comes from a Chinese source that names the tones of this pentatonic scale.[35] The same pentatonic scale is popular in countless musical cultures of the world, including my own. And for good reason. Its four upper tones are siblings, spawned by the consonant 5th, who have not yet wandered far from their parenting fundamental. Sounding together, they are a consonant family. As a result, any melody employing this pentatonic scale is essentially pleasing to the ear. The black notes of a piano keyboard comprise a pentatonic scale of this same pattern. Thus the black-note-glissandos and the up-and-down rolling-and-tapping ditty that children love to play with their fists on the black keys. Piano owners often flinch, but they ought to be grateful that these rudimentary improvisations are not being undertaken on the piano's non-pentatonic and therefore more

34. p.146.
35. Kuo-huang Han and Lindy Li Mark, "Evolution and Revolution in Chinese Music," in May, ed., *Musics of Many Cultures*, 11.

cacophonous white keys.

In Chinese culture this pentatonic scale is heard in a range of invention that far transcends the scale's apparent simplicity. (We must keep saying "this pentatonic scale," since there are others. Softly sound and sustain the descending five-note scale C B A F E, for example, and a different pentatonic scale transports us to Japan.).[36] We do not have to visit China to enjoy this pentatonic scale, however. "Amazing Grace" uses it, without sounding Asian in the least. Similarly the Scottish "Ye Banks and Braes O'Bonnie Doon" and "Auld Lang Syne," together with a host of British and American folk ballads, such as "Silver Dagger" and "Wildwood Flower." One reason that the tunes of many popular and country-and-western songs sound so similar is that a remarkable number of them – from "Tennessee Waltz" right down to guitar riffs in rock music – avoid melodic adventures that would carry them out far beyond the pentatonic safety net, while at the same time they often lack the distinctive melodic profiles that characterise the strongest traditional ballads. That the songs are nevertheless quite distinctive is owing less to their tunes than to their varied lyrics, to the highly characteristic timbres of different voices, to variations in arrangements and bands, and to producers' choices relating to mixing and recording.

Recalling that in the end we are relating this musical analysis to our theme of music's sacramental potential, let us add two more upward steps in the cycle of 5ths from the A where we left it, namely, E and B. The cycle has now produced the seven tones F, C, G, D, A, E, and B, and our hand has traversed a bit more than three octaves. If again we collect our notes into the range of a single octave and arrange them in ascending order, we obtain F G A B C D E. The cycle of 5ths has generated a seven-tone scale like the one we earlier derived from successive up-and-down applications of the 5th and the 4th within a single octave. We call this scale a diatonic scale (*dia*, "through," *tonic*, "the tones"), since its seven notes fill the octave with intervals more nearly the same size than is the case with the intervals of pentatonic scales. These seven notes are fundamental to most European-derived music, and to a great deal of the rest of the world's music as well. Maurice Ravel pays them ravishing homage at the opening of his ballet *Daphnis and Chloe*. The harp slowly plucks the first six ascending 5ths, which are sustained and accumulated by the orchestra's muted strings, as muted horns offer distant comment. Then the flute joins the harp to cap the cycle of 5ths with its seventh note, celebrating this diatonic completion with a shimmering new timbre.

Like the pentatonic, the diatonic scale is a far richer musical resource than might at first seem likely. In part this is because its seven notes produce not only the scale we have specified, the scale beginning on F, but a

36. See Malm, *Music Cultures*, 188.

scale beginning and ending on each of the other six notes as well. Thus we have seven species of diatonic scale with seven intervals each – or with eight notes each, since as we have said a scale is topped off with its beginning note repeated up an octave. Each of these seven-tone scales differs from the rest, since its pattern of intervals is unique. These various species of diatonic scale underlie the basic "modes" of western music (not, as we shall see in a moment, to be confused with modes of similar names in the music of ancient Greece):

F to F, Lydian Mode: F G A B C D E F
G to G, Mixolydian Mode: G A B C D E F G
A to A, Aeolian Mode: A B C D E F G A
B to B, Locrian Mode: B C D E F G A B
C to C, Ionian Mode: C D E F G A B C
D to D, Dorian Mode: D E F G A B C D
E to E, Phrygian Mode: E F G A B C D E

**Figure 4. Basic Musical Modes.**

The Ionian Mode we commonly call the major scale. The Aeolian Mode is one of a variety of minor scales, about which more in Chapter 4. The Myxolydian Mode, together with the Aeolian, characterises much Celtic music. The Phrygian Mode characterises much music of Moorish and Spanish derivation. The Dorian mode gives us the French carol, "Sing We Now of Christmas." And so on. In the history of Christianity, we hear some of these modes in the august tradition of plainchant. Beyond European-derived music, I have heard the Phrygian and Mixolydian modes in music of India, the Dorian mode in music of Senegal, the Mixolydian mode in music of Tanzania.

The further we go in our discussion, the more we shall come to appreciate that these musical modes are far from simple. Though the west inherited the names for its modes from ancient Greece, the musical scales we have tabulated here are not the modes for which the Greeks used the same names. Exactly what the ancient Greek modes were remains a matter of considerable debate. It seems that they were nearer to musical genres than to mere scales. In this respect the modes of ancient Greece were rather like the *raga* in the music of India: "The term *raga* . . . is both the basic scale and the basic melodic structure. The term is derived from a Sanskrit root, *rang*, which means to colour with emotion; thus the name implies many features beyond those of actual pitches."[37] Of ancient Greek music Eric Werner writes: "The tangle of the terminology concerning modes and modality is truly

37. Malm, *Music Cultures*, 98.

unbelievable."[38] For now all this need not concern us. Our concern here is to appreciate how the natural overtone series gives rise to the octave and the 5th as fundamental consonant intervals, and how a reiterative cycle of 5ths, regathered within a single octave, gives rise to the five-note and seven-note scales that structure a great deal of the music we hear, particularly the folk and popular and church music of the west.

Let us pursue the cycle of 5ths to its conclusion. We had reached the note of B, some three octaves above the fundamental tone of F. Resuming there, if we take five additional steps of a 5th up the keyboard we shall obtain two results. First, we shall accumulate five new tones, for a total of twelve. These five additional tones carry us through the various black keys of the piano, adding "sharps" and "flats" to the seven diatonic notes we generated previously. Second, with step number twelve, we arrive back at the beginning tone of F, seven octaves up the keyboard. (Or we would, if the keyboard extended far enough. The standard piano keyboard falls a 4th short of the required span, so we must extend it in imagination.) Thus the cycle of 5ths generates twelve tones on our keyboard, then reaches F again and begins a repetition of its cyclical pattern. We must emphasise "on our keyboard," since the keyboard is in reality a bit of a cheat and gives rise to unjustified expectations. A cycle of theoretically precise 5ths, defined by the Pythagorean ratio of 2:3, does not quite attain closure at its twelfth iteration. Instead it narrowly misses closure and continues in a spiral of new tones to infinity. As with the related question of fine tuning the scale within the octave, we shall save this complicated issue of the non-closure of the cycle of 5ths for later, namely, for our discussion of dissonance in Chapter 4 and of temperament in Chapter 5.

Here we may simply observe that while that the twelve tones generated by a "completed" cycle of 5ths comprise the fundamental repertory of tones we encounter in most of the world's musics, these twelve tones are fine tuned in widely varying fashions. In ornamented melodies, such as Indian *ragas*, Islamic *qawwali*, and American blues, the tones are "bent" or "warped" for colouristic and expressive effects. Still, most music draws upon a fundamental repertory of twelve distinct tones, or upon sub-repertories of seven or five. The only music I have heard that seems quite independent of a twelve-note repertory of tones comes from Korea. Players of the traditional Korean instrument, the *kayagum*, together with the singers they accompany, seem at times to lurch about within the octave with complete freedom from assigned pitches of any kind. To my ears, the effect seems slaphappy. I can imagine that to *kayagum* players, traditions of twelve-note music such as my own must sound straitjacketed. The music-ologist Kang-sook Lee writes that "Korean music-grammar . . . is totally

38. *The Sacred Bridge: The Interdependence of Liturgy and Music and Syna-gogue and Church during the First Millennium* (New York: Columbia University Press, 1959), 374.

different from that of any other country. Indeed, the differences are so great that Westerners might initially reject the validity of the system."[39] For all its unique qualities, however, Korean music is nonetheless dependent upon the identity of the octave and orients itself about a fundamental tone, and the *kayagum* is a zither of twelve strings, usually tuned pentatonically.

The basic repertory of twelve basic tones makes possible "chromatic" scales, so called because of the tonal colour (Gk: *chroma*) the five additional notes add to diatonic scales. In the European-derived music that we call "classical" – that is, harmonic music formalised by exact notation – use of the chromatic scale was taken to one kind of limit in the 19th century by Chopin, whose music maximises chromaticism to achieve exquisite colouristic effects. In the 20th century, the twelve-note repertory was taken to another kind of limit by "twelve-tone" composers such as Arnold Schoenberg, whose music democratises the tones in order to escape from traditional western harmony, which he regarded as exhausted and burdensome. In both these composers, however, the twelve tones yielded up by the cycle of 5ths remain axiomatic.

## *Melody and Harmony*

I have spoken of Schoenberg's revolt against traditional western harmony. The basis of traditional western harmony is the chord, that is, a group of tones that are simultaneous and sustained. From our discussion of the overtone series we may recall that every time a periodic tone sounds, a chord sounds with it, namely, the chord consisting of the tone and its overtones. We know that most of the overtones escape our conscious notice. Due to the human ear's capacities, and to the capacities of instruments designed and pitched to accommodate the human ear, only the lowermost ten to sixteen partials play significant roles in our musical experiences. For trained and sensitive musical ears, closest attention to a low note forcibly struck on the piano can discern no more than the first five or six partials. This does not mean that additional partials are insignificant, however. We have seen that their presence and relative strength help to determine a tone's timbre. Every tone, therefore, and especially every tone with colourful timbre, is a sounding chord.

What chord? The overtone series discloses the answer: a major chord. If the fundamental tone or "tonic" is C, as in Figure 3, the first six partials of its series are C G C E, a major chord. Indeed, all the sixteen partials represented in Figure 3, sounded together and sustained, produce an impression that is essentially major, albeit a bit muddy. In this sense, just as the first four partials of the overtone series produce the octave and the 5th as the most fundamental intervals, with the 4th also making an appearance

---

39. "Certain Experiences in Korean Music," in May, ed., *Musics of Many Cultures*, 32.

in their midst, so the overtone series produces the major as the most fundamental chord. Furthermore, if the 5th is sounded as a fundamental tone, its timbre also resonates with an accompanying major chord. So, too, with the 4th. These three chords – generated by the overtones of the tonic, the 5th, and the 4th – have proven to be the fundaments of western harmony. They are commonly labelled I, IV, and V.

Being predominantly chordal, European-derived music is regulated by the phenomena of consonance and dissonance. Consonance means "sounding together." Thus the concept of consonance presupposes simultaneous tones and implies that the chords are sustained long enough for their tones to interact audibly. More specifically, we usually take consonance to mean "sounding well together."

In contrast to the largely harmonic traditions of European-derived music, many other musical dialects of the world give predominance not to harmony but to melody. Where tones are transient and successive, rather than simultaneous and sustained, harmonic consonance and dissonance tend to be of less importance than other musical qualities, such as melodic and rhythmic variety and tonal and ornamental colour. Melodic music, being less tightly bound to principles of consonance grounded in fundamental acoustical laws, is more easily conditioned by its cultural settings, more various and locally distinctive, whereas harmonic music, being more closely bound to the universal overtone series, more easily crosses cultural boundaries without radical alteration. Music thus gains harmonic universality at the expense of melodic distinctiveness, and vice versa.

In his Charles Eliot Norton Lectures, delivered at Harvard University in 1973, Leonard Bernstein states that in Europe around 1700 "music reached its tonal adulthood. . .",[40] meaning by "tonal" what we are here calling "harmonic". But we must be circumspect. As with the attaining of any adulthood, some things are gained, but others are lost – namely, childhood with its freedoms, and alternative kinds of possible adulthood. As European music attained tonal adulthood, with its extraordinary wealth of harmonic resources, it lost certain freedoms and alternatives that characterise other musical traditions. Paul Hindemith, in his earlier turn at the Norton Lectures (1949-50), brings us closer to the full truth when he compares western harmonic tradition to the melodically richer traditions of much of the rest of the world: "When harmony was introduced to our Western music, this wealth of melody . . . shrank to forms of comparatively little significance."[41] Harmonic wealth in exchange for melodic riches may be a perfectly reasonable trade-off. But when European-derived music loses its harmonic wealth without significant enrichment in melodic, rhythmic, and colouristic variety, as has so widely happened in west-

40. *The Unanswered Question: Six Talks at Harvard* (Cambridge: Harvard University Press, 1976), 25.
41. *A Composer's World: Horizons and Limitations* (Cambridge: Harvard University Press, 1952), 116.

ern culture's popular musics, then the tradition is relatively impoverished.

Here we come to the amazing gravitational pull of the most rudimentary element of harmonic music, the sequence of chords constructed on the tonic, the 4th, the 5th, and back again to the tonic: I-IV-V-I. The history of western classical music offers examples of composers stuck in the rut of this rudimentary chordal progression, to the neglect of harmonic music's greater variety. Certain passages of Rossini, for example, are laughable in this respect. Beethoven also composes many pages of music within the compass of this basic harmonic pattern. He, however, compensates for harmonic constriction with monumental architectonic structure enriched with endless melodic and ornamental inventiveness and variation.

It is when we come to more popular music, I believe, that western musical impoverishment becomes most obvious. Beginning guitarists who can master the three fundamental chords, for example, have perhaps half of all country-and-western songs at their disposal. Similarly for beginning organists learning the most popular Christian hymns. Much of popular and rock music suffers a similar kind of harmonic agoraphobia. Only the uncommonly inventive popular artist enriches the three fundamental chords of western harmony with more than one or two in addition. Mirthless promotional photographs betray no sense of irony over rock groups who struggle to project individual disaffection and social non-conformity by endlessly reiterating our musical culture's three most conventional chords. Rhythmic compulsion, distortions of traditional timbres, and volcanic amplification offer compensations for this harmonic impoverishment, with, it must be admitted, remarkable popular success.

When popular music collapses into harmonic constriction without corresponding melodic compensation, it tends to become merely an occasion for exhibiting a personality or vociferating a message. The logical outcome is the rap genre of the 1990s. Rap can perhaps claim more integrity than most, however, since it pretends less musically and openly promotes declamation and self-aggrandisement to primary significance. In what remains for me a refreshing contrast among our culture's popular musical genres, jazz does best at transcending harmonic music's most rudimentary pull. Jazz is a cross-cultural art form, and as such, a treasury of harmonic as well as melodic, rhythmic, and colouristic riches.

Our point in all this is that the powerful gravitational pull of harmonic music's most basic chords is an empirical indication that the fundaments of music are grounded in acoustical realities, given and enduring. Those acoustical realities also shape the composition of harmonic music. In his masterful textbook of musical acoustics, Donald Hall specifies acoustical bases for a number of western music's standard harmonic progressions and cadences.[42] Hall also shows how the art of musical counterpoint, of

42. *Musical Acoustics: An Introduction* (Belmont, CA: Wadsworth, 1980), 471-
    3.

which Bach was the supreme master, and the art of orchestration, for which Bartok provides Hall's example, are grounded in acoustical realities:

> Here then is good acoustical reason for some traditional rules of orchestration and counterpoint. To keep two musical lines distinct, assign them to instruments of contrasting timbres or attack characteristics, and make the parts move in contrary motion. Smooth and similar timbres (especially on electronic organs) or parallel part motion (especially parallel octaves and fifths) make it too easy for voices to fuse together and lose their individuality. Occasionally, a composer may want two parts to fuse into a single musical line and so deliberately write for similar instruments in parallel. For a marvellous example, listen to the second movement ("Game of Pairs") of Bartok's *Concerto for Orchestra* (1944). I can almost hear each duet as a single melodic line played by some new instrument with a strange, exotic timbre.[43]

Hall is arguing – persuasively, I believe – that in setting compositional standards for western counterpoint and orchestration, Bach and Bartok were at once musical discoverers and musical inventors: discoverers of fundamental acoustical verities, given and enduring; inventors within the boundless universe of musical creativity arising out of those verities.

Even western atonal music, music that ignores or defies the traditions of western harmonic composition, is not exempt from grounding in acoustical verities. In his pathfinding *Three Pieces for Piano*, Opus 11, of 1908, Schoenberg deliberately abandoned the western tradition of harmonic progression and cadence by treating the twelve tones of the scale with equality. He gives no harmonic preference to the tonic, the 4th, and the 5th, for example. Still the twelve tones he uses are those generated by the cycle of 5ths, and the octave, given by the overtone series, is still absolute – that is, Schoenberg treats octave notes as identical or equivalent pitches. Pierre Boulez observes that in Schoenberg's *Pierrot lunaire*, Opus 21, of 1912, Schoenberg pushed still farther along the atonal path:

> I note three remarkable phenomena in the writing of these scores: the principle of constantly efficacious variation, or non-repetition; the preponderance of "anarchic" intervals – presenting the greatest tension relative to the tonal world – and progressive elimination of the octave, the tonal world par excellence; and a manifest attempt to construct contrapuntally.[44]

Yet as Hall has shown, acoustical laws set basic parameters for contrapuntal construction. Even more fundamentally, acoustical laws establish the atonal composer's very orientation: atonal paths are oriented in relation to tonality,

---

43. *Musical Acoustics*, 441.
44. *Notes of an Apprenticeship*, tr. Herbert Weinstock (New York: Alfred A. Knopf, 1968), 269.

defined as always *away*. In the words of Boulez, atonal music is defined by its "tension relative to the tonal world."

During the decades since Schoenberg, composers have explored a wide variety of musical alternatives to the basic harmonic system arising directly from the overtone series. Recently, however, some composers have reacted against these "wrong-note modernists." Music of "minimalist" composers has gained considerable public approbation by a deliberate return to fundamental harmonic chords, repeating and repeating them, with subtle alterations, variations, colourations, and borrowings from other musical cultures to impart new life. Thus recent compositional history serves to remind us that the overtone series is given and enduring. Indeed, it seems inescapable.

### *Musical Particularity and Universality*

Is the overtone series in fact inescapable? That is, do all musical systems come under the sway of its basic principles? I believe they do. The ways in which they do, however, vary immensely. We have already considered the complicated example of the Korean *kayagum*, which seems at times independent of the twelve notes of the chromatic scale and yet is dependent upon the identity of the octave, gravitates to a tonic key, and utilises pentatonic tuning. Let us explore this issue of musical particularity and musical universality with the aim of coming to analogous questions concerning issues of religious particularity and religious universality.

In 1977 archaeologists working in central China discovered a royal tomb dating from the 5th century BC. It contained percussion, string, and wind instruments, along with "the largest assemblage of bronze bells ever recovered."[45] Now restored, the bells are "the only musical instruments from the Bronze Age that still emit tones close, if not identical, to those heard in antiquity."[46] It appears that the bells' design rested on music theory very much like the Pythagorean theories we have been tracing:

> The inscriptions on Marquis Yi's bells and on his chime stones reflect an elaborate and mathematically elegant system of step intervals (do, re, mi, etc.) that could be related in multiple ways to fixed pitches or keys (C, D, E, etc.). The inscriptions indicate names for 12 notes per octave and sets of up to 12 pitch standards or keys. This system is superficially similar to the 12-tone system of Western classical music. It appears, however, that its principal attraction

---

45. Jenny F. So, "Bells of Bronze Age China," *Archaeology* 47 (January/February, 1994), 44.

46. Lothar von Falkenhausen, "The Sound of Bronze Age Music," *Archaeology* 47 (January/February, 1994), 49. The bells may be heard in composer Tan Dun's *Symphony 1997* (Sony CD SK63368, 1997), written for the ceremonies that reunited Hong Kong with China, 1 July 1997.

lay in its mathematical elegance, which enabled the learned minds
of the time to speculate about music in a complex network of cosmo-
logical correlations. Such musicological ideas, however, probably
had little impact on musical practice.[47]

Close study of the China bells – their design, their inscriptions, and their
sounds – indicates that they probably produced music based upon the pentatonic scale arising from the first five tones of the cycle of 5ths:

Bell chimes throughout the Bronze Age were clearly designed mainly
for playing pentatonic music, i.e. melodies using the five primary
notes do, re, mi, sol, and la. This comes as no surprise, as virtually all
known Chinese music, especially ritual music, is also pentatonic.[48]

These bells give us an indication of the widespread historical and cultural
sway of the overtone series and its associated acoustical and musical
principles.

The bronze-age bells constitute no proof of musical universality, of
course. No single cross-cultural comparison could do that. Discussions of
universality require patient listening to actual musical performances from
the world's myriad cultures. This is the work of ethnomusicologists, and
their discipline is still relatively young. As more and more of their studies
become available, however – and with them more and more recordings of
world music – we are able to make specific comparisons. In 1980 Bruno
Nettl asserted, "Today, after a period in which the particular character of a
music was stressed above all else, the search for universals is again important."[49] Though my experience with musics of the world is amateur and
limited and thus my conclusions must remain tentative, I am sympathetic
toward the conclusion expressed by David P. McAllester:

Let me venture the opinion, first, that there are probably no absolute "universals" in music. I say this simply on the grounds of
human variability and complexity. Any student of man must know
that somewhere, someone is doing something that he calls music
but nobody else would give it that name. That one exception would
be enough to eliminate the possibility of a real universal. But I
think there are plenty of near-universals and, even though such a
term contradicts itself, a near-universal is near enough for our purposes. I will be satisfied if nearly everybody does it.[50]

I would risk going one step further, joining George Herzog in the belief that
we may speak of music as a universal language in countless cultural dialects.[51]

Different musical systems of the world fine tune the notes of the diapason

47. p.49.
48. p.49.
49. "Ethnomusicology: Definitions, Directions, and Problems," in May, ed., *Musics
of Many Cultures*, 2.
50. "Some Thoughts on 'Universals' in Word Music," *Ethnomusicology* 15:3 (September 1971), 379.

with countless microtonal variations, yet as a general rule their melodies draw from a repertory of twelve discrete tones or fewer – specifically, seven or five. Malm notes these basic principles in the tunings and scales of Persian music:

> There are obviously more than twelve pitches in the Persian octave. In practice there are an infinite number (though only 7 are used at one time), for individual performers, like many jazz musicians, have their own interpretations of the "correct" pitches of a given or scale or piece. . . . In performance and in scale constructions, however, it is important to know that such tiny divisions, like the Indian *sruti*, are never actually used individually; rather, they are combined into various kinds of larger seconds to form seven-tone scales. Thus there is actually no microtonal "chromaticism" in pan-Islamic music, as is sometimes indicated in writings about such "oriental" music. This descriptive error is usually caused by the "out-of-tune" sound of Near Eastern Music (when in fact it is being played very accurately and artfully with the varied intervals mentioned above).[52]

Malm elaborates further on the Indian *sruti* or microtone:

> In ancient India, the smallest interval perceptible to the ear was called a *sruti*. Theoretically there were three different sizes of *sruti* and a total tonal vocabulary of 22 such nonequidistant units within an octave. Like Near Eastern theorists . . . , Indian music theorists did not consider the movement just from one *sruti* to an adjacent one as an interval. Rather, two to four *sruti* were combined to form a *svara*, an actual musical interval or step. In musical practice today the complete tonal vocabulary seems to include only twelve tones, though each has a fairly wide range of tolerance as to actual pitch.[53]

Electronic musical devices now easily generate quarter tones and other microtonal intervals at the touch of a key, and none of us can predict what our ears may learn to enjoy as music.[54] Ezra Sims, Harry Partch, and others compose microtonal music for traditional instruments such as cello, flute, and the human voice.[55] In his 1969 composition *Ramifications*, György Ligeti writes for traditional stringed instruments arranged in two small ensembles tuned approximately a quarter-tone apart. The result is a fascinating wash of sound. But such experimental compositions have not as yet established

---

51. Quoted in Bruno Nettl, *The Study of Ethnomusicology* (Chicago: University of Illinois Press, 1983), 43.
52. *Music Cultures*, 74.
53. *Music Cultures*, 95-6.
54. See Anthony Tommasini's review of the American Festival of Microtonal Music, "A Bit Off Key and Proud of It," *The New York Times*, 22 May 1997.
55. Allan Kozinn, "A Challenge for a Cellist: More Notes per Octave," *The New York Times*, 14 March 1998.

microtonal tuning as a widely accepted musical system. Ligeti's description of his intention in fact argues the opposite, namely, that microtonal tuning represents not a new harmonic system but rather "uncertain" harmony, harmony in a state of deliberate decomposition: "That is what I wanted: not music based on quarter-tones but mistuned music, 'uncertain' harmony. What interested me is the effect of music where the tuning systems clash; it is like a body in a state of gradual decomposition. *Ramifications* is an example of decadent art."[56]

One final consideration concerning musical particularity and universality directs us again to the divisive method of generating musical pitches, as contrasted with the cyclical. Microtonal variations of pitch that we hear in the world's different tunings of the twelve tone scale can be shown to arise naturally, like the twelve-tone scale itself, out of acoustical principles relating to the overtone series. In Figure 3 we have seen that the table of consonant intervals and their Pythagorean ratios, involving whole numbers from 1 to 10, is missing the number 7. In Figure 3 we see that the seventh partial of the overtone series produced by C falls between A and A-sharp in the major scale of western harmonic music. It is what we have been calling a microtone. To ears like mine, accustomed to harmonies based upon cyclical repetition of the 5th, this seventh partial sounds distinctly out of tune. To ears accustomed to intervals based upon repeated division of a string, however, this seventh partial may sound quite natural and musical. For example, in music of a traditional Javanese gamelan orchestra, with melodies composed upon a basic five-tone scale of the pattern B C E F and G, I have heard this seventh partial, between A and A-sharp, occasionally ring out as a sixth melodic tone. The musical effect is tingling.

The exotic effect is further heightened by what I hear as a sharpened tuning of F in this Javanese gamelan music. This may be an appearance of the eleventh partial of the overtone series, which is near but unmistakably different from the Pythagorean 4th. Traditional western harmonic music avoids the eleventh partial. Alternatively, however, since our ears do not usually discern elements of the overtone series beyond about the tenth partial, perhaps the sharpened F results not so much from the overtone series as from gamelan ensemble's abundance of tuned percussive instruments, such as gongs and metallophones. We have seen that such instruments are to varying degrees non-periodic and therefore emit non-harmonic overtones. From his research in musical acoustics John R. Pierce explains that in most bells and other bell-like instruments, "pitch is not the frequency of the lowest partial (the *hum tone*), but an average of the frequency separations between some higher partials of the sound of the bell."[57] In a word, bell-like tones and overtones are extremely complex. Like tones

56. Quoted by Stephen Plaistow, programme notes to *Ligeti*, Deutsche Grammophon CD 423 244-2, 1988.
57. *The Science of Musical Sound* (New York: Scientific American Books, 1983), 89.

of the overtone series in periodic instruments, the non-harmonic tones of bells are altogether natural. Unlike tones of the overtone series, however, they are irregular. Therefore they are less universal in their occurrence and far more subject to local variations. I am told that gamelan musicians are extremely sensitive to the subtleties of bell-like tones and tunings, and that gamelan ensembles take pride in their distinctive local variations. Yet local variations by no means place gamelan ensembles beyond the pale of fundamental acoustical laws. Gamelan ensembles play and sing what seems to me a particularly exotic dialect of musical language.

Let us summarise our discussion of musical particularity and universality. We have considered three factors that help us account for local variations among musical dialects. The first is whether the musical dialect is more amenable to analysis in relation to cyclical musical derivation, which generates the twelve tones of harmonic music, or in relation to a divisive musical derivation, which more easily incorporates more exotic members of the overtone series, such as the seventh or eleventh partial. Closely related, the second factor is whether music employs chiefly periodic instruments, such as those of western tradition, or chiefly non-periodic instruments, such as bells, gongs, and metallophones. The third factor in differentiating European-derived harmonic musical traditions from many other musical traditions of the world may be the most decisive of all. Namely, much depends upon whether music consists primarily of tones that are sustained and simultaneous or primarily of tones that are transient and successive, upon whether music is dominated by chords or by melody. We have been considering the hypothesis that music is a universal language expressed in cultural dialects. Those dialects differ greatly from culture to culture and vary from age to age. Their differences are not absolute, however, and Nettle observes that their variations occur within certain common parameters: "There are musical systems, there are musics, but they are readily connected, more readily understood at least in some respects by the novice, than are true languages. Despite the enormous variety of musics, the ways in which people everywhere have chosen to make music are more restricted than the boundaries of the imaginable."[58] Nettl expresses my own, more limited, experience. On first listening to recordings of Javanese gamelan music, I found it alien and impenetrable. In subsequent listenings I began to hear a basic pentatonic tonality emerging from the music's complex texture, and the texture itself began to strike me as colourful and intriguing rather than merely opaque and strange. Before long the seventh partial of the overtone series began to tickle my ear and dawn upon my awareness, and then what I take to be the non-periodic, bell-based tunings of certain other notes of the Javanese scale. I now attend to the gamelan ensemble's combining of universal elements and particular qualities with growing pleasure and appreciation.

58. *The Study of Ethnomusicology*, 43.

Tentative though it must be, my conclusion is that in all musical traditions, the overtone series and other acoustical principles, given and enduring, are present as formative constituents, acting as a necessary though not sufficient preconditions for musical experience. John A. Sloboda suggests additional "musical universals" or "underlying features which typify most music."[59] These include fixed reference pitches – tonics or drones – serving as points of orientation for melodies, and fixed pulses – repeating and emphasised – serving as a framework for metres. Underlying principles such as these provide inescapable parameters for my own tradition of western harmonic music. That tradition is complex and wonderful, and it is unique. But it is by no means exclusive. Related parameters regulate other, quite different musical traditions, themselves complex and unique but not exclusive. By way of analogy, we might say that wherever dance occurs, no matter how various its forms may be, gravity is present as an unavoidable and formative constituent. Yet the differences here are as illustrative as the similarities. Dancers experience gravity as an amorphous and finally unforgiving force. The overtone series, in contrast, is manifold in its structure, unlimited in its possibilities, and exceedingly hospitable to creative human choices. Hindemith summarises the principles involved here: "The intervals which constitute the building material of melodies and harmonies fall into tonal groupments, necessitated by their own physical structure and without our consent. . . . It seems to me that attempts at avoiding them are as promising as attempts at avoiding the effects of gravitation." Hindemith makes the significant addition, however, that although "in producing and perceiving music you must keep your feet on the solid ground of our earth, . . . with your imagination you may rove through the universe"[60]

## *Religious Particularity and Universality*

Hindemith's summary suggests certain analogies between music and religion. Both realms of experience involve the exercise of our human freedom and creativity, by which we may "rove through the universe," yet always within an abiding context of cosmic structure, given "without our consent." These analogies are important to appreciating Pythagorean contemplation of music as a sacramental exercise. Our considerations of contrasting tonal systems can aid our appreciation of contrasting religious systems, and considerations of particularity and universality in music

59. *The Musical Mind: The Cognitive Psychology of Music* (Oxford: Clarendon Press, 1985), 253. See also the suggestions concerning universal musical principles in Malm, *Music Cultures*, 214, and McAllester, "Some Thoughts on 'Universals' in World Music," 378-9.
60. *A Composer's World*, 55, 24.

suggest parallels to corresponding issues in religion.

One strand of modern Christian theology in particular has characterised religion in terms of our human freedom and creativity exercised within a context of given cosmic structure. I have in mind Schleiermacher's influential formulation that religion consists in the interplay between our sense of self-initiated "activity," on the one hand, and our sense on the other hand of "receptivity" that is in no way self-affected – that is, our sense of the ultimate dependence of all our activity upon the givenness of our cosmic context.[61] This interplay is pervaded by an accompanying sense that our receptivity or dependence is finally "absolute" in a sense that our freedom and creativity are not. Yet our freedom and creativity are actual. The analogy between this religious interplay of our human freedom and ultimate dependence on the one hand, and the interplay of our musical creativity and its given acoustical and harmonic foundations on the other, helps us appreciate a Pythagorean dimension to Schleiermacher's assertion that music is "the most sacred of the arts."[62]

For Schleiermacher, as for the mystical tradition stemming from Dionysius, God is the primordial, unfathomable "Whence" to which we feel our ultimate receptivity relating us. More particular names for that sacred Whence, as well as ritual expressions of our sense of ultimate receptivity, are as manifold and various in different religious traditions as the varieties of vocabulary and practice are in different musical traditions. As with the musics of the world, the religions of the world speak colourful, local, and exotic dialects of religious language. I believe that the world's great religions combine a sense of universal cosmic givenness with unique religious practices, in vital interrelation – much as skilful manifestations of music, as in jazz, combine universal principles of harmony with unique melodic invention. Schleiermacher makes this comparison specific:

> Were I to compare religion in this respect with anything it would be with music, which indeed is otherwise closely connected with it. Music is one great whole; it is a special, a self-contained revelation of the world. Yet the music of each people is a whole by itself, which again is divided into different characteristic forms, till we come to the genius and style of the individual. Each actual instance of this inner revelation in the individual contains all these unities. Yet while nothing is possible for a musician, except in and through the unity of the music of his people, and the unity of music generally,

---

61. *The Christian Faith* 4.1, 13.
62. "Rede am Sarge Zelters," in Walther Sattler, "Vergessene Dokumente aus dem musikalischen Leben Schleiermachers," *Zeitschrift für Musikwissenschaft* 7 (October, 1924-September, 1925), 540. See my article "The Role of Music in Schleiermacher's Writings," in *Internationaler Schleiermacher-Kongreß Berlin 1984*, ed. Kurt-Victor Selge, vol.1, *Schleiermacher-Archiv*, ed. Hermann Fischer et al. (Berlin: Walter de Gruyter, 1985), esp. 445-6.

he presents it in the charm of sound with all the pleasure and joy-ousness of boundless caprice, according as his life stirs in him, and the world influences him. In the same way, despite the neces-sary elements in its structure, religion is, in its individual manifes-tations whereby it displays itself immediately in life, from nothing farther removed than from all semblance of compulsion or limita-tion. In life, the necessary element is taken up, taken up into freedom.[63]

Theologically, what have we proven by these analogies between musical experience and religious experience? Nothing, of course. Not only do analysis and analogies fail to constitute proofs; our age has learned that mature theol-ogy avoids most talk of proof. Schleiermacher knew this well. In his treatise *On Freedom* he introduces an analogy between artistic experience and moral experience with these careful words: "Allow me to show this by means of an example. Our way of forming judgements and experiencing sentiments in the aesthetic realm has so much similarity to our mode of dealing with the moral realm that I believe I am entirely justified in taking recourse there – not to prove something about the moral realm, but rather to present a possibility."[64] In this spirit, our comparisons here of musical experience and religious expe-rience are not for the purpose of proving something, but rather for the purpose of appreciating theological possibilities and likelihoods.

In earlier ages of Christianity, it is true, musical analogies, along with analogies of many other kinds, were put forward as arguments for God's existence from cosmic design. Writing in the 4th century, Athanasius pro-vides a classic example of theological argument by musical analogy:

Just as though one were to hear from a distance a lyre, composed of many diverse strings, and marvel at the concord of its sym-phony – in that its sound is composed neither of low notes exclu-sively, nor high nor intermediate only, but all combine their sounds in equal balance – and would not fail to perceive from this that the lyre was not playing itself, nor even being struck by more persons than one, but that there was one musician, even if he did not see him, who by his skill combined the sound of each string into the tuneful symphony; so, the order of the whole universe being perfectly harmonious, and there being no strife of the higher against the lower or the lower against the higher, and all things making up one order, it is consistent to think that the Ruler and King of all Creation is one and not many.[65]

Athanasius writes beguiling rhetoric, and it will convince those ready to

63. Schleiermacher, *On Religion: Speeches to Its Cultured Despisers*, tr. John Oman (New York: Harper Torchbooks, 1958), 51.
64. Tr. Albert L. Blackwell (Lewiston, NY: Edwin Mellen Press, 1992), 43-4.
65. *Against the Heathen*, tr. Archibald Robertson, in A Select Library of Nicene and Post-Nicene Fathers of the Christian Church: Second Series, ed. Philip Schaff and Henry Wace (Grand Rapids: Eerdmans, 1957), 24.

be convinced by it. For modern religious seekers, however, I believe that Weil discusses artistic and religious analogy in terms that are more appropriate. "The proof of the existence of God by the order of the world," she writes, "in the manner which it is usually put forward, is a wretched one."[66] In a remarkable passage, Weil speaks of the impossibility of drawing theological proofs from tangible evidence; of analogies as sources not of empirical verification but of theological encouragement; of redirecting religious attention from speculations concerning a designer of the universe to appreciation for the universe's holy design; of the transcendent God's eminence in creation; and of love, not argument, as the true centre of both artistic and religious experience:

> One can never find enough visible finality in the world to prove that it is analogous to an object made with a view to a certain end. It is even manifest that this is not the case. Yet the analogy between the world and a work of art has its experimental verification in the very feeling itself of the beauty of the world, for the beautiful is the only source of the sense of beauty. This verification is valid only for those who have experienced that feeling, but those who have never felt it, and who are doubtless very rare, cannot perhaps be brought to God by any path. . . . Art is thus the unique legitimate term of comparison. Moreover, this comparison alone leads to love. One can use a watch without loving the watchmaker, but one cannot listen with attention to a faultlessly beautiful song without love for the composer of the song and for the singer. In the same way the watchmaker does not need love to make a watch, whereas artistic creation . . . is nothing but love.[67]

Thus Weil sets aside theological traditions of rationalistic proof, turning instead to more subtle comparisons of art and religion that appeal to mind and heart alike.

## *Beyond Contingency: Trusting Divine* Logos

Forewarned by Weil against both overconfidence and oversimplification, we are prepared to take a step beyond analogy to a further kind of relation between musical experience and religious experience, the relation of theological inference. The kind of theological inference I have in mind involves neither arguing to ostensible fact nor rationalising to inflexible dogma. Rather it involves arriving at grounds for religious faith as reasonable, or at least not unreasonable, commitment and trust.

Some contemporary philosophers and literary critics dismiss not only the possibility of arriving at reasonable grounds for religious commitment

66. *Notebooks*, 1:240.
67. *Intimations of Christianity*, 90-1.

and trust, but also the very concept of such grounds or foundations. Among these anti-foundational thinkers I wish to focus here on Richard Rorty because I find him so clear, consistent, and uncompromising, and because his influence is so widespread. Yet I believe that in the end Rorty is not persuasive in insisting that our foundational commitments are utterly contingent, purely historical and social phenomena, with no ascertainable foundation in anything that is given and enduring, with no dependency that is ultimate. And I believe that reflections on musical experience can illumine this theological point.

In *Philosophy and the Mirror of Nature*, Rorty studies the foundational assumptions of modern philosophy with the intention of "making clear that they are optional":[68]

> The aim of the book is to undermine the reader's confidence in "the mind" as something about which one should have a "philosophical" view, in "knowledge," as something about which there ought to be a "theory" and which has "foundations," and in "philosophy" as it has been conceived since Kant.[69]

Though Rorty's book is about modern philosophy, it casts a wider net. By the end Rorty is describing his aim in terms that encompass all our experiences, or supposed experiences, of knowing: "The point is always the same – to perform the social function which Dewey called 'breaking the crust of convention,' preventing man from deluding himself with the notion that he knows himself, or anything else, except under optional descriptions."[70]

Rorty conceives of knowledge as what we are "justified" in believing. And what justifies our believing? Rorty asserts that what we call justifications of knowledge are completely historical and cultural phenomena, free of dependence upon or constraint by any given and enduring foundation:

> If we have a Deweyan conception of knowledge as what we are justified in believing, then we will not imagine that there are enduring constraints on what can count as knowledge, since we will see "justification" as a social phenomenon rather than a transaction between "the knowing subject" and "reality."[71]

In a subsequent work, *Contingency, Irony, and Solidarity*, Rorty writes again that criteria for choosing among possible beliefs are optional because our beliefs always arise from contingent social conditions and conditionings. Criteria for justifying beliefs are not intrinsic to human nature or to the nature of the world, he insists, for human beings and the world have no intrinsic nature: "The temptation to look for criteria is a

68. *Philosophy and the Mirror of Nature* (Princeton: Princeton University Press, 1979), xiii.
69. p.7.
70. p.379.
71. p.9.

species of the more general temptation to think of the world, or the human self, as possessing an intrinsic nature, an essence."[72] In this connection Rorty invokes an idea he claims to find expressed in European Romanticism, the idea that truth is made rather than found: "I can sum up by redescribing what, in my view, the revolutionaries and poets of two centuries ago were getting at. What was glimpsed at the end of the eighteenth century was that anything could be made to look good or bad, important or unimportant, useful or useless, by being redescribed."[73]

Rorty summarises his study of intellectual history, naming some of his anti-foundationalist mentors, and then states his conclusion:

> I can crudely sum up the story . . . by saying that once upon a time we felt a need to worship something which lay beyond the visible world. Beginning in the seventeenth century we tried to substitute a love of truth for a love of God, treating the world described by science as a quasi divinity. Beginning at the end of the eighteenth century we tried to substitute a love of ourselves for a love of scientific truth, a worship of our own deep spiritual or poetic nature, treated as one more quasi divinity. The line of thought common to [Hans] Blumenberg, [Friedrich] Nietzsche, [Sigmund] Freud, and [Donald] Davidson suggests that we try to get to the point where we no longer worship *anything*, where we treat *nothing* as a quasi divinity, where we treat *everything* – our language, our conscience, our community – as a product of time and chance.[74]

It is significant, I believe, that nowhere in his argument does Rorty make more than passing reference to music, musical experience, or musical imagery. Music presents a substantial problem for anti-foundational thinkers. Think of instrumentalists tuning for a performance of Bach or Schoenberg or Ligeti; think of a chorus of accomplished singers burnishing their intonation; think of parents suffering through a recital of the lower-school strings class; or think of Bach and Schoenberg and Ligeti themselves at their work of composing music: are any of these persons apt to agree with Rorty that the world has no intrinsic nature, that the Pythagorean octave and 5th are contingent ratios, products of time and chance? Are they apt to agree that the overtone series can, in Rorty's phrase, "be made to look good or bad, important or unimportant, useful or useless, by being redescribed"? I do not think so.

One possible rejoinder to my rhetorical questions here is that music is not philosophy, and that musical experience does not constitute knowledge. This brings us back to the question of whether musical experience can illumine theological inferences. Can music help us find a way of theo-

---

72. (Cambridge: Cambridge University Press, 1989), 6.
73. p.7.
74. p.22. Rorty's emphases.

logical inference that is different from outmoded traditions of argument
for God's existence from cosmic design, and also different from Rorty's
recommendation "that we try to get to the point where we no longer worship *anything*"? Can we find theological paths between dogmatic "apologetics" and post-modernist "hermeneutics of suspicion."

Most constructive in this regard is an article by Donald Walhout titled
"Augustine on the Transcendent in Music."[75] Music is central to his
philosophical discussion: "music is said to be a way of bringing the listener
into a communion with, and strengthening the union with, transcendent
reality. It is this claim that I am particularly interested in exploring."[76] To
this end Walhout suggests a "newly named discipline" that he calls
"propaedeutics". Propaedeutics derives from the Greek *pro*, "before," and
*paideuein*, "to teach," and means "preliminary teaching," or less literally,
rational inquiry preparatory to some discipline of art or science. In our
present instance the discipline is theology, the art and science of religious
commitment and trust.

Walhout's use of "propaedeutics" differs from that of certain Christian
figures of an earlier age. In 1893, for example, the church historian Philip
Schaff published an impressive volume with an imposing title: *Theological
Propaedeutic: A General Introduction to the Study of Theology, Exegetical,
Historical, Systematic, and Practical, Including Encyclopaedia, Methodology, and Bibliography.*[77] By "Propaedeutic" Schaff means an all-inclusive
survey introductory to more thorough study. But new occasions teach new
duties. Walhout's late-20th-century usage denotes an enterprise that is more
preliminary than Schaff's, more tentative, more modest, and I believe more
suitable for our age. Walhout defines that enterprise by contrasting
propaedeutics with "apologetics" and "hermeneutics."[78] Apologetics, he
writes, is "post-commitment" defence of our beliefs. Hermeneutics is "mid-
commitment" interpretation of our beliefs. Propaedeutics, in contrast, is
"pre-commitment" preparation for beliefs. More specifically, propaedeutics
is rational preparation for religious convictions, giving support to "the
belief that having such convictions has an initial rationality."[79] Walhout's
"propaedeutics," then, is the art and science of reasonable grounding, and
it promises to be an alternative way of theological inference between the
apologetics argued in traditional Christian theology and the hermeneutics
of suspicion advanced by Rorty.

Whether or not propaedeutics becomes a "newly named discipline," as
Walhout recommends, the fundamental concept is by no means new. In

75. *Philosophy and Theology* 3, no.3 (Spring 1989): 283-92.
76. p.283.
77. New York: Charles Scribner's Sons, 1893. I am grateful to the late Professor
    Theron D. Price for acquainting me with this volume.
78. p.284.
79. p.284.

the 3rd century, Origen wrote to a fellow ecclesiastic concerning Christianity's "propaedeutic" use of Greek philosophy and the liberal arts, including the study of music:

> I would wish that you take from Greek philosophy that which has the capacity, as it were, to become encyclical and propaedeutic studies for Christianity, and whatever of geometry and astronomy might be useful in the interpretation of the Holy Scriptures, so that just as the children of the philosophers speak of geometry and music, grammar, rhetoric and astronomy as being ancillary to philosophy, we too may say this of philosophy itself in relation to Christianity.[80]

Walhout's essay brings this tradition of propaedeutics into the 20th century. He addresses a theme we have encountered in Rorty, the question of what we are justified in believing. We have seen that Rorty rejects the concept of transcendent reality. Instead he advocates justifying our convictions as a purely "social phenomenon rather than a transaction between 'the knowing subject' and 'reality.'" Walhout's advocacy is the opposite, and contemplation of music plays a propaedeutical role:

> In this article I am concerned with whether this claim to a transcendent dimension in music is justified. I believe there is a perfectly straightforward way of maintaining that the claim is indeed justified, and I want to give an argument to that effect. Of course, human expressions of this kind can and will continue as matters of belief or conviction regardless of justification by philosophers. But then they may not carry the assurance of being rational rather than irrational, and they are open to the charge by critics of being irrational. I am assuming that it is better to have a rational procedure than an irrational one.[81]

Walhout commences his argument with a consideration of Augustine's treatise *On Music*. Routley has described Augustine's treatise as "the single example in all history of independent and original theoretical thinking by a theologian upon music . . . , an application of Christian theology, not to the use of music in the church, but to the science of music itself."[82] In the terms of our study, Augustine's work is a Christian treatise on music as a liberal art in the Pythagorean tradition. The treatise has come down to us incomplete, however, as Walhout explains: "Its six Books deal largely with meter and rhythm, whereas another six Books were supposed to deal with harmonics. Moreover, the first five Books discuss mainly poetic meter, so that his thoughts on music are limited to Book VI in the main."[83] Walhout summarises the central musical insight of Augustine's treatise, an insight

---

80. *Letter to Gregory* 1, in McKinnon, *Music in Early Christian Literature*, 37.
81. p.284.
82. *The Church and Music*, 55-6.
83. "Augustine on the Transcendent in Music," 285.

that we have no difficulty recognising as the Pythagorean sacramental tradition:

> What is Augustine's main insight in all this talk about musical
> numbers? It is, I believe, that a musical composition, although part
> of the most temporal of arts, is nevertheless inexplicable without
> reference to abstract properties whose instantiability and indeed
> very existence are not limited to that temporal product but have a
> timeless status as objects of rational discourse.[84]

After supplementing Augustine's argument with some "amplifications" of his own, Walhout arrives at his propaedeutic summation, namely, that we are reasonably justified in believing that music manifests transcendent realities. Walhout states his conclusion in modest terms: "I am content here to claim only that we can speak meaningfully of the transcendent in music provided it is legitimate to think of abstract objects in general as existents other than natural things in the empirical order – a reasonable enough intuition, it seems."[85] By "existents," if I understand him correctly, Walhout means acoustical laws and musical principles that transcend history and culture – foundational realities, such as Pythagorean ratios and the overtone series, that are given and enduring. Writing in the 19th century, critic Eduard Hanslick coined the lovely phrase for music, "sonorous forms in motion."[86] Walhout is making the essentially Pythagorean argument that music's sonorous forms in motion are moving images of eternity.

Upon this propaedeutical foundation, Walhout then offers some graceful Augustinian reflections upon music as a path of human and divine meeting, which in Chapter 1 of this study we have taken as central to our understanding of the term sacramental:

> We might note some ways in which Augustine himself thought the
> soul was brought toward God by music. Music can, through its
> abstract core of numbers, bring the soul to contemplate the eternal,
> and this leads to God, since eternity is a central attribute distin-
> guishing God from mortal things. Again, musical numbers exhibit
> beauty and order in their arrangement, and beauty and order are of
> divine origin. So music brings the soul toward God through the
> beauty and order of its elements. Again, the very notion of music
> being immaterial in a central dimension of its being will bring the
> soul in the end to a contemplation of the most pre-eminent of
> immaterial things, God. Perhaps Augustine had all of these facets
> in mind when he said that "with a restored delight in reason's
> numbers, our whole life is turned to God."[87]

84. p.286.
85. p.289.
86. *"Tönend bewegte Formen." Vom Musikalisch-Schönen*, 16th ed. (Wiesbaden, Breitkopf and Härtel, 1966), 59.
87. p.291. Walhout quotes from Augustine, *On Music* 6.11.33, 358.

Walhout ends his reflections with a cautionary note concerning what propaedeutical contemplation of music may and may not appropriately claim:

> All of these kinds of expression are, let us recognise, convictional expressions of Christian belief when applied to music. They are not philosophical proofs. But they illustrate the kinds of expression that might be forthcoming in accordance with the kind of Augustinian rationale reviewed above. . . . The role of propaedeutics is to exhibit basic rationalities in logical preparation for conviction, and not to engage in that convictional form of utterance itself.[88]

Let us draw some conclusions from this juxtaposition of Rorty and Walhout. Rorty's hermeneutics of suspicion advances an ironic relation with a contingent world. Propaedeutical reflections in a musical mode suggest the rational legitimacy of what Steiner calls an "initial act of trust,"[89] a covenant relation with the world, analogous to a musician's covenant with the overtone series. Rorty describes all of our concepts as personal or cultural "redescriptions" of previous relativities. Propaedeutical reflections in a musical mode imply foundations for abiding principles and values, analogous to the Pythagorean ratios of octave and 5th and to the overtone series. Rorty insists upon the "notion of a culture as a conversation rather than as a structure erected upon foundations." Propaedeutical reflections in a musical mode encourage us to ask why culture should not be conceived as *both* social conversation *and* structure erected upon common foundations. A model here might again be the jazz ensemble, where each player innovates and creates, but upon given acoustical foundations and toward common musical goals. In summary, Rorty maintains that our world is contingent, without enduring foundation. Propaedeutical reflections in a musical mode entitle us to venture religious trust in the poetry of Job where, amidst stupendous mystery, divinity measures and proportions the world's enduring foundation to the accompaniment of joyful song:

> Where were you when I laid the foundation of the earth?
> Tell me, if you have understanding?
> Who determined its measurements – surely you know!
> Or who stretched the line upon it?
> On what were its bases sunk,
> or who laid its cornerstone
> when the morning stars sang together,
> and all the heavenly beings shouted for joy? (Job 38.4-7)

We come, then, to the fundamental theological point of this chapter's musical analysis. The religious faith into which Pythagorean contemplation

---

88. pp.291-2.
89. *Real Presences*, 89.

of music helps us venture involves a sense of trust in cosmic order, basic trust that the world is grounded in and permeated by rational pattern and principle. In the language of Christian theology, contemplation of the given and enduring logic of music contributes to trust in the second person of the Trinity, God's *logos*, the foundational logic of the world. To recall our basic definitions from Chapter 1, music thus serves as a path of human and divine meeting, a finite reality through which the divine is perceived to be disclosed and communicated. Pythagorean contemplation of music is in this sense a sacramental exercise.

## Music, Mathematics, and Transcendence

Before turning in Chapter 3 to music's sacramental sounds, let us devote a few pages to mathematics, that silent intimate of music. We have seen that Augustine refers to music as "sounding numbers," and Pythagorean appreciation rests upon the principle that whether or not we are conscious of the fact, music involves mathematics via the ear. Insofar as this is the case, music shares whatever foundational claims mathematics can make.

Though Rorty does not address the subject of music, he admits that mathematics makes it difficult to shake off the "Platonic Principle" that differences in our certainty are founded upon differences in reality. Nevertheless Rorty wishes to shake off all vestiges of such Platonism. He speaks of mathematical truths as he speaks of all claims to truth. Right down to plane geometry's Pythagorean theorem, he asserts, mathematical principles are contingent outcomes of historical "conversation":

> It is so much a part of "thinking philosophically" to be impressed with the special character of mathematical truth that it is hard to shake off the grip of the Platonic Principle. If, however, we think of "rational certainty" as a matter of victory in argument rather than of relation to an object known, we shall look toward our inter-locutors rather than to our faculties for the explanation of the phe-nomenon. If we think of our certainty about the Pythagorean Theo-rem as our confidence, based on experience with arguments on such matters, that nobody will find an objection to the premises from which we infer it, then we shall not seek to explain it by the relation of reason to triangularity. Our certainty will be a matter of conversation between persons, rather than a matter of interaction with nonhuman reality.[90]

I believe that Rorty's final sentence here employs an absolute distinc-tion that weakens his argument. It is his either/or disjunction between "per-sons" and "nonhuman reality." If, in contrast to Rorty, we assume that as persons we are immersed in given and enduring realities, and that these

90. *Philosophy and the Mirror of Nature*, 156-7.

realities permeate our lives as persons, then we shall have no difficulty understanding why the members of a string quartet, let us say, are able to agree as they tune their octaves. Their agreement on tuning is not merely conversational – not, in Rorty's words, "based on experience with arguments on such matters, that nobody will find an objection." Rather, their agreement is based on the mathematical ratio 1:2, given and enduring, immanent in the dynamics of their instruments, their recital hall, their ears, and the ears of their audience. We come again to Augustine's principle of the eternity and immutability of numbers: "Whether they are considered in themselves or applied to the laws of figures, or of sound, or of some other motion, numbers have immutable rules not instituted by men but discovered. . . ."[91]

John D. Barrow opens a book on mathematics with these provocative words:

> A mystery lurks beneath the magic carpet of science, something that scientists have not been telling, something too shocking to mention except in rather esoterically refined circles: that at the root of the success of twentieth century science there lies a deeply "religious" belief – a belief in an unseen and perfect transcendental world that controls us in an unexplained way, yet upon which we seem to exert no influence whatsoever.[92]

Let us grant Barrow the rhetorical excesses of this opening flourish, and let us grant also that some mathematicians will disagree with his assertions. I nonetheless concur with Barrow's correction of Rorty's mistake of separating the "transcendental world" from our lives as persons. Barrow understands that the two are interpenetrating and inseparable. "We no longer need to think of mathematical entities as abstractions that our material minds are battling to make contact with in some peculiar way," he writes. "We exist in the Platonic realm itself."[93]

> Our minds and the world of tangible things have not sprung ready-made into the world. They have evolved by a gradual process in which the persistent and the stable survive over long periods of time. These persistent structures are manifestations of the mathematical structure of the world long before they could become re-creators of it.[94]

Concerning philosophers of mathematics Barrow writes: "We find ourselves being drawn towards deep questions which were once the sole preserve of the theologians."[95] Perhaps Barrow will not mind, therefore, if we

91. *On Christian Doctrine* 2.38.56, p.73.
92. *Pi in the Sky: Counting, Thinking, and Being* (Oxford: Clarendon Press, 1992), 1.
93. p.282.
94. p.294.
95. p.4.

paraphrase him in theological terms. He seems to be saying that mathematicians inquire into the divine *logos*, to which The Wisdom of Solomon alludes:

> For it is he who gave me unerring knowledge of what exists,
> to know the structure of the world and the activity of the elements.
> (Wis 7.17)

One of the "deep questions" concerning divine *logos* immanent in our world relates to the mystery of child prodigies in mathematics and in music. Hearing a recital performed by violinist Sarah Chang at the age of ten suggests to me that musical genius involves both what Rorty calls cultural conversation and some kind of immediate participation in reality's *logos*. "We feel," writes Rothstein in his book devoted to music and mathematics, "that music teaches itself."[96] Such musical maturity in such a bright and well-adjusted child is more than an occasion for pleasure and amazement. For me it is religiously propaedeutical. Young Sarah Chang's musical gift has sacramental implications.

Mathematical precocity is similarly uncanny and religiously suggestive. Oliver Sacks reports on autistic twins "in whom there is something exceedingly mysterious at work, powers and depths of a perhaps fundamental sort, which I have not been able to 'solve' in the eighteen years that I have known them":[97]

> They were seated in a corner together, with a mysterious, secret smile on their faces. . . . I crept up quietly, so as not to disturb them. They seemed to be locked in a singular, purely numerical converse. John would say a number – a six-figure number. Michael would catch the number, nod, smile and seem to savour it. Then he, in turn, would say another six-figure number, and now it was John who received, and appreciated it richly. They look, at first, like two connoisseurs wine-tasting, sharing rare tastes, rare appreciations. I sat still, unseen by them, mesmerised, bewildered.[98]

Sacks wrote down the twins' numbers and later researched their possible meanings: "I already had a hunch – and now I confirmed it. *All the numbers, the six figure numbers, which the twins had exchanged, were primes* – i.e., numbers that could be evenly divided by no other whole number than itself or one."[99] As Sacks concludes his account, he leaves the twins chuckling together over twenty-digit numbers. Sacks could only assume those numbers to be primes also, as he had access to no reference volumes listing prime numbers of greater than ten digits.

Sacks summarises the twins' mathematical delight in sacramental terms,

96. *Emblems of Mind*, 120.
97. *The Man Who Mistook His Wife for a Hat and Other Clinical Tales* (New York: Summit Books, 1985), 186.
98. p.191.
99. p.192. Sacks's emphasis.

as a kind of communion with the real, analogous to a musician's communion with consonance:

> I observed them in countless other sorts of number games or number
> communion, the nature of which I could not ascertain or even guess
> at. But it seems likely, or certain, that they are dealing with "real"
> properties or qualities – for the arbitrary, such as random numbers,
> gives them no pleasure or scarcely any at all. It is clear that they
> must have "sense" in their numbers – in the same way, perhaps, as
> a musician must have harmony.[100]

Finally, Sacks expresses his conclusions by invoking Pythagorean tradition:

> The twins, I believe, have not just a strange "faculty" – but a sen-
> sibility, a harmonic sensibility, perhaps allied to that of music. One
> might speak of it, very naturally, as a "Pythagorean" sensibility –
> and what is odd is not its existence, but that it is apparently so
> rare.[101]

To me Sacks's observations suggest a significant if unorthodox dimension
for the New Testament prayer of Christ: "I thank you, Father, Lord of
heaven and earth, because you have hidden these thing from the wise and
the intelligent and have revealed them to infants. . ." (Mt 11.25).

Mathematical and musical sensibilities differ in significant ways, of
course. Mathematics has a vast universal vocabulary; music has a universal grammar expressed in a myriad of cultural vocabularies. Mathematics
is more objective; music is more expressive. Mathematics is more dictatorial of results. Barrow writes that mathematics "allows freedom of thought,
but only in the sense that it is your fault if you want to think the wrong
thoughts."[102] Music is more congenial to human creativity and
inventiveness.

As for comparisons between religious sensibilities and those of mathematics, I believe that Barrow draws the distinction a bit too rigidly: "The
mystic leans towards celebration; the mathematician to cerebration."[103]
Many mathematicians celebrate the mysteries their minds explore, and
some mystics have become what they are as a result of cerebration. The
difference between mathematicians and mystics is not the difference between cerebration and celebration, but the different ranges of experience
they include in their cerebration and celebration. Christian Pythagoreans
of the Middle Ages prized the science of mathematics, but they named
theology the queen of the sciences. Why? Because theology is the most
comprehensive of disciplines and brings us to highest ends. In theological
inference every human experience is relevant, and the result can be

100. p.194.
101. p.197.
102. *Pi in the Sky*, 264.
103. p.294.

communion with the divine.

As a religious mystic, Weil maintains that every experience of cerebration is also an occasion for theological celebration. She begins with mathematics, which she considers "first, before all, a sort of mystical poem composed by God"[104]:

> Our intelligence has become so crude that we no longer conceive that there could be an authentic, rigorous certainty concerning the incomprehensible mysteries. Upon this point there would be an infinitely precious use for mathematics, which is irreplaceable in this respect.[105]

Bringing music into her considerations, Weil writes that if mathematics "should again become faithful to its origin and its destination, demonstrative rigour in mathematics would be to Charity what musical technique is to Charity in the Gregorian melodies."[106]

For all his quasi-theological sympathy, Barrow finally shies from the queen of sciences, adopting as his own a cryptic sentence he attributes to Christopher Morley: "'My theology, briefly, is that the universe was dictated but not signed.'"[107] Weil is a bolder theologian. Her Pythagorean contemplation of mathematics and music discloses a flourish of divinity's signature:

> To be precise, there is here below but one single beauty, that is the Beauty of the World. All other beauties are reflections of that one, be they faithful and pure, deformed and soiled, or even diabolically perverted. . . . This cluster of marvels is perfected by the presence, in the necessary connections which compose the universal order, of divine verities symbolically expressed. Herein is the marvel of marvels, and as it were, the secret signature of the artist.[108]

104. *Intimations of Christianity*, 193.
105. p.165.
106. p.171-2.
107. *Pi in the Sky*, 159.
108. *Intimations of Christianity*, 191.

# III. Creation: Manifesting Transcendence

*Die Sinnen sind im Geist all ein Sinn und Gebrauch;*
*Wer Gott beschaut, der schmeckt, fühlt, riecht und hört ihn auch.*

The senses in the Spirit are one and have one use;
Who sees God, tastes, feels, smells and hears God too.

## *The Incarnational Tradition: Music's Sacramental Sound*

In Chapter 2 we entered what we are calling the Pythagorean tradition of sacramental encounter by way of the West Portal of Chartres Cathedral, where Pythagoras sits in stone. We may enter our second great sacramental tradition, which we are calling the Incarnational tradition, through the West Portal of the Abbey Church of Saint Denis near Paris. It too is a triple portal, symbolic of the Trinity.[1] In the central arch, the 12th-century doors of gilded bronze were dedicated to the crucifixion, resurrection, and ascension of Christ. The doors bore an inscription in versified Latin, including the famous line:

*Mens hebes ad verum per materialia surgit.*

The dull mind rises to truth through that which is material.[2]

As the figure of Pythagoras on the West Portal of Chartres reminds us of the Nicene Creed's assertion that God is Creator of all things invisible, including the mathematics of music, this inscription from the West Portal of Saint Denis reminds us of the Creed's assertion that God is Creator of all things visible, including the perceptible sounds of music, which may serve as a sacramental path to encounter with God.

Abbot Suger, who presided over the 12th-century design, decoration, and dedication of the church at Saint Denis, was an important influence in the development of Gothic style. Erwin Panofsky writes that Suger "was frankly in love with splendor and beauty in every conceivable form," and he speculates that Suger's response to ecclesiastical ceremony was "largely aesthetic."[3] Historians seem to agree that Suger was not a great religious thinker. He developed no elaborate theological rationale for incorporating beauty into the spaces and ceremonies of worship. Yet he was heir to a tradition of scriptural interpretation and theological thinking that has valued palpable beauty as a sacramental incarnation of God's grace. That tradition

---

1. Sumner McKnight Crosby, *The Royal Abbey of Saint-Denis* (New Haven: Yale University Press, 1987), 181.
2. Erwin Panofsky, ed., *Abbot Suger on the Abbey Church of St.-Denis and Its Art Treasures*, 2d ed. (Princeton: Princeton University Press, 1979), 23.
3. p.14.

is known by the term "anagogical," from the Greek meaning "upward leading" (*an*: "up"; *agogos*: "leading"). Suger uses the words "grace" and "anagogical" in his best known passage on material beauty as a path to God:

> When – out of my delight in the beauty of the house of God – the loveliness of the many-coloured stones has called me away from external cares, and worthy meditation has induced me to reflect, transferring that which is material to that which is immaterial, on the diversity of the sacred virtues: then it seems to me that I see myself dwelling, as it were, in some strange region of the universe which neither exists entirely in the slime of the earth nor entirely in the purity of Heaven; and that, by the grace of God, I can be transported from this inferior to that higher world in an anagogical manner.[4]

Suger bases this passage upon an anagogical interpretation of a verse from the biblical prophet Ezekiel:

> You were in Eden, the garden of God; every precious stone was your covering, carnelian, chrysolite, and moonstone, beryl, onyx, and jasper, sapphire, turquoise, and emerald; and worked in gold were your settings and your engravings. On the day that you were created they were prepared. (Ezek 28.13)

The sacramental means of Suger's heavenly transport were not limited to visual experience. He heard the simultaneous performance of twenty masses in the church of Saint Denis as a "symphony angelic rather than human."[5]

## On Balancing the Pythagorean and Incarnational Traditions

The Incarnational tradition of sacramental sights and sounds that Suger represents is, I believe, an essential counterpoise to the tradition of sacramental contemplation of music's invisible and inaudible principles, rooted in Pythagoreanism. Plato slights this incarnational counterpoise. In his *Republic*, Plato mocks musicians of the audible tradition who "vex and torture the strings and rack them on the pegs," and who attempt to base their judgements of musical intervals on the perceptions of their ears rather than the calculations of their minds:

> They talk of something they call minims and, laying their ears alongside, as if trying to catch a voice from next door, some affirm that they can hear a note between and that this is the least interval and the unit of measurement, while others insist that the strings now render identical sounds, both preferring their ears to their minds.[6]

4. p.21.
5. p.14.
6. *Republic* 531a, tr. Paul Shorey (London: William Heinemann, 1969), 191-3.

Similarly, a treatise *On Music* which the Middle Ages attributed to the classical biographer Plutarch portrays Pythagoras as uninterested in musical judgements based upon the ear rather than the mind: "The grave Pythagoras rejected the judging of music by the sense of hearing, asserting that its excellence must be apprehended by the mind. This is why he did not judge it by the ear, but by the scale based on the proportions, and considered it sufficient to pursue the study no further than the octave."[7]

The generation following Plato broke with this Pythagorean tradition of disdain for the ear. After the cognitive severity of Pythagorean musical analysis, what a change we sense – and for me it is a most welcome change – in Aristotle's broader endorsement of music's various roles in education, amusement, and entertainment:

> Our first inquiry is whether music ought not or ought to be included in education, and what is its efficacy among the three uses of it that have been discussed – does it serve for education or amusement or entertainment? It is reasonable to reckon it under all of these heads, and it appears to participate in them all. Amusement is for the sake of relaxation, and relaxation must necessarily be pleasant, for it is a way of curing the pain due to laborious work; also entertainment ought admittedly to be not only honourable but also pleasant, for happiness is derived from both honour and pleasure; but we all pronounce music to be one of the pleasantest things, whether instrumental or instrumental and vocal music together.[8]

What is more, Aristotle's pupil Aristoxenus taught that we must trust our ears as well as our minds in evaluating musical consonances:

> We endeavour to supply proofs that will be in agreement with the phenomena – in this unlike our predecessors. For some of these introduced extraneous reasoning, and rejecting the senses as inaccurate, fabricated rational principles, asserting that height and depth of pitch consist in certain numerical ratios and relative rates of vibration – a theory utterly extraneous to the subject and quite at variance with the phenomena. . . . Our method rests in the last resort on an appeal to the two faculties of hearing and intellect. . . .
> We must in matters of harmony accustom both ear and intellect to a correct judgement of the permanent and changeable element alike.[9]

McClain describes the revolutionary importance for the future of western

---

7. *Plutarch's Moralia* 1144f, tr. Benedict Einarson and Phillip H. De Lacy (London: William Heinemann, 1967), 441.

8. *Politics* 8.5.1 (1339b), tr. H. Rackham (London: William Heinemann, 1950), 653.

9. Aristoxenus, *Harmonic Elements*, in Strunk, *Source Readings in Music History*, 26-7.

musical development when "the umbilical cord which tied tone to number" was cut by Aristotle and his pupil Aristoxenus: "The ear rules the universe of tone, they declared, at a time when Plato and the Pythagoreans had mastered the insights number provided acoustical theory. By that radical act they preserved for music the flexibility of definition – a certain elasticity in intervals – which the evolving science of mathematics could no longer tolerate."[10]

Following upon this philosophical respect for music as sounds in our ears as well as ratios in our minds, western tradition was to embrace a perennial conviction that music, of all our sensual experiences, affects our souls most deeply. Ovid gives the conviction classic expression in his telling of the legend of Orpheus in the underworld, where music brings tears even to the cheeks of the Furies:

> As he sang these words to the music of his lyre, the bloodless ghosts were in tears: Tantalus made no effort to reach the waters that ever shrank away, Ixion's wheel stood still in wonder, the vultures ceased to gnaw Tityus' liver, the daughters of Danaus rested from their pitchers, and Sisyphus sat idle on his rock. Then for the first time, they say, the cheeks of the Furies were wet with tears, for they were overcome by his singing. The king and queen of the underworld could not bear to refuse his pleas.[11]

In Christian tradition, Augustine, recalling the time of his conversion, composes a memorable image to express his sense of music's influence upon his heart – irresistible as the ocean, surging, seeping, overflowing, and streaming down:

> The tears flowed from me when I heard your hymns and canticles, for the sweet singing of your Church moved me deeply. The music surged in my ears, truth seeped into my heart, and my feelings of devotion overflowed, so that the tears streamed down. But they were tears of gladness.[12]

This Augustinian tradition echoes in Calvin's "Foreword" to the *Geneva Psalter*: "And in truth we know by experience that song has great force and vigour to move and inflame the hearts of men to invoke and praise God with a more vehement and ardent zeal."[13]

Hans Urs von Balthasar writes of the need for balance between the two great traditions, Platonic and Aristotelian, in Christian spirituality:

> The consequences of a balanced philosophy of man – not exclusively platonic or aristotelian – and of its full realisation in the mysteries of Christ's incarnation, death and resurrection are very

10. *The Myth of Invariance*, 4.
11. *Metamorphoses*, tr. Mary M. Innes (Harmondsworth: Penguin, 1955), 226.
12. *Confessions* 9.6, 190.
13. In Strunk, *Source Readings*, 346.

far-reaching for Christian contemplation. A profound cleavage runs through the history of Christian spirituality. On the one hand, we have the protagonists of a platonic kind of contemplation which strives after contact with the "naked" truth, a direct "touching" of the essence of God, albeit in the night of the senses and spirit and in a simple non-conceptual awareness of God's presence; it aims at a corresponding abstraction from the sensible, first from the external senses, then from the imagination, and finally from all finite ideas bound up, as they are, with the world. On the other hand, we have the advocates of a contemplation dependent on the sensible images and concepts of the Gospel and the whole historical course of salvation. St. Bernard and St. Francis, to some extent, and St. Ignatius in particular, were opposed to the dominant traditional conception, and insisted on a concrete type of contemplation using the imagination and, indeed, the five senses.[14]

Our aim in this third chapter is to add musical explorations of the Incarnational tradition to the Pythagorean explorations of Chapter 2, in the spirit of Balthasar's commendation of balance.

## *Emotion and Meaning, Musical and Religious*

The tradition that regards material, sensual, audible experiences as potentially sacramental traces its heritage from biblical scripture through Dionysius, the mystical theologian for whom the Abbey Church of Saint Denis is named. Dionysius opens his treatise *The Celestial Hierarchies* with a quotation from the New Testament book of James: "Every good gift and every perfect gift is from above and cometh down from the Father of Lights" (Jas 1.17).[15] Emphasising the qualifier "every," Dionysius comments on the sacramental importance of sensual experiences:

> For the mind can by no means be directed to the spiritual present-
> ation and contemplation of the Celestial Hierarchies unless it use
> the material guidance suited to it, accounting those beauties which
> are seen to be images of the hidden beauty, the sweet incense a
> symbol of spiritual dispensations, and the earthly lights a figure of
> the immaterial enlightenment.[16]

Dionysius then states his broad concept of sacramental encounter quite plainly: "Holy contemplations can therefore be derived from all things."[17]

Our present question is how holy contemplations derive from sounding

---

14. *Prayer*, tr. A. V. Littledale (New York: Sheed and Ward, 1961), 210.
15. *The Mystical Theology and the Celestial Hierarchies*, 2d ed. (Surrey: The Shrine of Wisdom, 1965), 21.
16. p.22.
17. p.26.

music. A beloved hymn of Christendom, "For the Beauty of the Earth,"
includes the following stanza:

> For the joy of ear and eye,
> for the heart and mind's delight,
> for the mystic harmony
> linking sense and sound and sight,
> Christ our God, to thee we raise
> this our hymn of grateful praise.[18]

This simple stanza suggests our not-so-simple question. It is the question
of how religious "sense" is linked to "sound and sight." What is the "mystic
harmony" that joins ear and eye to heart and mind? What is the sense of
music's sounds? Particularly, can music convey religious meaning? Music
with religious texts can do so, of course. But music *per se*, apart from
texts?

Let us return to religious meaning at its deepest level in the theological
tradition of Schleiermacher. For Schleiermacher religion is grounded in
"sense and taste for the infinite,"[19] or, in his later formulation, in "the
consciousness of being absolutely dependent, or, which is the same thing,
of being in relation with God."[20] In this understanding, religion is grounded
in a sense of the ultimate givenness of our lives and of the abiding context
and conditions amidst which we live. Unlike more specific emotions that
come and go with various occasions of our lives, this religious sense of
final dependence is inescapable. This does not mean that we are always
conscious of our ultimate dependence. It means rather that such awareness is always appropriate and never inappropriate. A contrary sense –
that we are ourselves the ultimate bestowers of our own lives and of the
ultimate conditions and context of our lives – is never appropriate.
Reflection always discloses the inappropriateness of such a sense. Thus
the assertion concerning God in the King James Version of the Psalter:

> It is he that hath made us,
> and not we ourselves. (Ps 100.3)

Many people find such a religious sense elusive, and the divine object
of such sentiment (the "he" of the Psalter verse) more elusive still. Let us
consider an example of particular celebrity. In 1927 Sigmund Freud sent
Romain Rolland a copy of Freud's book *The Future of an Illusion*, calling
it a "small book that treats religion as an illusion." Freud reports Rolland's
reply:

> He answered that he entirely agreed with my judgement upon
> religion, but that he was sorry I had not properly appreciated the
> true source of religious sentiments. This, he says, consists in a

18. *The Hymnal 1982*, #416.
19. *On Religion*, tr. Oman, 39.
20. *The Christian Faith* 1.4, 12.

> peculiar feeling which he himself is never without, which he finds confirmed by many others, and which he may suppose is present in millions of people. It is a feeling which he would like to call a sensation of "eternity," a feeling as of something limitless, unbounded – as it were "oceanic." . . . One may, he thinks, rightly call oneself religious on the ground of this oceanic feeling alone, even if one rejects every belief and every illusion.[21]

Rolland's "oceanic" feeling recalls the oceanic imagery Augustine uses to express sounding music's effect upon his ears and heart and tears at the time of his religious conversion.

Freud finds Rolland's oceanic feeling foreign to himself. Yet he characterises that feeling with accuracy:

> If I have understood my friend rightly, he means the same thing by it as the consolation offered by an original and somewhat eccentric dramatist to his hero who is facing a self-inflicted death. "We cannot fall out of this world." That is to say, it is a feeling of an indissoluble bond, of being one with the external world as a whole.[22]

Freud's characterisation of the oceanic feeling is in fact very close to Schleiermacher's characterisation of the fundamental religious awareness of absolute dependence, except that Schleiermacher evokes the name of God:

> The sum total of religion is to feel that, in its highest unity, all that moves us in feeling is one; to feel that aught single and particular is only possible by means of this unity; to feel, that is to say, that our being is a being and living in and through God.[23]

Our question now is whether sounding music is capable of conveying such a profound and elusive religious sensibility as the fundamental feeling characterised by Schleiermacher and Freud. Anthony Storr suggests that music cannot convey such sensibility: "music can cause intense emotional arousal followed by feelings of relaxation and satisfaction; but this common response to being moved by musical performance is far removed from the uncommon oceanic state."[24] Yet to me music has conveyed this profound and elusive religious sensibility. As with theological arguments and proofs, I suspect that music can convey profound religious sensibility only to persons who are empathetic to such sensitivity and thus attuned to perceive musical expression in this way. In speaking of religious sensibility Schleiermacher seems at times to suggest that the cosmos ultimately compels our admission of its abiding and inescapable givenness, and with

21. *Civilization and Its Discontents*, tr, James Strachey (New York: W. W. Norton, 1961), 10-11.
22. p.12.
23. *On Religion*, tr. Oman, 49-50.
24. *Music and the Mind*, (New York: The Free Press, 1992), 96

that admission compels a religious feeling of absolute dependence as well. Freud respectfully disagrees, as I believe he has a right to do:

> I cannot discover this "oceanic" feeling in myself. . . . I may remark that to me this seems something rather in the nature of an intellectual perception, which is not, it is true, without an accompanying feeling-tone, but only such as would be present with any other act of thought of equal range. From my own experience I could not convince myself of the primary nature of such a feeling. But this gives me no right to deny that it does in fact occur in other people.[25]

If Freud convinces us to acknowledge that the cosmos itself does not have the unexceptionable capacity to impart, still less to compel, religious sensibility, we certainly cannot claim that capacity for music. I have argued that in the Pythagorean tradition of music's mathematics, the overtone series compels our intellectual attention as something given and enduring, and we have considered certain theological inferences from that fact, inferences that I believe to be plausible. In the Incarnational tradition of sounding music, however, where musical experience is richer, more inward, and correspondingly more complex, matters become less compelling and more subjective. Storr is correct, I think, when he observes that the oceanic feeling of religious mysticism "is almost invariably a solitary experience."[26] We can therefore expect that musical occasions for the feeling will also be solitary experiences. One can only describe them in the hope that others may sense some recognition, experience some sympathetic resonance.

In this spirit, let me attempt a description. Music in which I have sensed an intense oceanic feeling comes in the second movement of Brahms's *Fourth Symphony*. The movement ends in the key of E major. In many of its passages, however, beginning with the movement's opening bars, Brahms uses the Phrygian mode, neither quite major nor quite minor, giving the music an antique atmosphere and a disquieting mood of uncertainty. Sombre horns and woodwinds intensify this impression, and strings play the movement's principal theme pizzicato, making it sound tentative and halting.

The movement is some twelve minutes in duration (118 bars). After about four minutes of the principal theme in Phrygian, major, and minor, the cellos introduce a new, expressive melody (bar 41). The melody is in the key of B major, B being the 5th or "dominant" of E. Following the principal theme's harmonic ambiguity as it does, this new melody's more conventional harmony brings a sense of welcome and relief. Marked "expressively" (*espressivo*) and moving in diatonic steps and small intervals of the 3rd and 4th, this soft cello melody is accompanied by sustained chords in higher strings, marked "sweetly" (*dolce*). Above all the other

25. *Civilization and Its Discontents*, 11, 12.
26. *Music and the Mind*, 95.

strings, the first violins play placid arpeggios, as in a lullaby. The lowest
strings, together with the rest of the orchestra, are silent. The melody lasts
for only a minute or so (10 bars) and then gradually sublimates. It has been
a brief haven in the movement's larger flow, conveying a sense of calm,
tenderness, intimacy. The effect is not oceanic. The passage has prepared,
however, for something to come.

The movement returns to its principal theme and again develops it in
major, minor, and Phrygian. Then, about eight minutes into the movement
(bar 84), the music builds to its loudest passage: insistent triplets ham-
mered out by the entire orchestra, again ambiguous as to major or minor,
suggesting something of crisis or panic. After a final orchestral stroke (bar
87), the woodwinds, in a highly condensed modulation, bring the movement back to its home key of E major. There, about nine minutes into the
movement (bar 88), the expressive melody returns. This time, however,
Brahms gives it to the first violins, supported by all the lower strings,
where every desk divides into two or three parts for the richest possible
texture and harmony. The whole is marked "strong" (*forte*) and "rather
expressive" (*poco espressivo*). The double basses are asked to play their
notes with connection (*legato*), and are helped to this end by notes tied
across the strong first beat of the bar. The melody's original ten bars are
prolonged by half, in which the full orchestra joins the theme, adding sonic
strength and rhythmic vigour. The melody's earlier tenderness and intimacy are transfigured into the full orchestra's power, vastness, and cohesiveness.

On me, when I am in a suitable listening mood, the effect of this passage is oceanic. Exactly in the terms of Rolland's religious sensibility and
Schleiermacher's theological exposition, the music evokes an engulfing
sense of indissoluble bond, of intimacy with the overpowering vastness of
the world. My skin crawls – even at the moment of this writing, when I am
merely recollecting the music's sound. Thus I appreciate Ludwig
Wittgenstein's exclamation: "The musical *strength of thoughts* in Brahms"
("Die musikalische *Gedankenstärke* bei Brahms").[27] I would exclaim also:
"The *religious* strength of thoughts in Brahms."

We must clarify several things about such exclamations, however. First,
we have no reason to believe that Brahms intended any explicitly
conceptual, still less any explicitly religious, interpretation of this symphonic
passage. We have good reason, in fact, to believe that he did not. Brahms
rarely wrote music with conceptual, pictorial, or programmatic intent. Typically
his compositions are pure, or abstract, music. Wittgenstein, who as a child
knew Brahms as a close friend of his family, illumines this point:

---

27. *Culture and Value*, ed. G. H. von Wright, tr. Peter Winch (Chicago: University
     of Chicago Press, 1980), 23. Wittgenstein's emphasis.

In the days of silent films all kinds of classical works were played as accompaniments, but not Brahms. . . . Not Brahms, because he is too abstract. I can imagine an exciting scene in a film accompanied by Beethoven's or Schubert's music and might gain some sort of understanding of the music from the film. But this would not help me to understand Brahms's music.[28]

We cannot assume that Brahms composed his music to give rise to religion's oceanic feeling. The feeling is the hearer's, is mine. Yet I am entitled to believe that the feeling is not purely random or idiosyncratic. Quite particular musical qualities and characteristics occasion it: richness of harmony, vigour of rhythm, prolongation of melody, and orchestral power, vastness, and cohesiveness. Given appropriate conditions one might expect a not dissimilar response on the part of other hearers, and indeed even on the part of the composer. Yet the stimulating qualities and characteristics are musical, not conceptual or psychological.

This example, I believe, illustrates the sacramental miracle of sounding music. Music's sounds can occasion strong thoughts and deep feelings, including religious thoughts and feelings. Music's sounds can convey human meanings, including religious meanings. Such sonic-to-spiritual transubstantiation, in the phrase of Schleiermacher we considered earlier, "belongs to the mysteries."[29] No one can fully account for such musical experiences. They come by way of an immediacy of feeling that eludes analysis – certainly Pythagorean and Freudian analysis. Yet for those who sense them, such musical experiences can be life-forming. Numerous theories of causation and correlation between particular kinds of music and particular kinds of emotion have been suggested as explanations of how music "manages to *sound* the way emotions *feel*,"[30] and most of those theories have been widely discredited as crude and unconvincing. Much to be preferred, I believe, is the simplicity of Wittgenstein's observation: "Feelings accompany our apprehension of a piece of music in the way they accompany the events of our life."[31]

We have been discussing musical and religious emotion and meaning in relation to a most fundamental religious feeling, the oceanic feeling of absolute dependence and indissoluble bond. Music also occasions more particular emotions, of course. Walhout writes: "People regularly describe musical compositions as dancing, serene, agitated, sad, ecstatic, sombre, death-like, joyous, restless, pensive, deep, exultant, and by a thousand other adjectives and adjectival phrases."[32] In an essay occasioned by his study of Aristotle, Thomas Twining, the 18th-century classicist, writes

28. p.25.
29. *On Religion*, tr. Crouter, 166.
30. Jim Holt, "Roll Over, Pythagoras," *The New Yorker*, June 5, 1995, 92.
31. *Culture and Value*, 10.
32. "Augustine on the Transcendent in Music," 287.

with uncommon finesse concerning music's evocations of particular emotions and meanings:

> Music is capable of raising ideas through the medium of those *emotions* which it raises *immediately*. But this is an effect so delicate and uncertain – so dependent on the fancy, the sensibility, the musical experience, and even the temporary disposition, of the *hearer*, that to call it *imitation* is surely going beyond the bounds of all reasonable analogy. Music, here, is not *imitative*, but if I may hazard the expression, merely *suggestive*. But, whatever we may call it, this I will venture to say: that in the *best* instrumental music, expressively *performed*, the very indecision itself of the expression, leaving the hearer to the free operation of his emotion upon his *fancy*, and, as it were, to the free *choice* of such ideas as are, to *him*, most adapted to react upon and heighten the emotion which occasioned them, produces a pleasure, which nobody, I believe, who is able to feel it, will deny to be one of the most delicious that music is capable of affording.[33]

Twining quotes with approval Aristotle's conclusion: "Music, even *without words, has expression*."[34] Many agree, among them Søren Kierkegaard on the overture to Mozart's *Don Giovanni*:

> It is powerful like a god's idea, turbulent like a world's life, harrowing in its earnestness, palpitating in its desire, crushing in its terrible wrath, animating in its full-blooded joy; it is hollow-toned in its judgement, shrill in its lust; it is ponderous, ceremonious in its awe-inspiring dignity; it is stirring, flaring, dancing in its delight.[35]

## Divine Artistry and Human Artistry

Against Pythagoreans who valued music primarily for its silent, abstract, cerebral significance, Aristotle undertook "to refute those who assert that the practice of music is vulgar."[36] Christian tradition went further. Beyond merely freeing the sounds of music from a reputation of vulgarity, the church embraced appropriate sounding music as spiritually edifying and as a suitable medium of worship. This was not a simple process, however. In our next chapter we shall consider the church's long history of suspicions

---

33. *Aristotle's Treatise on Poetry, Translated: with Notes on the Translation, and on the Original: and Two Dissertations, On Poetical, and Musical, Imitation*, 2d ed. (London: 1812). Twining's emphases. In Weiss, *Music in the Western World*, 294.
34. p.294. Twining's emphasis.
35. *The Immediate Erotic Stages Or The Musical-Erotic. Either/Or, Part I*, tr. Howard V. Hong and Edna H. Hong (Princeton: Princeton University Press, 1987), 127
36. *Politics* 8.6.2 (1340b), 663.

concerning the inappropriateness and even sacrilege of certain kinds of music. Yet at no point in history did the mainstream traditions of the church reject sounding music. How could they possibly have done so, with the Psalter at the heart of their sacred scriptures?

> It is good to give thanks to the LORD,
>> to sing praises to your name, O Most High;
> to declare your steadfast love in the morning,
>> and your faithfulness by night,
> to the music of the lute and the harp,
>> to the melody of the lyre.
> For you, O LORD, have made me glad by your work;
>> at the works of your hands I sing for joy. (Ps 92.1-4)

Indeed, Jewish and Christian traditions portray the Creator God as a musical artist, and Christian tradition portrays Christ as God's divine instrument and human musicianship as echoing divine. Let us consider these three portrayals in turn.

First, God as artist, whose creative expression is the world, is a recurrent biblical theme. The Wisdom of Solomon portrays God as the world's "artisan" (13.1) and as "the author of beauty" (13.3). Both Isaiah and Jeremiah compare God to a sculptor working in clay:

> O LORD, you are our Father;
> we are the clay, and you are our potter;
> we are all the work of your hand. (Is 64.8)[37]

Augustine applies this prophetic simile to resurrection bodies sculpted by the "Almighty Artist":

> An artist who has for some reason produced an ugly statue can recast it and make it beautiful, removing the ugliness without any loss of the material substance. And if there was any displeasing excess in some parts of the first figure, anything out of proportion to the rest, he does not have to cut it off or throw away any part of the whole; he can simply moisten the whole of the material and remix it, without producing any ugliness or diminishing the quantity of material. If a human artist can do this, what are we to think of the Almighty Artist?[38]

The biblical prophet Zephaniah portrays God as a specifically musical artist – namely, a festival singer:

> He will rejoice over you with gladness,
>> he will renew you in his love;
> he will exult over you with loud singing
>> as on a day of festival. (Zeph 3.17)

A related theme appears in an anonymous 2nd-century text traditionally

---

37. See also Jeremiah 18.5-6.
38. *The City of God* 22.19, 1060-1. See also 22.30, 1087-8.

misattributed to Justin Martyr. It is the theme of the Almighty Artist as instrumentalist, playing upon an ensemble of compliant prophets:

> For neither by nature nor by human understanding is it possible for men to know things so great and divine, but by the gift descending from above at that time upon those holy men, to whom there was no need of verbal artifice nor of saying anything in a contentious or quarrelsome way, but to present themselves pure to the working of the divine Spirit, so that the Divinity itself, coming down from heaven like a plectrum and using those just men as an instrument like the cithara or lyre, might reveal to us the knowledge of divine and heavenly things. Therefore, as if from one mouth and one tongue, in conformity and harmony with one another, they have taught us about God, about the creation of the world, about the fashioning of man.[39]

Second, in the most elaborate of all early Christian treatments of divine artistry, Clement of Alexandria shifts the accent from God to Christ. Christ is God's holy wisdom, word, and instrument: "Assuredly He Himself is an all-harmonious instrument of God, melodious and holy, the wisdom that is above this world, the heavenly Word."[40] Clement extends his metaphor to portray Christ not only as God's instrument but also as himself a musical artist. Christ is God's "minstrel" and "new song," who composes cosmic harmony out of dissonant elements and tunes the universe and humankind to be his own harmonious instruments:

> See how mighty is the new song! . . . Furthermore, it is this which composed the entire creation into melodious order, and tuned into concert the discord of the elements, that the whole universe might be in harmony with it . . . as one might blend the Dorian mode with the Lydian . . . thus melodiously mingling these extreme notes of the universe. . . . By the power of the Holy Spirit He arranged in harmonious order this great world, yes, and the little world of man too, body and soul together; and on this many-voiced instrument of the universe He makes music to God, and sings to the human instrument.[41]

Third, as for human artistry, biblical scripture portrays arts and crafts of all kinds as gifts of God's spirit:

> The LORD spoke to Moses: See, I have called by name Bezalel son of Uri son of Hur, of the tribe of Judah: and I have filled him with divine spirit, with ability, intelligence, and knowledge in every kind of craft, to devise artistic designs, to work in gold, silver, and

39. Pseudo-Justin, *Hortatory Address to the Greeks* 8, in McKinnon, *Music in Early Christian Literature*, 21.
40. *The Exhortation to the Greeks*, tr. G. W. Butterworth (London: William Heinemann, 1953), 15.
41. p.13.

bronze, in cutting stones for setting, and in carving wood, in every
kind of craft. (Ex 31.1-6)

Augustine regards musical artistry as a particularly intimate marriage of
human and divine spirit. He speaks of an *occulta familiaritas*[42] ("hidden
affinity") between music and the soul, and from his characterisation of the
octave he draws the theological inference we encountered earlier: "the
harmony between the single and the double . . . which has been naturally
so implanted in us (by whom indeed, if not by Him who created us?). . . ."[43]

These interpretations of musical experience remind us that we are created
creators. We find ourselves in a created world of given and enduring acoustical
conditions and musical principles that ultimately we did not choose and
cannot change. Yet our relation to these musical principles is artistic interaction. We may alter, shape, and direct musical realities in ways that are
highly creative and profoundly significant. Analogously, the tradition of
religious experience that Schleiermacher represents leads us to acknowledge both the ultimate givenness of the world and our creative significance within it.

Our musical and religious creativities disclose our conjunctive relation
with creation and the Creator. As this sense of cosmic conjunction is near
the fundamental religious feeling that Schleiermacher describes, so it is
near the heart of religious worship. Like the faith it expresses, worship is
both complex and risky. Mature worship, I believe, acknowledges our
finitude in relation to beauty, goodness, and truth. Mature worshippers
confess that extraordinary beauty in our liturgies, for instance, never ex-
hausts the beauty of holiness. Yet we are nevertheless able to create religious ceremonies that resound with the sacred beauty, goodness, and truth
that are manifest in creation. Weil calls such ceremonial echoes of creation not only beautiful but "marvellously beautiful":

> It is a fact that the purity of religious things is almost everywhere
> to be seen in the form of beauty, when faith and love do not fail.
> Thus the words of the liturgy are marvellously beautiful; and the
> words of the prayer issued for us from the very lips of Christ is
> perfect above all. In the same way Romanesque architecture and
> Gregorian plainchant are marvellously beautiful.[44]

In worship, human artistry may echo the divine artistry that underlies,
enables, and inspires it.

42. *Confessiones* 10.33, ed. W. H. D. Rouse, 2 vols. (London: William Heinemann,
        1968), 1:166.
43. *The Trinity* 4.2.4, 134.
44. *Waiting for God*, 187.

## *Mozart and Deconstruction*

But does the world really manifest divine artistry for our creativity to echo? May we really trust that our music resounds with transcendence? Some contemporary musicologists answer these questions in the negative. In their understanding, human creativity expresses cultural conditions, conventions, practices, and conversations. Talk of artistic creativity as expression of transcendent order is outdated at best. At worst, such talk represents ideological presumption cloaked as aesthetic taste.

These contemporary critics of a sacramental approach to music demand attention. We have considered Rorty's criticisms of the kind of foundationalism that I believe we can infer from Pythagorean appreciation of music's sacramental silence. Susan McClary is similarly critical of claims of transcendent meaning in sounding music. Challenging "the notion that music shapes itself in accordance with self-contained, abstract principles",[45] McClary and fellow musicologists wish to deconstruct the traditional canon of musical masterpieces. In an article on the music of Bach, McClary writes: "It seems to me quite inescapable that Bach was (among many other things) a Christian; but regardless of how strong his belief, his music remains a human, social construct."[46]

> Thus we must *confront* Bach and the canon and resituate him in such a way as to acknowledge his prominence in musical and nonmusical culture while not falling victim to it. What I am suggesting here is deconstruction as a political act. . . . The claim to transcendental truth that attaches to Bach and Mozart especially will continue to undercut our efforts until we can begin to define all these various kinds of artistic production as social practice.[47]

That the musical compositions of Bach and Mozart are imbued with the cultural contexts of their times seems to me self-evident. McClary's claim that "all" their various kinds of artistic production are "social practice," however, requires substantiation.

McClary applies her interpretation of artistic production as social construct in an engaging article on the second movement of Mozart's Piano Concerto in G Major, K.453.[48] She indicates impatience with fellow deconstructive critics who "still seem reluctant to let go of the classical music through which we yet have (the illusion of) access to transcendental truth:

45. Richard Leppert and Susan McClary, eds., *Music and Society: The Politics of Composition, Performance and Reception* (Cambridge: Cambridge University Press, 1987), xi.

46. "The Blasphemy of Talking Politics during Bach Year," in *Music and Society* (Cambridge: Cambridge University Press, 1987), 58n.

47. p.60. McClary's emphasis.

48. "A Musical Dialectic from the Enlightenment: Mozart's *Piano Concerto in G Major, K.453*," *Cultural Critique* 4 (Fall 1986), 129-69.

truth that seems not to have been put together by human hand."[49] McClary's analysis "seeks to perform a cultural critique on the 'perfect order' of Mozart's music."[50] She states her premises clearly. First, she assumes that the complex "codes" through which music communicates meaning – "specific repertories of gestures, rhetorical devices, associations, and so on"[51] – are "produced, shaped, transmitted, and declared meaningful only through social interaction."[52] Second, she similarly assumes that the "formal procedures" of musical composition, "even those abstract, seemingly self-contained formal procedures that regulate rhythm, melody, and harmony – that seem so insulated from the workings of the outside world – are social constructs."[53] Like Rorty, McClary is a clear, uncompromising, and influential critic of traditional modes of interpretation.

McClary deconstructs three of Mozart's musical conventions in particular: tonality, sonata procedure, and concerto format. Tonality refers to harmonic syntax, sonata procedure to compositional architecture, and concerto format to the interplay between solo piano and accompanying orchestra.[54] In relation to tonality, McClary observes that tonal compositions, such as Mozart's, are "strongly goal oriented,"[55] that is, are governed by the strong pull of the tonic key. The tonic's strong pull was one of our subjects in Chapter 2. But whereas my argument was that the tonic's pull is gravitational, as it were, with given and enduring foundations in Pythagorean intervals and the overtone series, for McClary the pull of the tonic is a manifestation of 18th-century bourgeois ideology:

> Early twentieth-century composers sought to banish tonality and
> its attendant "bourgeois" ideology altogether. If we today want to
> identify with and uphold these values (and the music of the eight-
> eenth century), well and good. But universals they are not.
> Recognising Mozart's participation in this ideological landscape
> is essential if we are to understand the terms upon which hinge his
> compositional strategies.[56]

Similarly, McClary asserts that basic bourgeois structures of "confrontation and eventual resolution" characterise the tonal and thematic architecture of Mozart's sonata procedure, as well as the dynamics between soloist and orchestra in the concerto format. According to McClary's interpretation, tonality, sonata procedure, and concerto format all manifest the "conflict and struggles for dominance" characteristic of 18th-century culture and politics:

49. p.131.
50. p.131.
51. p.131.
52. p.132.
53. p.132.
54. p.134.
55. p.135.
56. p.136.

Indeed, the problematics addressed in tonality, sonata procedure, and concerto are the familiar issues of the late eighteenth century: the narrative construction of identity and the threat of alterity, relationships between individual freedom and collective order, between objective reason and subjectivity, between stability and dynamic progress.[57]

With her premises clear, McClary turns to detailed analysis of Mozart's music. In addressing the perennial problems associated with trying to express analysis of sounding music in verbal language, she once again reveals her basic intention, namely, to dismantle the illusion of transcendent universals in music:

> This process may seem tedious, frustrating, or inconvenient; yet the alternative is to continue to exempt music from critical scrutiny – to let it have its way without our having the tools to question it. When the verbal going gets rough, just remember that we are trying to dismantle a highly resistant cultural barrier: one of the last toeholds of a universalist metaphysics.[58]

I confess that I do not find McClary's analysis "tedious, frustrating, or inconvenient" in the least. Her unfolding of the particular means by which Mozart develops his musical drama of confrontation and resolution is both dramatic and convincing. Rather than attempting to condense McClary's analysis here, I recommend her original as a model of clarity, and fascinating as well. The problem is not with McClary's musical analysis, I believe, but with the relation of the analysis to her deconstructionist conclusions. I find that the article's conclusions simply restate its premises, privileging historical and cultural reduction over given and enduring musical principles, but without significant argumentative support from the intervening analysis. That is, the article concludes what it assumes, namely, by asserting that Mozart's music expresses no kind of order except "the product of another struggle over cultural meaning":

> To acknowledge Mozart's music itself, then, as the product of another struggle over cultural meaning – a struggle that left its imprint on, that is enacted in the very musical processes themselves – is to place it on the same methodological footing as other repertories: all would have to be defined as products of particular social discourses, grounded in the priorities of the groups that create, preserve, and transmit them.[59]

Yet McClary's intervening musical analysis does little to support this uncompromising conclusion. The analysis concerns itself with questions of how Mozart's musical choices express the movement's basic drama of

57. pp.138-9.
58. p.140.
59. p.164.

conflict and resolution. This the article does beautifully. To substantiate its conclusions, however, the analysis would have to show that Mozart's musical choices arise solely from his "ideological landscape,"[60] and not from any additional influences, such as given physical laws that govern musical acoustics or enduring physical, physiological, and psychological laws that govern musical consonance and dissonance. This the analysis does not undertake. What is more, the analysis would have to show that Mozart's musical choices are nowhere "cloaked in mystery" and have in them nothing of "music's reputed 'ineffability'" – mystery and ineffability being notions that McClary has rejected in her premises.[61] This again the analysis both assumes and concludes but does not demonstrate.

Let us consider one of McClary's assumptions in more detail. Her article asserts that "eighteenth-century musical procedures purport to be based on the premise that harmony between social order and individual freedom is possible," but McClary argues that despite what those musical procedures purport to be, they in fact reflect "the authoritarian force that social convention will draw upon if confronted by recalcitrant nonconformity."[62] Her musical analysis claims to show this authoritarian dynamic at work in the tonal architecture of Mozart's movement, most particularly at the point of Mozart's "abrupt, under-motivated" modulation from C-sharp minor back to the prevailing key of C major, bridging from the movement's third section to its fourth.[63] McClary concludes that Mozart's abrupt modulation is a musical expression of 18th-century social convention, as represented by conventional harmony in the orchestra, suppressing nonconformist individuality, as represented by harmonic adventures on the part of the piano. But to support this conclusion, the analysis would need to show that a similar musical dynamic of sudden modulation does not appear elsewhere else in musical history, amidst social conditions different from the ideology of Mozart's culture of the late 18th century. This, again, the analysis does not do. In fact, Big Band music of the 20th century expresses much the same dynamic of conflict and forced resolution as that which McClary discovers in Mozart's movement: the band presents a standard tune, various soloists stretch the tune in more and more nonconformist dimensions, the drummer improvises a cadenza of wild individuality, and all are then jerked back to conventionality in an instant by the full band's abrupt reentry with the original tune. It seems to me more convincing to assume that there is something intrinsically satisfying in this musical pattern of statement, departure, and return, than to assume that the ideological conditions of Mozart in the 18th century and those of jazz-band leader

60. p.136.
61. p.139.
62. p.151.
63. p.152.

Buddy Rich, let us say, in the 20th century are as nearly alike as their similar musical architectures would indicate. I think we must agree with Steiner: "The construct of theme and variation, of quotation and *reprise*, is organic to music, particularly in the West."[64] Or with Malm, who includes "a basic need for musical tension and release, with all their melodic or rhythmic implications" among his provisional list of "universal principles in music."[65]

Besides particular lacunae of argument, McClary's hermeneutic of deconstruction shares with Rorty's what seems to me a general deficiency. Both authors insist upon a disjunctive view of what I observe to be an abundantly conjunctive world. For Rorty the disjunction is between historical opinions to redescribe, which he endorses, and given and enduring truths to discover, which he rejects. For McClary the disjunction is between musical procedure generated by cultural context, which she endorses, and composition engendered by given and enduring musical principles, which she rejects. Both authors present the disjunction as rigid and absolute. Neither seems willing to countenance both possibilities in conjunction.[66] Their insistence upon the contingent and cultural, together with their corollary rejection of the given and enduring, is categorical.

In contrast to McClary's deconstructive approach, a reconstructive appreciation of Mozart such as I would recommend recognises his music as a conjunction of cultural influences with transcultural, transhistorical acoustical laws and musical principles. Reconstructive appreciation embraces cultural and sociological analysis while at the same time acknowledging that musical genius such as Mozart's is finally ineffable. Such appreciation hears in Mozart's music expressions of his time and place as well as disclosures to many times and places. Deconstruction demands "reasons for keeping a piece in the collective cultural baggage."[67] Reconstruction approaches Mozart's compositions not as baggage but as transport.

McClary reports that she has been "told outright by prominent scholars that Bach . . . had *nothing* to do with his time or place, that he was 'divinely inspired,' that his music works in accordance with perfect, universal order and truth."[68] Surely we must join McClary in rejecting such silly overstatement. It is unfortunately true that lovers of music are often careless in

64. *Real Presences*, 20.
65. *Musical Cultures*, 214.
66. Elsewhere McClary speaks of both the mathematical and the social foundations of music, but again in disjunctive terms, as if the choice were either/or: "Afterword" to Jacques Attali, *Noise: The Political Economy of Music* (Minneapolis: University of Minnesota Press, 1985), 150.
67. McClary, "A Musical Dialectic," 161.
68. "The Blasphemy of Talking Politics during Bach Year," 14. McClary's emphasis.

speaking of great works as "eternal" or "timeless" without sufficient attention to exactly what such characterisations must mean. We may welcome David Tracy's exactness when he defines the timelessness of classics not as reified eternity but as "permanent timeliness":

> The classical text is not in some timeless moment which needs mere repetition. Rather its kind of timelessness as permanent timeliness is the only one proper to any expression of the finite, temporal, historical beings we are.[69]

In this study let us understand "eternity" to mean permanent timeliness.

Bach and Mozart are finite, temporal, historical beings, and their art has a great deal to do with their time and place. It is quite another thing, however, to claim as McClary does that Bach and Mozart have to do with nothing besides their time and place. I believe that to reduce musical experience to cultural experience is, in Tracy's phrase, to "disown the original experience of art and replace it with some other kind of experience."[70]

Before we continue with some reconstructive explorations into the second movement of Mozart's piano concerto, let us consider an analogous process of reductionism – disowning an original experience and replacing it with some other kind of experience – as it relates to the study of religion. In his book *Religious Experience*, Wayne Proudfoot carefully distinguishes between two different kinds of reduction. The first is "descriptive" reduction, which Proudfoot finds unacceptable:

> *Descriptive reduction* is the failure to identify an emotion, practice, or experience under the description by which the subject identifies it. This is indeed unacceptable. To describe an experience in nonreligious terms when the subject himself describes it in religious terms is to misidentify the experience, or to attend to another experience altogether. . . . This might properly be called reductionism. In any case, it precludes an accurate identification of the subject's experience.[71]

Our earlier example from Freud might illustrate Proudfoot's point. Rolland writes about the "oceanic" feeling that is the source of his "religious energy," and according to Proudfoot's analysis Freud is justified in responding to Rolland as he did. Freud accepts and acknowledges Rolland's description, yet at the same time confesses that he himself does not know such experience at first hand: "From my own experience I could not convince myself of the primary nature of such a feeling. But this gives me no right to deny that it does in fact occur in other people."[72]

69. *The Analogical Imagination*, 102.
70. *The Analogical Imagination*, 113.
71. (Berkeley: University of California Press, 1985), 196-7.
72. *Civilization and Its Discontents*, 12.

The second kind of reduction is "explanatory" reduction, and this reduction Proudfoot endorses for the study of religion:

> *Explanatory reduction* consists in offering an explanation of an experience in terms that are not those of the subject and that might not meet with his approval. This is perfectly justifiable and is, in fact, normal procedure. . . . The explanation stands or falls according to how well it can account for all the available evidence.[73]

To continue our illustration, Freud comments about Rolland's religious experience: "The only question is whether it is being correctly interpreted."[74] Proudfoot seems to suggest that Freud is justified in interpreting and attempting to account for religious experience in his own terms of explanation – whatever those terms may be, and whether or not his friend Rolland would find the terms an acceptable explanation of his original experience.

It is a difficult question just how adequate in fact our explanations of religious experience can be. I can appreciate Proudfoot's ambivalence on this issue. At one point he acknowledges the likelihood that no explanation can fully account for the original force of a religious or an artistic experience: "It is likely that no general account can be given which is adequate to capture the force or impressiveness of different kinds of experience."[75] Yet elsewhere Proudfoot suggests that good explanation may account for the force of an original experience, rendering it understandable to a person who has not shared the experience: "An explanation must satisfy in that it must account for the force of the experience. It is not necessary for the analyst to share the experience, however, to understand its force. It is the account which must satisfy, and an account can satisfy if it makes clear why the experience has the power it has for the subject."[76] The question remains: how far can "explanatory reduction" make the power of an experience clear to someone who has not shared the experience?

In an illustrative example of his own, Proudfoot writes of Schleiermacher's religious sense of the infinite:

> To explain Schleiermacher's sense of the infinite, his feeling of absolute dependence, and his apprehension of all events as miracles one would need to know more about his early years among the Moravians, his study of Spinoza, and the circle of friends in Berlin for whom he wrote *On Religion*. Each of these instances requires acquaintance with the Christian tradition and with the particular forms of that tradition which shaped the person and his experience.[77]

73. *Religious Experience*, 197.
74. *Civilization and Its Discontents*, 12.
75. *Religious Experience*, 212.
76. p.210.
77. p.224.

But just how much more would we need to know about Schleiermacher's personal and intellectual biography in order to explain his religious experiences and convey their original force in other terms? How much would we have to know to ascertain that Schleiermacher's fundamental religious sense arose from nothing except what those other terms express? Is it wiser to assume that his biography shaped, or that in association with given and enduring principles and structures of the world his biography co-shaped Schleiermacher's religious experiences?

I remain persuaded that our various descriptive and explanatory disciplines can illumine our profound religious and artistic experiences but never account for them fully. This is what I understand Kierkegaard to mean in his cryptic formulation, "I am convinced that if Mozart ever became entirely comprehensible to me, he would then become completely incomprehensible to me."[78] Our particular histories shape our religious beliefs and our artistic creations, but only partially. We cannot escape our placements in history and culture, nor should we wish to. Rorty is correct: our lives are contingent. McClary is correct: our musics are "products of particular social discourses."[79] Yet within our particular times and places, we also cannot escape principles and structures that are given, enduring, infinite in complexity, and finally irreducible, nor should we seek to.

## *Mozart and Transcendence*

In the midst of his particular context and our universal contexts, I believe, Mozart has composed music of permanent timeliness, the sublimity of which is cloaked in mystery and resounds with transcendence. Such ineffable conjunctions of time and transcendence go by various names. In religion we speak of "inspiration" and "incarnation," in art of "inspiration" and "genius." For me these conjunctions of time and transcendence are most admirable in religious saints and in the morally valiant. I find these conjunctions most palpable, however, in musical compositions, and supremely palpable in the music of Mozart.

To speak of Mozart's inspiration, or of his genius, as an incarnation of transcendence, is to transgress McClary's assumption that Mozart's music is solely a cultural construct, a product of 18th-century social discourse. Yet I believe that this augmentation is warranted by close attention to Mozart's music itself – attention that discloses not a single-cause, disjunctive explanation, but rather far richer conjunctions among contingent social contexts, given acoustical laws, enduring musical principles, and the ineffability of musical genius. In a word, I believe that the sounding presence of Mozart's music renders all our explanatory reductions paltry.

78. *The Immediate Erotic Stages*, 61.
79. "A Musical Dialectic," 164.

By way of seeking to establish this belief persuasively, let us return to the second movement of Mozart's piano concerto. Mozart constructs his movement upon a principal musical theme or "motto" occuring five times (at bars 1, 30, 64, 90, and 123). This recurring motto marks five musical sections within the movement. The first section opens with what McClary characterises as a "contemplative," even "votive," orchestral statement of the motto. The orchestra pauses, then proceeds to state and expand upon a second theme that, in comparison with the opening motto, McClary finds merely "stereotypical" – "pleasant if vacuous."[80] The second section of the movement then begins with the piano in its first solo entrance. The piano restates the principal motto, then pauses, just as the orchestra has done in the first section.

McClary describes the high drama of what happens next. In a startling departure from conventional expectation, the piano "strikes out" against the orchestra's earlier "prettiness." It does so "by pivoting to another – minor – key and by plunging headlong in the contrary affective direction, defining itself immediately in terms of anguish or sorrow."[81] McClary mentions in passing the "wide leaps" of the piano's new melodic theme as a sign of "grief." Let us concentrate our reconstructive appreciation on those wide melodic leaps. Can we go beyond deconstructive reduction of them to mere products of Mozart's cultural setting? Do they disclose given acoustical laws, enduring musical principles? Do they express ineffable genius? Do they manifest permanent timeliness? I believe that analysis will support affirmative answers to all these questions.

We may begin with the question of how Mozart's wide melodic leaps are able to sing of grief with such poignancy. In this second section of the movement, the right hand of the piano part has two dramatic leaps in succession. The interval of each leap is a 12th. The first is from G up an octave and a 5th to D, while a simultaneous B flat in the left hand defines a G minor chord. The leap's wide span, the minor key, and the deliberate pacing of its two notes suggest something of terrible determination. The second leap follows in the next bar, also the interval of a 12th, but this time from A flat to E flat, with a simultaneous C in the left hand defining an A flat major chord. The second leap is up a chromatic step from the first and is thus coloured with harmonic tension. The piano's melodic line then descends from its high point into a diminished chord. That chord is fraught with ambiguity, as the conventions of 18th-century harmony al-low such a chord to resolve in a number of different ways. Mozart chooses to resolve it into the placid key of D major. Has the piano's theme been exhausted by its expressions of grief, or has its grief been seduced by the orchestra's conventional comforts? We are not sure.

80. "A Musical Dialectic," 145.
81. p.146.

The movement's third section begins with the orchestra again stating the principal motto. Again a pause. Then the piano answers with a melody which McClary describes as "melancholy":

> This time, however, it is less deliberately theatrical in style. It is expressive now of melancholy. Many of the same signs reappear (the throbbing, reiterated harmonies – which now seem like a dull, persistent ache – the leaps, the turns), but they all fold back on themselves. It is as though the piano is no longer concerned with public display (to say nothing of the facile escapism offered by the orchestra), but rather with genuine expressions of loss.[82]

As McClary notes, again in passing, the leaps in the piano's melodic line reappear in this third section. How do the leaps contribute to the greater intensity, the "genuine expressions of loss," in this section's passage? They are again wide leaps of a 12th. But whereas in the movement's second section their pacing was deliberate, this time the two melodic leaps come suddenly. The rhythm of each is quick and irregular, and the second follows instantly upon the first. The stabbing effect is like an alarming arrhythmia, a hurtful stitch in the heart. What is more, the two leaps are this time without harmonic ambiguity. They lie within a single chordal harmony, a dominant 7th, that leads with a sense of inevitability to a minor cadence.

This brings us to the movement's fourth section. We noted above that McClary emphasises Mozart's "abrupt, under-motivated" modulation back to the tonic key, bridging from the movement's third section to its fourth. She suggests that the orchestra's highly compressed return from the harmonically distant key of C sharp minor to the tonic key of C major represents an authoritarian overpowering of the piano's individual grief. McClary regards this modulation as a social construct, a typical Enlightenment attempt to affirm "some principle that *transcends* both the social order and individual subjectivity."[83] She dismisses this 18th-century affirmation, however, as utopian:

> This finally, then, is a world that contains transcendental ideals, social order, and subjective alienation. A world that professes equal dedication to individual freedom and social harmony, that demands originality of expression and yet the unvarying affirmation of a pre-determined bottom line. A world in which all these elements, these contradictions appear to be reconciled through effortless, rational means – a Utopia.[84]

McClary's interpretation of the orchestra's compressed modulation exemplifies a hermeneutics of suspicion. It leads to an ironic "reading" of the piano passage that opens the movement's fourth section by restating the principal motto:

82. p.148.
83. pp.152-3. McClary's emphasis.
84. p.155.

The formerly resistant, newly converted soloist not only acquiesces to convention, it even takes the lead – embracing warmly and confidently the opening motto. . . . [I]t apparently concurs wholeheartedly with whatever the motto stands for and is even willing to elaborate on it. Then, after the usual pause, the piano plunges not into its previous forms of melancholy but into the most declaratively affirmative material in the entire composition.[85]

Here a hermeneutics of appreciation may part company, for non-ironic interpretations of this fourth section are also possible, and they seem to me more complete and more convincing. In the orchestra's extraordinarily condensed modulation that Mozart uses to bridge the third and fourth sections, we might hear an harmonic inventiveness that transcends, rather than enforces, the orchestra's bland conventionality. We might hear unexpected resolution of musical tension and reconciliation of musical difference. One need not number Pollyanna among the saints to believe that inexplicable resolutions of tension and unexpected reconciliations of difference are possible. A hermeneutics of appreciation might enable us to hear in this movement from Mozart's music neither utopian illusions exclusive to the 18th century, nor irresponsible denials of grief and loss that would be unforgivable in the 20th, but rather support for hope and encouragement to faith. Mozart, from his time and place, might thus compose music that offers revelatory potential for many times and places.

In this fourth section of the movement Mozart's melodic leap makes a final appearance. How might Mozart's melodic leap support an interpretation of the kind I am suggesting? Specifically, how is the melodic leap, which has earlier reinforced moods of grief and loss, able to enhance this fourth, most affirmative of the movement's five sections? First, for this fourth appearance of the movement's principal motto Mozart chooses a fresh and refreshing key, E flat major. Second, he restricts the harmony of the piano passage to the most basic major pattern of I-IV-V-I, mellowing the IV-chord with a 6th. Third, Mozart has the melodic voice sing not in the alto and soprano ranges, as in the previous two leaps, but rather in the piano's warm tenor range. The combined effect of key, harmony, and range is a sense of serene, autumnal resolution.

Then the melodic leap occurs. In its pacing we hear neither the terrible deliberateness of the first occurrences, nor the mortal panic of the second, but rather a moderated, natural resolve. Instead of two successive leaps we hear only one. In comparison with the drama of the earlier double leaps, is the effect of this single leap not therefore anticlimactic? By no means. Mozart's musical genius compensates – whether by intention or intuition, who can say? He expresses his music's new sense of serenity and resolve by increasing the leap's span. The earlier melodies leapt by 12ths. This final melody takes the extraordinary melodic leap of a 17th,

85. p.153.

up two whole octaves and a 3rd. It then cascades in the rapids of a scale
back to the piano's deep tenor range and the section's tranquil home key
of E flat major. In this fourth section, the piano expresses a sense of resolution, leaps to its extreme limit, tests it through its entire range, and finds
it trustworthy. The movement's earlier grief and loss are not forgotten or
suppressed, for in the piano's very next phrase the mood of grief returns to
colour the nostalgic turns of melody in a wistful minor key. But the mood
has been appropriated and transfigured.

What are the origins of Mozart's compositional choices of the kind we
have been considering: the fresh key of E flat major; the simplification of
earlier harmonies; the autumnal voice of the piano's tenor range; the single
leap instead of a double; the capacious interval, followed by the melodic
cascade back down through its extraordinary range? Do these compositional
choices originate from Mozart's cultural context? From given laws of
acoustics? From enduring principles of musical harmony? From Mozart's
musical genius, where intention and intuition are finally inseparable and
inscrutable? Surely from none of these alone. Rather from all of them in
conjunction.

Mozart is a created creator. He composed within 18th-century culture,
and the musical conventions of his time and place profoundly shape his
music, as McClary is right to emphasise. Yet these conventions are themselves shaped by acoustical laws – determining the timbre of the piano's
tenor range, for example – and by principles of harmonic relationships
originating in the overtone series. At the same time, Mozart's musical
genius transcends and transforms these cultural and natural contexts and
conditions. What analysis – descriptive or explanatory – could ever predict
Mozart's musical gestures or account for their sublime expressiveness?

Still less can description and explanation reproduce or stand in for our
immediate experiencing of Mozart's sounding music. This brings us back
to Proudfoot's issue of the significance of immediate experience. We do
not have to accept Aristotle's entire philosophy of art as "imitation" of
reality to hear in Mozart's music the truth of Aristotle's observations
concerning the expressiveness and impressiveness of music:

> Rhythms and melodies contain representations of anger and mild-
> ness, and also of courage and temperance and all their opposites
> and the other moral qualities, that most closely correspond to the
> true natures of these qualities (and this is clear from the facts of
> what occurs – when we listen to such representations we change in
> our soul).[86]

Music does not change our souls inevitably, of course, or always, or all
alike. Much depends upon our cultural, social and psychological situations.
Given propitious times and places and states of mind and heart, however,

---

86. *Politics* 8.5.6 (1340a), 657.

Mozart's music has the potential to effect changes in our souls, namely, to engender a sense of resolve, hope, reconciliation, or transfiguration.

This expressiveness and impressiveness are finally a matter of immediate, palpable experience of sounding music, which no description or explanation can adequately reduce, still less convey. In my experience no substitute of any kind can evoke the thrilling sense of rightness that transfixes our hearing of Mozart's musical choices. Paradoxically, he makes them sound not like choices at all but like musical inevitabilities, even as we are fully aware that Mozart's compositional inventiveness – and probably his improvisational inventiveness as well, if only we could have heard it – seems capable of alighting upon any number of alternative musical choices that we might find equally convincing and transfixing.

Plotinus (3rd century) marvels over the immediate sense of such evident rightness: "something which we become aware of even at the first glance; the soul speaks of it as if it understood it, recognises and welcomes it and as it were adapts itself to it."[87] Wittgenstein likewise wonders over the sense of musical rightness that accompanies our immediate experiences of sounding music in the absence of any analytical paradigm, and he acknowledges the genuine novelty of musical inspiration:

> "The repeat is *necessary*." In what respect is it necessary? Well, sing it, and you will see that only the repeat gives it its tremendous power. – Don't we have an impression that a model for this theme already exists in reality and the theme only approaches it, corresponds to it, if this section is repeated? Or am I to utter the inanity: "It just sounds more beautiful with the repeat"? . . . Yet there just *is* no paradigm apart from the theme itself. And yet again there *is* a paradigm apart from the theme: namely, the rhythm of our language, of our thinking and feeling. And the theme, moreover, is a *new* part of our language; it becomes incorporated into it; we learn a new *gesture*.[88]

Wittgenstein recognises the incapacity of reductive analyses to account for the elusive and unlimited variability of sounding music's expressiveness:

> Tender expression in music. It isn't to be characterised in terms of degrees of loudness or tempo. Any more than a tender facial expression can be described in terms of the distribution of matter in space. As a matter of fact it can't even be explained by reference to a paradigm, since there are countless ways in which the same piece may be played with genuine expression.[89]

---

87. *Enneads* 1.6.2, tr. A. H. Armstrong (London: William Heinemann, 1966), 237.
88. *Culture and Value*, tr. Peter Winch, 52. Wittgenstein's emphases.
89. p.82.

It was Elbert Green Hubbard, I believe, who said that masterpieces of art are cloud-capped. Our analyses, however subtle or poetic, and our explanations, however descriptive or explanatory, finally fail to clear away the heights of original inspirations or original experiences of music.

Our reconstructive appreciation has finally to consider the fifth and concluding section of Mozart's movement. The fourth section of the movement has culminated in a cadenza for the piano. Thereupon Mozart opens the fifth section by giving the principal motto's final presentation to the orchestra alone. The motto is significantly altered, however. It is still contemplative. But for the first time it includes a chromatic, downward progression – a progression of the kind that has earlier coloured the piano's expressions of loss. Also for the first time, the motto's cadence is not by way of a conventional dominant 7th chord. The orchestra's cadence is rather by way of an ambiguous diminished chord, such as has earlier expressed the piano's sense of grief. It is as if the orchestra has learned from, indeed has come to share, the piano's expressions of grief and loss. The piano has also learned from the orchestra's earlier tone of amiability. For the first time, the principal motto is not followed by an ambivalent pause. Rather, the piano straightaway presents a musical theme that, in McClary's phrase, "answers and completes" the orchestral motto – which seems this time in need of solace rather than mere continuation. The piano sings its musical theme in the warmth of the movement's subdominant key of F, leading at last to a conventional cadence into the tonic key of C major.

Neither McClary's deconstructive analysis nor my reconstructive one is likely to evoke a response anything like what McClary describes upon actually hearing this concluding section of Mozart's music:

> The question then is not whether I personally find Mozart's music beautiful or not. (I have to restrain myself from weeping every time the piano in this concerto movement answers and completes the motto, both because of the glory of that illusion of certainty and because I know what that "certainty" cost.)[90]

I share McClary's experience of tears, but tears born from a different interpretation. McClary concludes that Mozart's movement ends in a costly "illusion of certainty," since according to her analysis the reconciliation of piano and orchestra is either authoritarian or utopian, in accordance with 18th-century ideology. What I hear is reconciliation achieved through mutual interaction, the orchestra learning to share the piano's grief, the piano learning to share the orchestra's congeniality. My tears well at the movement's sheer musical fulfilment, but also at the suggestion of resolution and reconciliation achieved through individual suffering and social sharing. At the movement's end McClary hears the illusory certainty of pseudo-Enlightenment. It is possible to hear human grief transfigured.

90. "A Musical Dialectic," 168.

## *Creativity as Covenant*

To say that Mozart transcends his time and culture is not to say that Mozart is divine or that his music is holy. To speak in these ways invites musical silliness and religious idolatry. Yet to honour Mozart as a created creator may enhance our religious appreciation. Music and mathematics, writes Rothstein, "remain mysteries, seeming too close to Truth to be merely human, too close to invention to be divine."[91] Thus we are prompted to think of Mozart's creativity as the image and likeness of divine creativity and of his music as having a sacramental dimension. An ineffable conjunction of historical and trans-historical realities, Mozart's art constitutes an incarnation as characterised by Hocking: "This is the primitive motive of honest art – not imitation, not invention, but an ever-continuing appropriation of the real through one's own begetting."[92]

Hocking's lovely phrase here, "appropriation of the real through one's own begetting," expresses a significant part of what biblical tradition includes in the idea of covenant relationship between divine Creator and human creature. Steiner laments the "break of the covenant between word and world . . . which defines modernity itself."[93] With Steiner, I believe that an appreciation of musical creativity can help restore a sense of covenant. Let us therefore conclude this chapter with some considerations of covenant as relationship between transcendent reality and human freedom, with special reference to musical creativity.

In particular, let us consider biblical traditions of covenant in three aspects. Natural covenant includes human creativity as a process of discovering. Historical covenant includes human creativity as a process of synthesising. Eternal covenant includes human creativity as a process of transcending. The biblical tradition of the first of these, natural covenant, traces back to the rainbow covenant between God and the family of Noah. Itself a work of divine art, the rainbow signifies God's pledge that nature's abiding structures and forces are for the support, not the destruction, of humankind. Begbie explicitly relates this biblical tradition of natural covenant to human artistry: "if we regard the orderliness of creation chiefly as gift, it will not be seen as a cramping constraint, a strait-jacket to which we yield grudgingly, but rather as a framework provided and sustained by the covenant love of God, as something which is given to stimulate rather than restrict authentic creativity."[94] Natural laws of acoustics and persisting principles of melody and harmony constrain tonal composing. In music such as Mozart's, however, these natural structures and forces are little more confining than the rainbow arch that signifies them. Intuiting the

91. *Emblems of Mind*, 242.
92. *The Meaning of Immortality*, 247.
93. *Real Presences*, 93.
94. *Voicing Creation's Praise*, 211.

inmost secrets of acoustics and harmony, Mozart becomes a covenant partner with creation, begetting music that echoes and celebrates divine creativity.

Second, the tradition of historical covenant traces back to God's covenant with the biblical ancestors Abraham and Sarah, and it takes on specific content with Moses' transmission of ethical and ritual laws. The stories of these ancestral figures arise from particular times and places. The laws these stories transmit are profoundly conditioned by their historical context. Many are synthesised from neighbouring traditions and limited to local applications. Yet as heirs of this covenantal tradition, Jews, Christians, and Muslims, as well as others outside these faiths, find ethical and religious values for many ages. Analogously, Mozart is a figure of his time and place. His heritage of musical conventions and his syntheses from other composers are innumerable. Yet he is a covenant partner with history, begetting music that touches minds and hearts in times and places other than his own.

Third, the natural and historical covenants of biblical tradition are also portrayed as eternal covenants. God's natural covenant is called everlasting and universal: "When the bow is in the clouds, I will see it and remember the everlasting covenant between God and every living creature of all flesh that is on the earth" (Gen 9.16). God's historical covenant is likewise called everlasting: "I will establish my covenant between me and you, and your offspring after you throughout their generations, for an everlasting covenant. . ." (Gen 17.7). A historical covenant, however, is by definition particular. Thus God's covenant with the biblical ancestors acknowledges the frictions of particularity that are inevitable in history: "I will bless those who bless you, and the one who curses you I will curse." Yet the covenant concludes with an eschatological promise of universality: "and in you all the families of the earth shall be blessed" (Gen 12.3).

These biblical traditions of covenant between humanity and God raise a cluster of perennial theological issues. I have expressed disagreement with contemporary critics who take a disjunctive view of what I experience as a conjunctive world. Now I must acknowledge that Christian tradition has frequently made what I judge to be a similar mistake. I believe that Christian revelation is particular and unique. Christians have tended, however, to confuse particularity and uniqueness with exclusivity. We have tended to regard our particular revelations as excluding possible revelations of truth in other places. We have tended to regard our unique revelations as excluding possible revelations of truth in other times.

Biblical prophets urged their fellows to broaden the pride of their exclusivism by expanding it into the hopes of true universalism. To Israelites prone to consider themselves God's only chosen people, Amos addresses words of a radical universalism:

> Are you not like the Ethiopians to me,
>   O people of Israel? says the LORD.

Did I not bring Israel up from the land of Egypt,
  and the Philistines from Caphtor
  and the Arameans from Kir? (Amos 9.7)

Similarly Isaiah employs the musical image of "a new song . . . from the end of the earth" to disturb the complacency of Israelites who assume that their traditions are exclusive and unchanging throughout eternity:

See, the former things have come to pass,
  and new things I now declare;
before they spring forth,
  I tell you of them.
Sing to the LORD a new song,
  his praise from the end of the earth! (Is 42.9-10)

These prophetic traditions continue in New Testament writings that jolt exclusivism in its peculiarly virulent form of Christian self-righteousness: "He [Christ] also told this parable to some who trusted in themselves that they were righteous and regarded others with contempt. . ." (Lk 18.9).

Among contemporary echoes of these prophetic voices (if they will tolerate such a designation) we may include deconstructionist critics like Rorty and McClary who reject the particular claiming to be universal and the temporal claiming to be eternal. We do not have to follow these critics, however, all the way to their categorical rejection of concepts such as the universal and the eternal. I believe that we may embrace these concepts as what philosophy calls regulative ideas and religion calls eschatological hopes – ideals and norms to which the particular and the temporal may aspire. Our historical strivings towards these ideals may be better or worse. At any point in history our concepts may be more or less adequate, our practices more or less proximate. At no point in history are our concepts and practices congruent with our ideals. Our criteria for judgement in these matters must arise from social conversation, as Rorty suggests, including conversation with hallowed traditions, which Rorty suspects. Unlike Rorty, however, I believe that we may conduct our conversations under a propaedeutic postulate of possible agreement. In a word, we may reasonably hope that our historical approaches to the universal and the eternal are asymptotic. We are justified in aspiring. We must remain satisfied with never attaining. This is our historical covenant with the universal and the eternal.

Particular traditions, and particular figures within traditions, may be unique embodiments of this covenant relation, but they cannot be exclusive embodiments. Here again musical analogy may serve us. When we say that Mozart's music is unique, we can mean only that it is radically distinctive and that it cannot be replaced by descriptions or reduced to explanations. But in no sense can we mean that Mozart's music excludes other music.

On this point my son was once my critic and teacher. A friend and I were extolling the uniqueness of Mozart, and my son, then a teenager with his own musical tastes, demanded to know what we meant. His tendentiousness was justified. My friend and I had been cavalier in our expressions of praise for Mozart. The three of us thus found ourselves, over pizza, calling up Aristotle's definition of a perfect work as one we would not change, and agreeing that music has many perfect works in many genres. My friend and I conceded that our praise of Mozart had meant only that we found his music to consist mostly of perfect works. We also discussed my idea of a classic as a work rewarding repeated exposure with new disclosure, agreeing that music offers many classics in many genres. My friend and I conceded that our praise of Mozart had meant only that we found Mozart's music to include mostly classics. If not exactly won over to Mozart at that point, my son seemed at least mollified. When later he told me that Paul Simon's album *Graceland* was great, I listened, appreciating its gentleness and its internationalism, even hearing in it more of perfection and more of the classic than I might otherwise have done.

I have said that musical incarnations such as Mozart's Piano Concerto in G major are cloud capped. The theological mystery of sanctity's incarnation, in religious saints and the morally valiant, is more obscure still. The Christian doctrine of God uniquely incarnate in Christ is so paradoxical as to render even Dante – after one hundred Cantos of *The Divine Comedy* – speechless:

Thither my own wings could not carry me. . .
High phantasy lost power and here broke off.[95]

Dante is wise not to attempt description or explanation of the mystery of divine incarnation. Nonetheless, the paradox and marvel of Mozart's creativity leads Küng to suggest an extended analogy between Mozart's music and Christ's life, asserting that both exceed our descriptions and explanations, both fully embody yet ineffably transcend their times and places:

In the music of Wolfgang Amadeus Mozart we can observe the roots of his style and all the points at which he is dependent on Leopold Mozart, on Schobert, Johann Christian Bach, Sammartini, Piccinni, Paisiello, Haydn and so many others; but we have not thereby explained the phenomenon of Mozart. Although he was intensely occupied with the whole musical environment and the whole available musical tradition, we find in amazing universality and differentiated balance all styles and genres of music of his time; we can analyse "German" and "Italian" elements, homophony and polyphony, the erudite and the courtly, continuity and contrast of themes, and nevertheless lose sight of the new, unique specific Mozartean feature: this is the *whole* in its higher unity rooted in the freedom of the spirit, it is *Mozart himself* in his music.

95. *The Divine Comedy*, "Paradise" 33.139, tr. Dorothy L. Sayers and Barbara Reynolds (New York: Penguin, 1962), 142.

So too in Jesus' ethos all possible traditions and parallels can be detected and again brought together in unity, but this does not explain the phenomenon of Jesus. And we can emphasise the pre-eminence and universality of love in Jesus' message and bring out the radicality of the theocentrism, of the concentration, intensity, spiritualising of the ethos of Jesus by comparison – for instance – with Jewish ethics; we can distinguish also the new background of meaning and the new motivations: but we are still far from grasping clearly what is new, unique, about Jesus. What is new and unique about Jesus is the *whole* in its unity; it is this *Jesus himself* in his work.[96]

As manifestations of transcendence, Mozart's music and Christ's life are unique, but their followers need not claim that they are exclusive. The Nicene Creed can scarcely be accused of undervaluing Christ's significance: "the only-begotten (*monogenes*) Son of God, begotten from the Father before all time, Light from Light, True God from True God, begotten not created, of the same essence as the Father. . . ." Yet we have already noted that the Creed does not confine God's Holy Spirit to Christ, asserting that the spirit also "spoke through the prophets."[97] Biblical scripture asserts that God's spirit is active universally, presiding over the world's creation (Gen 1.2) and immanent in the world's sustenance (Ps 104.30). God's wisdom – also "only-begotten" (*monogenes*: "unique" in the NRSV) – is omnipresent: "she pervades and penetrates all things" (Wis 7.22, 24).

Cautioned by deconstructive criticism, but not limited to its assumptions or conclusions, I believe that we can celebrate "the unique miracle of genius, which . . . posits a spiritual transcendence."[98] With 19th-century precursors of deconstruction in mind, Kierkegaard speaks with acerbity against the "paltry disbelief" that considers every conjunction of artistic expression and artistic genius "accidental and sees nothing more in it than a very fortunate conjunction of the various forces in the game of life":

It considers that . . . many a composer [has lived] who would have been just as immortal as Mozart if the opportunity had offered itself. This wisdom contains considerable consolation and balm for all mediocrities, who thereby see themselves in a position to delude themselves and like-minded people into thinking that they did not become as exceptional as the exceptional ones because of a mistaken identification on the part of fate, a mistake on the part of the world. This produces a very convenient optimism. But it is abhorrent, of course, to every high-minded soul, every optimate, to whom it is not as important to rescue himself in such a paltry manner as it is to lose himself by contemplating greatness. . . .[99]

96. *On Being a Christian*, 549-50. Küng's emphases.
97. Leith, *Creeds of the Churches*, 33.
98. Bloch, *Essays on the Philosophy of Music*, 123.
99. *The Immediate Erotic Stages*, 47-8.

Kierkegaard goes on to deprecate the folly of his own wishing to rank persons of transcendent genius:

> And although it makes no difference . . . whether one ranks highest or lowest – because in a certain sense everyone ranks equally high, since all rank infinitely high – and although it is just as childish to argue about first and last places here as it is to argue about the place assigned in church on confirmation day, I am still too much of a child, or more correctly, I am infatuated, like a young girl, with Mozart, and I must have him rank in first place, whatever it costs.[100]

Josef Krips is reported to have remarked that whereas Beethoven's music aspires to heaven, Mozart's music was written from there.[101] Of course the great conductor's remark is a joke, but not a joke without significance. It reflects a judgement that on the asymptotic curve of musical genius, Mozart's music is farthest from subjectivism, from mannerism, from egocentrism. It is correspondingly nearer to universality and permanent timeliness. To agree with this comparison of Mozart and Beethoven is not to suggest that Mozart is divine or that his music is holy. It is to suggest that his music uniquely, though not exclusively, manifests transcendent principles – that in Mozart's music the sacred sounds.

100. p.46.
101. I have been unable to document this attribution.

# IV. Fall: Enduring Time

*Die Schönheit lieb ich sehr; doch nenn ich sie kaum schön,*
*Im Fall ich sie nicht stets seh untern Dornen stehn.*

Beauty I dearly love; but I scarcely name it well,
If constantly beneath the thorns I do not see it dwell.

## *From Harmony to Babel*

In the preceding two chapters our subject has been music in relation to the theological doctrine of Creation. In Chapter 2 we considered the Pythagorean tradition of music's silent sacramental role in transcending historical and cultural contingencies, and in Chapter 3 we considered the Incarnational tradition of music's sounding sacramental role in manifesting transcendence amidst our histories and cultures. In this chapter we turn to music in relation to the theological doctrine of the Fall. According to the biblical archetype, we are created in the image of the Creator, but we are tempted to mistake similitude for identity. Made in God's likeness (Gen 1.26; 5.2), we seek to become like God (Gen 3.5). We overstep our creaturely bounds. The result is a fallen world – in John Milton's language, a consonant creation rendered dissonant:

disproportion'd sin

Jarr'd against natures chime, and with harsh din
Broke the fair musick that all creatures made
To their great Lord, whose love their motion sway'd
In perfect Diapason, whilst they stood
In first obedience, and their state of good.[1]

The patterned language and structure of the creation account in Genesis 1 express a creation that is fundamentally proportionate and harmonious. The narrative of God's creative activity closes with a summary evaluation: "God saw everything that he had made, and indeed, it was very good. And there was evening and there was morning, the sixth day" (Gen 1.31). The subsequent narrative of Genesis, however, uses aural imagery to portray humanity's fallen state in comparison to the archetypal ideal. In the story of individual fall, the sound of God's approach frightens Adam: "'I heard the sound of you in the garden, and I was afraid. . .'" (Gen 3.10). In the story of familial fall, Abel's blood cries out: "And the LORD said, 'What have you done: Listen; your brother's blood is crying out to me from the

---

1. "At a solemn Musick" 19-24, *The Poetical Works of John Milton*, 2 vols., ed. Helen Darbishire (Oxford: Clarendon, 1952-5), 2:133.

ground!'" (Gen 4.10). In the story of social fall at the tower on the Plain of Shinar, common language becomes unintelligible noise: "Therefore it was called Babel, because there the LORD confused the language of all the earth. . ." (Gen 11.9).

We follow Calvin here in understanding our fallen condition as the result of our "seeking more than was granted":

> Knowledge of ourselves lies first in considering what we were given at creation and how generously God continues his favour toward us, in order to know how great our natural excellence would be if only it had remained unblemished; yet at the same time to bear in mind that there is in us nothing of our own, but that we hold on sufferance whatever God has bestowed upon us. Hence we are ever dependent on him. . . . But thereafter ambition and pride, together with ungratefulness, arose, because Adam by seeking more than was granted him shamefully spurned God's great bounty, which had been lavished upon him. To have been made in the likeness of God seemed a small matter to a son of earth unless he also attained equality with God – a monstrous wickedness.[2]

Calvin understands the Fall as an event within history, with historical consequences for all humanity:

> The Lord entrusted to Adam those gifts which he willed to be conferred upon human nature. Hence Adam, when he lost the gifts received, lost them not only for himself but for us all. . . . For the contagion does not take its origin from the substance of the flesh or soul, but because it had been so ordained by God that the first man should at one and the same time have and lose, both for himself and for his descendants, the gifts that God had bestowed upon him.[3]

Schleiermacher, along with much of modern theology, diverges from earlier theological understandings of the Fall as an event within history. A pioneer of post-Enlightenment theology, Schleiermacher values the story of the Fall not for its presumed historicity but for its perennial truths. Schleiermacher does not regard the Fall as a historical introduction of sin by the first human pair: "we have no reason for explaining universal sinfulness as due to an alteration in human nature brought about in their person by the first sin."[4] Defining sin as misuses of human freedom that disrupt "harmony with God-consciousness,"[5] Schleiermacher articulates the suggestion that was epoch making for modern theology, namely, that the Fall is a doctrine portraying our abiding human condition, not a doctrine describing a moment of human history:

2. *Institutes* 2.1.1,4, 242, 245.
3. *Institutes* 2.1.7, 249-50.
4. *The Christian Faith* 72, 291.
5. *The Christian Faith* 68.2, 277.

> For the contrast between an original nature and a changed nature
> we substitute the idea of a human nature universally and without
> exception – apart from redemption – the same; and . . . for the
> contrast between an original righteousness that filled up a period
> of the first human lives and a sinfulness that emerged in time . . .
> we substitute a timeless original sinfulness always and everywhere
> inhering in human nature and co-existing with the original perfec-
> tion given along with it.[6]

For Schleiermacher the doctrine of the Fall expresses Christian experience that all of human life embodies a tension between human sin and
divine grace. The Fall is a myth conveying this profound and abiding truth
about our human situation.

We shall consider the second component of Schleiermacher's dialectic
between human sin and divine grace in our discussion of the Christian
doctrine of salvation in Chapter 5. The theme of this present chapter is the
former component of Schleiermacher's dialectic: "a timeless original sinfulness always and everywhere inhering in human nature and co-existing
with the original perfection given along with it." Our thesis will be that
music is unexcelled in its power to express our fallen world's unavoidable
mixture of harmony and disharmony.

## *Christian Ambivalence toward Music*

First, let us think of music as instantiating our fallen condition. Perhaps
Steiner is correct: "There was, presumably, no need of books or art in
Eden."[7] He is certainly accurate when he adds that after Eden, art "has
communicated the urgency of a great hurt." Part of this great hurt in relation
to music is manifested in Christianity's continual struggle with questions
of music's spiritual value. The church's ambivalence concerning music in
a fallen world dates from the time of its birth. From the beginning, Christian life included music. Before going out from the Last Supper, Jesus and
his disciples sang a hymn (Mt 26.30; Mk 14.26), and Christian singing
probably stems from "Jewish and pagan customs of singing at gatherings
around a meal."[8] The Apostle Paul exhorts his fellow Christians to make
music: "Let the word of Christ dwell in you richly; teach and admonish
one another in all wisdom; and with gratitude in your hearts sing psalms,
hymns, and spiritual songs to God" (Col 3.16; also Eph 5.18-19).

Though music was among Christians from the first, the Christian move-

6. *The Christian Faith* 72.6, 303.
7. *Real Presences*, 224.
8. Margot Fassler and Peter Jeffery, "Christian Liturgical Music from the Bible to
   the Renaissance," *Sacred Sound and Social Change: Liturgical Music in Jewish
   and Christian Experience*, ed. Lawrence A. Hoffman and Janet R. Walton
   (Notre Dame: University of Notre Dame Press, 1992), 84.

ment debated the proper kinds of music for worship, as well as for other occasions of Christian life. The early church had several worries about music. For one thing, many kinds of music were inseparably associated with pagan practices, including kinds of worship and carnality that Christians felt called to avoid. For another, being a sensual pleasure of great appeal, music was suspect as a temptation, a distraction from the communal sharing and divine worship it was supposed to serve. Augustine gives the second of these concerns eloquent expression in his *Confessions*. Eve and Adam were tempted by fruit (Gen 3.3-6). Augustine was likewise tempted by fruit, in his famous childhood incident of the stolen pears,[9] and also by music. We have seen that music played a significant role in Augustine's conversion to Christianity, and we have appreciated Augustine's metaphorical description of music's irresistible effects upon his soul. After his conversion, however, Augustine found music a source of temptation, a potential addiction, precisely because of its capacity to penetrate him so deeply and move him so irresistibly. Addressing his words to God, as he does throughout the *Confessions*, Augustine describes his struggle to resolve this paradox:

> I used to be much more fascinated by the pleasures of sound than the pleasures of smell. I was enthralled by them, but you broke my bonds and set me free. I admit that I still find some enjoyment in the music of hymns, which are alive with your praises, when I hear them sung by well-trained, melodious voices. But I do not enjoy it so much that I cannot tear myself away. I can leave it when I wish. But if I am not to turn a deaf ear to music, which is the setting for the words which give it life, I must allow it a position of some honour in my heart, and I find it difficult to assign it to its proper place. For sometimes I feel that I treat it with more honour than it deserves. I realise that when they are sung these sacred words stir my mind to greater religious fervour and kindle in me a more ardent flame of piety than they would if they were not sung.[10]

In this passage we see the "sacred words" of worship emerging as Augustine's primary concern. He goes on to speak of music's tendency to distract him from the sacred texts it is supposed to serve, and of his tendency to overreact against this temptation:

> But I ought not to allow my mind to be paralysed by the gratification of my senses, which often leads it astray. For the senses are not content to take second place. . . . Sometimes, too, from overanxiety to avoid this particular trap I make the mistake of being too strict. When this happens, I have no wish but to exclude from my ears, and from the ears of the Church as well, all the melody of

9. *Confessions* 2.4, 47.
10. *Confessions* 10.33, 238

those lovely chants to which the Psalms of David are habitually sung.[11]

Then Augustine relents, wavers, and arrives at an opinion that was destined to shape western Christian attitudes ever after. It is the opinion that music's primary role in Christian worship is to serve the meaning of sacred texts, with a secondary role – more a concession to human weakness than a mandate – of "indulging the ears" of "weaker spirits," that they might "be inspired with feelings of devotion":

> But when I remember the tears that I shed on hearing the songs of
> the church in the early days, soon after I had recovered my faith,
> and when I realise that nowadays it is not the singing that moves
> me but the meaning of the words when they are sung in a clear
> voice to the most appropriate tune, I again acknowledge the great
> value of this practice. So I waver between the danger that lies in
> gratifying the senses and the benefits which, as I know from expe-
> rience, can accrue from singing. Without committing myself to an
> irrevocable opinion, I am inclined to approve of the custom of
> singing in church, in order that by indulging the ears, weaker spir-
> its may be inspired with feelings of devotion. Yet when I find the
> singing itself more moving than the truth which it conveys, I con-
> fess that this is a grievous sin, and at those times I would prefer not
> to hear the singer.[12]

"This, then, is my present state," Augustine concludes.

In fact, the principles Augustine states in this passage from the *Confessions* have proven perennial to western Christian thinking about liturgical music. Writing more than a millennium later, for example, Calvin gives the Augustinian tradition classic expression:

> And surely, if the singing be tempered to that gravity which is
> fitting in the sight of God and the angels, it both lends dignity and
> grace to sacred actions and has the greatest value in kindling our
> hearts to a true zeal and eagerness to pray. Yet we should be very
> careful that our ears be not more attentive to the melody than our
> minds to the spiritual meaning of the words. Augustine also ad-
> mits in another place that he was so disturbed by this danger that
> he sometimes wished to see established the custom observed by
> Athanasius, who ordered the reader to use so little inflection of the
> voice that he would sound more like a speaker than a singer. But
> when he recalled how much benefit singing had brought him, he
> inclined to the other side. Therefore, when this moderation is main-
> tained, it is without any doubt a most holy and salutary practice.
> On the other hand, such songs as have been composed only for

11. p.238.
12. p.239.

sweetness and delight of the ear are unbecoming to the majesty of
the church and cannot but displease God in the highest degree.[13]

The mainstream liturgical position defined and exemplified by Augustine and Calvin leaves many particular questions to be resolved, however. Augustine recommends "well-trained, melodious voices," but how well trained and melodious should they be? He recommends that sacred texts be sung to "the most appropriate tune," but what constitutes appropriateness? Calvin endorses church music of gravity, dignity, and grace, and rejects music "composed only for sweetness and delight of the ear," leaving church musicians in every generation to struggle anew with this subtle differentiation. There are also larger questions. What texts are appropriate for musical settings in sacred worship? What instruments, if any? Is instrumental music without texts liturgically acceptable? In his recent book *Te Deum: The Church and Music*, Paul Westermeyer provides a survey of the early church's struggles with questions such as these, documenting attitudes of deep ambivalence towards the music that was nonetheless ubiquitous in the life and worship of early Christians.[14]

## *Time's Terrible Beauty*

Early Christian ambivalence toward music illustrates the biblical tradition that we are creators in the image of God, yet historical creatures living in a fallen world. Ecclesiastes observes that we are creatures of time with eternity in our minds (Eccl 3.11). Analogously, music is a temporal art with eternity at its core – namely, its abiding acoustical and harmonic principles, its *logos*. It is natural that T. S. Eliot should choose the musical title *Four Quartets* for his poetic soundings into our human situation as temporal creatures with eternity in our minds. He writes of the irremediable temporality of our poetry and music, and yet expresses a paradoxical sense of eternity coexisting with temporality in our artistic forms and patterns:

Words move, music moves
Only in time; but that which is only living
Can only die. Words, after speech, reach
Into the silence. Only by the form, the pattern,
Can words or music reach
The stillness, as a Chinese jar still
Moves perpetually in its stillness.
Not the stillness of the violin, while the note lasts,
Not that only, but the co-existence,
Or say that the end precedes the beginning,

---

13. *Institutes* 3.20.32, 2:895-6.
14. See the third section, "The First Centuries," Chapters 5 and 6, and the note of critique, p.76n.

> And the end and the beginning were always there
> Before the beginning and after the end.
> And all is always now. . . . [15]

Eliot's final lines echo traditional theological language of God's *logos* and *sophia*, pre-existing, perduring, and permeating time.

Most characterisations of music acknowledge its temporal essence. Gilbert Rouget writes that "music is in essence movement . . . , by definition sound is actualised in the unfolding of time."[16] We sometimes hear a distinction drawn between temporal arts and static arts. Temporal arts, such as music, dance, and the verbal arts of poetry, prose, and drama, require the passage of time for their presentation. Static arts, such as painting, sculpture, and architecture, present themselves with simultaneity. If we consider not only presentation but also creation and appreciation, however, we realise that this distinction is far from absolute. To appreciate architecture requires a lot of time, and an early biographer claimed that Mozart visualised entire symphonies in a moment.[17] Rouget combines the static and temporal categories in his characterisation of music as "an architecture in time."[18] This image need not be a mere commonplace. It reminds us that as architecture's value is not in merely enclosing space but more importantly in distinguishing, elaborating, and celebrating space, so music's value is not in merely occupying but also in distinguishing, elaborating, and celebrating time.

Our lives are dramas within the existential mystery of time, and for this reason the temporal art of music is well suited to accompany and express our lives. Some songs, for example, are "strophic," consisting of relatively simple and lyrical verses, repeated with different words but only minimal musical variations. So too with certain lives, or with certain periods of our lives. Such, we may suppose, was life in mythical Eden, where diurnal repetition brought new occasions for recurrent service and praise, marked by the sabbath's refrain. Schubert's "Das Wandern" ("Wandering") is often cited as a perfect strophic song – though in fact it harbours an existential restlessness that bodes poorly for the enduring contentment of the song's young protagonist. Apparently Adam and Eve knew a similar restlessness in Eden. In contrast to strophic songs, "through-composed" songs continually vary. Their verses are usually more complex and dramatic, and their stories more linear, leading often to ambiguous or tragic ends. Schubert's "Erlkönig" ("The Erlking") is a classic example. We listen to the song's breathless narrative, anxious for the outcome of a father's race against his

---

15. "Burnt Norton" 5, *T. S. Eliot: Collected Poems 1909-1962* (New York: Harcourt Brace Jovanovich, 1984), 180.
16. *Music and Trance: A Theory of the Relations between Music and Possession*, tr. Brunhilde Biebuyck (Chicago: University of Chicago Press, 1985), 121.
17. Maynard Solomon, *Mozart: A Life* (New York: HarperCollins, 1995), 117
18. *Music and Trance,* 121.

son's dying, though the opening bars have in fact foreshadowed the entire song's fateful pattern. Such are our lives in a fallen world. We are born amidst pain, forced to toil among thorns and thistles, and fated to return to dust – indentured to resistant matter and victims of destructive time.

Because of intrinsic similarities such as these, music is unsurpassed in its capacity to suggest what William Butler Yeats calls the "terrible beauty" of life's realities.[19] Yeats's later compatriot, playwright Brian Friel, provides a moving instance of this capacity. One character of Friel's play *Wonderful Tennessee* is an accordion player, George, who has been rendered almost mute by a frustrated career, a troubled marriage, and a terminal illness. Only his music remains to him for expression, communication, and consolation. In a catharsis late in the play, George pours forth the desperate disappointment of his life, wordlessly. These are Friel's stage directions:

> Silence. George looks at each of them in turn. Then he plays the first fifteen seconds of the Third Movement (Presto) of Beethoven's Sonata No. 14 (Moonlight). He plays with astonishing virtuosity, very rapidly, much faster than the piece is scored, and with an internal fury; so that his performance, as well as being dazzlingly dexterous and skilful and fast – because of its dazzling dexterity and skill and speed – seems close to parody. And then in the middle of a phrase, he suddenly stops. He bows to them all very formally, as if he had given a recital in a concert hall.[20]

In a review of the play Frank Rich describes the moment's theatrical impact:

> Giving expression to the inexpressible on stage is the most difficult imaginable task, and, for all the play's second-hand mythological and religious parables, there are still instances when Mr. Friel creates sacred drama in his own original terms. When the dying accordionist played by Mr. [Robert A.] Black, badgered by his friends to tell a story, responds by ripping through a Beethoven sonata, the flaming intensity and tragic futility of an entire life are compressed into a single burst of demented music. There will be better plays than *Wonderful Tennessee* this season, but how many of them will take us, however briefly, to that terrifying and hallowed place beyond words?[21]

Rich's phrasing is significant for our study of music's sacramental potential. The accordionist's music has power to create "sacred drama." His music gives "expression to the inexpressible," taking us, "however briefly, to that terrifying and hallowed place beyond words" – the terrible beauty of a human life.

19. "Easter 1916," *The Collected Poems of W. B. Yeats* (New York: Macmillan, 1938), 208.
20. *Wonderful Tennessee* (Loughcrew, Ireland: Gallery, 1993), 48.
21. "Futile Wait for a Ferry to a Mystical Island," *The New York Times*, 25 October 1993.

## *Music's Dark Resources*

What are music's resources that make possible such expression of life's terrible beauty? Confining our discussion to harmonic music, let us consider four of music's dark resources: tonal tension, harmonic dissonance, acoustical interference, and minor modes.

**Tonal Tension.** Levarie and Levy begin their book on musical acoustics with an epigram that reads as follows: "TONE, from Greek *tonos*: rope, cord, tension, stretching, exertion of force."[22] Thus the very word "tone" implies tension. In Chapter 2 we explored some Pythagorean rudiments of tonal harmony, confining our attention to the first eight partials of the overtone series and the consonant intervals arising from them. Once music ventures beyond these rudiments, however, tension joins consonance as a powerful partner. For example, in the overtone series generated by C, as in Figure 3, the ninth harmonic partial is D, the major 2nd of the C scale. Simply to play the tonic and then the major 2nd alongside it is to establish harmonic tension. The incipient melody begun by these two tones seems to require continuation, resolution, completion. The melody may fall back to the tonic, as in the principal motto of that most tranquil of church motets, Palestrina's *Sicut Cervus* (*Like as the Hart*). Or it may rise to the 4th, F, establishing a pentatonic scale on that tone, as in the placid folk hymn, "The Lord into His Garden Comes." The incipient melody may progress in innumerable ways. Our point is the melody's perceived need to progress. So long as its progression is deferred, tension exists. The same is true for other notes of the basic scales of harmonic music, particularly the minor 2nd and the major and minor 7ths. If a composer chooses not to continue, resolve, or complete such a melodic progression, then tension becomes a powerful expressive protagonist. Deryck Cooke offers the example of unresolved yearning in George Gershwin's bluesy minor 7th: "Some day he'll come a-*long*, the man I *love.* . . ."[23] Cooke provides such a wealth of illustrations of these harmonic effects, in fact – albeit not without controversy – that no one after him need proliferate examples. Suffice it to say that one key to music's expressiveness is the "controlled ambiguity"[24] of melodic tension.

**Harmonic Dissonance**. A second of music's resources for expressing terrible beauty is the dissonance of certain intervals. In the requisite harmonic context, most intervals can sound dissonant. Some intervals, however, have

---

22. *Tone: A Study in Musical Acoustics*, vi.
23. *The Language of Music* (London: Oxford University Press, 1959), 73.
24. Bernstein, *The Unanswered Question*, 107.

an intrinsic dissonance that we can isolate as examples. Acousticians have established that a sustained minor second is relatively displeasing to almost all auditors. Pierce summarises their findings.[25] He accounts for this aural phenomenon of dissonance first in terms of a "critical bandwidth" separating the frequencies of an interval's two tones. Most auditors hear intervals smaller than a minor third as dissonant. Second, Pierce accounts for consonance and dissonance by analysing the harmonic partials of each of the two tones. The more nearly congruent the various partials of any two tones, the more consonant the interval the tones define. Conversely, if the various partials of the two tones are widely divergent, the interval will sound dissonant. The most notorious interval in this latter regard is the tritone – B up to F, for example. The interval is considerably wider than the critical bandwidth defining the region of dissonance, and so the tritone's span does not account for its discordance. The two tones of the tritone are extremely distant from each other in the overtone series, however. The upper tone is the forty-fifth partial of the lower.[26] The problematic eleventh partial of the overtone series comes close to the tritone's upper pitch, but for ears accustomed to western harmonies, it is excruciatingly out of tune. In either case, the respective partials of the tritone's two pitches are so greatly out of congruence that the interval seems to jangle in the ear. Medieval musical theorists included the tritone among the clashing intervals they called *diabolus in musica*, the "devil in music," and its diabolical dissonance haunts harmonic music with powerful expressiveness.

Our perceptions of consonance and dissonance are immensely complicated. First of all, musical chords involve not just two notes but many, and every chord thus involves a number of intervals sounding simultaneously. Furthermore, our perceptions of consonance and dissonance involve cultural context, degree of musical sensitivity, extent of musical training, and the like. Pierce acknowledges the view that we encounter in deconstructive analyses of music, namely, that perceptions of consonance and dissonance are solely cultural artifacts. In the end, however, Pierce judges our perceptions of musical consonance and dissonance to be grounded in acoustical properties as well as cultural histories:

> Of consonance, dissonance, and chords, there can be several views. One might be that we simply learn to regard certain combinations of notes as consonant, others as dissonant. Composers of our century present us with an extraordinary range of combinations of notes, and with some rules for making such combinations. Can consonance and dissonance spring from nothing more than rules and customs? As will be seen, in a sense they can. I believe, however, that to look at experiences of consonance and dissonance as

25. *The Science of Musical Sounds*, 74-93.
26. Levarie and Levy, *Tone*, 202.

arising from rules is to look at things the wrong way round. Rather, I believe that the rules and customs are based on experiences of consonance and dissonance that are inherent in normal hearing.[27]

Pierce's conclusions find support among other experimenters. One empirical study of the perception of musical intervals takes as a thesis question, "Are harmonic preferences of American college students different from harmonic preferences of students in Japan, where the traditional oriental musical culture is distinctly different from Western musical culture?"[28] The study concludes that "agreement across cultures seems overwhelmingly to be the rule in the present instance."[29] The experimenters frame their conclusions in terms of the ancient debate between Pythagoras and his critic Aristoxenus, student of Aristotle, whom we encountered in Chapter 3:

> Are aesthetic judgements to be attributed to the workings of natural laws of consonance and dissonance, or can they be attributed to the impingement on man of his own cultural history? Pythagoras would uphold the former viewpoint, Aristoxenus the latter. The data from the present study would tend to favour a Pythagorean viewpoint: there were no significant differences in preferential judgements between the cultural groups.[30]

The study goes on to acknowledge the complex interactions of given acoustical laws and contingent cultural histories that generate our actual musical judgements:

> However, it may be that our results were a function of "isolated sensory experience." Judgements made about it might be under the jurisdiction of natural laws – i.e., a Pythagorean viewpoint. On the other hand, judgements about the more complex whole, about the "more complex systems of tonal relations" might be subject to the influence of the history of human cultural development – i.e. an Aristoxenian view. Where there is a functional use of harmony, we find man's cultural history a determinant of his judgments. Thus, no differences between cultures on judgments in the isolated sensation might be expected, but differences in judgments involving more complex tonal systems might be expected. This conclusion is quite consistent with that of others.[31]

The Pythagorean component of these empirical findings concerning the role of acoustical properties in our perceptions of consonance and disson-

---

27. *The Science of Musical Sounds,* 74-5.
28. Janet Wydom Butler and Paul G. Daston, "Musical Consonance as Musical Preference: A Cross-Cultural Study," *The Journal of General Psychology* 79 (1968), 131.
29. p.138.
30. p.140.
31. p.140.

ance is part of what we are calling music's *logos*, pre-existing, perduring, and permeating our musical experience.

However we account for it – and no one has accounted for it fully – musical dissonance is a powerful expressive resource. I recently heard a fine performance of Benjamin Britten's *War Requiem*. Britten steeps his setting of the Requiem Mass in harmonies involving the tritone. Several people I spoke to afterward had perceived an ominous ambivalence in Britten's musical treatment of the traditional liturgical texts. Though most of them could not have defined its source, they seemed to find Britten's harmonic ambivalence even more deeply disturbing than his interspersed settings of poems by Wilfred Owen that depict war and expressly condemn it.

**Acoustical Interference.** A third musical resource for expressing terrible beauty is the phenomenon of tonal interference or "roughness." It is a ramification of the "critical bandwidth" enclosing dissonant intervals that we noted above. Acoustical experiments and physiological research, still preliminary, indicate that our perception of roughness in musical intervals is a mechanical and electrical phenomenon of the inner ear. "In essence, the critical bandwidth results from the way that the ear resolves frequencies. At low and moderate sound levels, frequency components lying farther apart than a critical bandwidth send signals to the brain over separate nerve fibres, but frequency components lying within a critical bandwidth send a mixed signal over the same fibres."[32]

Acoustical experimenters agree that the critical bandwidth for interference is not the same for all frequency ranges. It is narrower at higher frequencies and wider at lower frequencies. That is to say, at higher frequencies our ears accept smaller musical intervals as consonant, whereas at lower frequencies our ears require that consonant intervals be larger. Anyone can share this observation at a piano by playing a minor third, C to E flat, let us say, first an octave above middle C and then two octaves below middle C and noting which interval growls the more. Or try tritones, C to F sharp, say, in the same two ranges.

Thus it is no accident that Bach generally employs wider intervals among the lower notes of chords than among the higher notes. In general, the lower the lowest notes go, the wider the intervals Bach chooses to write just above them, as a glance through a book of Bach chorales will confirm. A young organist friend of mine, a scarred veteran of recent composition classes, once complained to me that she had been forced to stick to this pattern "just because Bach did it." Well, yes. But Bach did it – to what degree by intention or intuition we can no more say than in the case of Mozart's genius – to avoid tonal interference or roughness.

Other composers have intentionally resorted to tonal roughness as a

32. Pierce, *The Science of Musical Sound*, 76.

means of conveying life's terrible beauty. What beauty could be more terrible than the opening of the Scottish ballad "Edward," on the theme of patricide, as composed in German by Johann Gottfried von Herder? The mother is speaking:

*Dein Schwert, wie ists von Bluth so roth?*
*Edward, Edward!*
*Dein Schwert, wie ists von Bluth so roth,*
*Und gehst so traurig her? – O!*[33]

Thy sword, how is't so red with blood?
Edward, Edward!
Thy sword, how is't so red with blood,
And thee so dismal moving? – O!

What a challenge the young Brahms set for himself, when, in one of his nearest approaches to pictorial music, he elected to evoke this grisly ballad in piano music without words. In his *Ballade* "After the Scotch Ballad 'Edward'," Opus 10, No. 1, Brahms establishes a morbid tone in the opening measures by violating two principles of classical composition at once. First, he roughens the bass chords of the left hand by filling in their octaves with various smaller intervals – 3rds, 4ths, and 5ths. Second, he has those roughening notes move in parallel with the same notes in the right hand, two and three octaves above, thus shunning the principle of contrary motion that gives counterpoint its clarity of texture. Then at just the right moments Brahms removes the filler notes in both hands, leaving only the octaves, stark, empty, and moving in parallel. The effect is extraordinary, at once growling and hollow (". . . so dismal moving? – O!").

**Minor Modes.** Brahms's growling 3rds in "Edward" are of course minor 3rds, not major. This brings us to the last of music's dark resources we shall consider: minor modes. Minor modes come a number of varieties. What we call the "natural" minor is identical with the Aeolian mode of Figure 4. The "harmonic" minor raises the seventh tone of the natural minor by a half step. The harmonic minor is closely related to still other variants, such as the "Gypsy" mode, which raises the fourth tone as well, and which infuses marvelous power into the violin's opening flourish in Brahms's *Violin Concerto* and into the piano's closing flourish in the "Gnomus" movement of Mussorgsky's *Pictures at an Exhibition*. Despite their variations, however, all these minor modes share the minor 3rd.

We may see from Figure 3 that in relation to the fundamental tone of C, the *major* 3rd, E, occurs as the fifth partial of the overtone series, the first new interval after the octave, 5th, and 4th. In contrast, the *minor* 3rd in relation to C, E flat, does not occur in the overtone series until the nine-

33. *Herders Werke* 1.2, ed. Heinrich Meyer (Tokyo: Sansyusya, 1974), 303.

teenth partial, well above the discernable range of our hearing. This contrast probably contributes to the difference in sound between the major and minor modes. In almost every musical tone we hear, the major mode is implicit in the accompanying overtone series, and is audible, either consciously or subliminally. This is not the case for the minor mode. No wonder, then, that the two modes sound different.

It is sometimes said that the major seems happier and the minor seems sadder, and that this difference too stems from the fact that the major occurs in the lower realm of the overtone series, whereas the minor does not. Major is the natural mode, it is said, and minor modes are unnatural. But Cooke shrewdly points out that this theory could apply only among people who assume happiness to be a natural human condition, namely, among heirs of the European Enlightenment, and he observes that some systems of music – African, Asian, Balkan, and others – express happiness "by music of a decidedly minor character."[34] So we are left asking not only what gives major and minor such different moods, but also what the contrasting moods of major and minor are. Finally, the really difficult question is not why the major and minor sound so different or engender different moods, but why the harmonic functions of major and minor 3rds are so similar. For all their acoustical differences, within the basic chordal structures of traditional harmonic music the two kinds of 3rds are in many ways interchangeable.

The minor mode's enigmas are fascinating, and we shall not resolve them here. Leonard Meyer believes that we should not even try:

> Attempts to explain the effect of the minor mode of Western music . . . in terms of consonance and dissonance or in terms of the harmonic series have resulted in uncontrolled speculations and untenable theories. Even those not thus haunted by the ghost of Pythagoras have contributed little to our understanding of musical meaning and its communication.[35]

Meyer's warning notwithstanding, the ghost of Pythagoras goads me to risk a few observations. Let us begin with the question of why the major and minor 3rds function so similarly in harmonic music. The simplest answer may be that the minor 3rd is in some ways more nearly related to the major 3rd than to any other interval in diatonic scales. That is, for all their differences, the major 3rd and minor 3rd share three characteristics. First, surprisingly, their general consonance, as determined by the degree of congruence among the partials of their respective overtone series, has been discovered to be very nearly the same.[36] Second, in the middle range of human voices and instruments, the minor 3rd, like the major, is an inter-

34. *The Language of Music*, 53.

35. *Emotion and Meaning in Music* (Chicago: University of Chicago Press, 1956), 5-6.

36. Pierce, *The Science of Musical Sounds*, 79.

val wide enough to lie outside the critical bandwidth of acoustical interference or roughness. In this sense also the minor 3rd shares consonance
with the major 3rd. Finally, both the major and the minor 3rd are intervals
small enough to fall short of the more consonant Pythagorean 4th. In sum,
major and minor 3rds function similarly because their consonances are
similar and because both are neither a dissonant 2nd nor a consonant 4th.

Why do major and minor convey different moods? Let us consider two
possible factors. First, while in relation to the fundamental tone of C the
minor 3rd, E flat, does not appear in the overtone series until the nineteenth
partial, the 5th and 6th partials, E and G, define a minor third between
them. We may recall from Figure 2 that a pure minor third is defined by
the Pythagorean ratio 5:6, which is simply the ratio of these 5th and 6th
partials. The next interval up the overtone series is that between the 6th
and 7th partials, G and B flat, with a ratio of 6:7. These two tones constitute an interval approaching a minor third. Because of the problematic
nature of the 7th partial, however, it is badly out of tune as compared with
the precise Pythagorean minor 3rd just below it. What is more, these two
neighbouring intervals together span a tritone, E to B flat, that in addition
to its intrinsic harmonic dissonance is also out of tune, due again to the
seventh partial. Perhaps this problematic cluster of intervals, within the
range of our aural discernment and intimately involving the minor 3rd,
gives rise to a sense of harmonic ambivalence and tension in association
with that interval.

A second consideration. Two tones played loudly together give rise not
only to two sets of harmonic partials or overtones, but also to other ancillary
tones known as "combination tones." These come in several varieties, but
let us confine our attention to what acousticians call the "simple difference tone." Difference tones are less frequently discussed than overtones,
and yet under proper conditions we can hear them. At a piano keyboard –
a grand piano, if possible, and in a location that is absolutely quiet – using
no pedal, sharply strike the minor 3rd, C to E flat, two octaves above
middle C, and hold it. Listen intently for the simple difference tone, sounding
in the ear like a momentary rebound or ricochet just after the 3rd is struck.
In this case it will be the A flat below middle C. The experiment may require
several tries. One can help it along by softly playing and releasing the A flat
just before striking the minor 3rd, to sensitise the ear. (This is not cheating,
since softly playing and releasing other notes will not lead to similar results, unless the notes happen to be other, more complex difference tones.)

Difference tones are said to have been discovered in the 18th century
by violinist Giuseppe Tartini, who reported sometimes hearing a third note
when he played two notes loudly.[37] We call them "difference tones" because, as ascertained by the great physiologist and acoustician of the 19th
century, Hermann von Helmholtz, the frequency of the perceived tone is

37. Hall, *Musical Acoustics*, 422.

equal to the difference between the frequencies of the two tones that are sounded.[38] Researchers still disagree as to what exactly gives rise to difference tones. Some attribute them to non-periodic characteristics of the sounding source – the piano, in our experiment. A larger number of researchers assign them to distorting or "nonlinear" mechanisms of the ear: "The eardrum, middle ear, and inner ear are all candidates to contribute nonlinearity; indeed it would be surprising if any of them had entirely linear response to loud sounds. It is still hard to pin down exactly which components in the chain contribute most, but the existence of some non-linearity in the ear has long been accepted."[39] In any case, together with the minor third (C to E flat in our experiment), there sounds also, more than two octaves below, the simple difference tone: A flat, a minor 6th of the C scale. This difference tone may serve to give the minor 3rd additional timbre and thus colour its mood.

With every interval we hear, in fact, an indefinite number of additional combination tones sound in our ears, either audibly or subliminally. And there are other kinds of tones as well – such as "residue tones," ancillary to intervals played softly as well as loudly – of even more obscure characteristics and origin. An interval, then, is not a simple duality. It is a sounding complex. Chords are resonating worlds of intervals. Orchestras are resounding universes. A universe is the greatest of wonders. Small wonder, then, that our responses to musical harmony are complicated, varied, and subtle.

As for our final question concerning what moods the major and minor modes convey, we may be brief. Most people seem to sense a response to minor music that is different from their response to major. Yet different people seem to respond differently to each. It seems safe to say that to most people the major sounds more settled, the minor more unsettling. It does not simply follow that the major sounds happy and the minor sad, however. Some people feel threatened by the thought of being settled. Yet in the history of harmonic music, as Cooke illustrates so exhaustively in *The Language of Music*, composers in the European-derived harmonic tradition have most commonly used minor mode for expression ranging from pensiveness and wistfulness to melancholy, depression, anger, and despair.

## *Music as Virtual Life*

Kandinsky writes that music "uses its own media to express the artist's emotional life and, out of these media, creates an original life of musical tones."[40] Not everyone agrees with Kandinsky's opinion that music ex-

38. For an elegant mathematical accounting for "difference" and "summation" tones see James Jeans, *Science and Music* (New York: Macmillan, 1937), 51-2, 232-40.
39. Hall, *Musical Acoustics,* 423.
40. *On the Spiritual in Art,* 71

presses the composer's emotional life, but the second half of his assertion seems more nearly self-evident. When we enter into the original life of a musical composition, it can also become for us a kind of virtual life, paralleling, echoing, enhancing, informing, even altering our own. Thus Shakespeare's defeated Richard II muses in a musical mode upon his political failure and imminent death:

> Music do I hear?
> Ha, Ha! keep time. How sour sweet music is
> When time is broke and no proportion kept!
> So is it in the music of men's lives.
> And here have I the daintiness of ear
> To check time broke in a disorder'd string;
> But for the concord of my state and time
> Had not an ear to hear my true time broke.[41]

Steven G. Smith, in a philosophical work that seems to have no place for the idea of music's sacramental potential that I am developing here, nevertheless gives beautiful expression to the idea that music represents a kind of virtual life:

> The deepest mystery of experience is the solidarity between intentional, spiritual, and material quality. I listen to a piano piece by Mozart and the rising and falling, tripping and gliding, swelling and fading, thickening and thinning, hurrying and tarrying just are the very shape of an exhilarating piece of living, the order of lived time turned inside out for my ear and proved real.[42]

Even the atonalist Schoenberg makes an inventory of qualities that give harmonic music its peculiar life, admitting that not all of them can be accomplished by his new twelve-tone technique: "It cannot replace all that harmony has performed in music from Bach – and his predecessors – unto our time: limitation, subdivision, connection, junction, association, unification, opposition, contrast, variation, culmination, declination, ebbing, liquidation, etc." At the same time, Schoenberg goes on to point out that music is more than harmony, and predicts that new dissonances will take their place among music's expressive means: "Today's ear has become as tolerant to these dissonances as musicians were to Mozart's dissonances. It is in fact correct to contend that the emancipation of the dissonance is at present accomplished and that twelve-tone music in the near future will no longer be rejected because of 'discords.'"[43] I would state Schoenberg's point somewhat differently. Our Age of Anxiety has

41. *Richard the Second* 5.5.41-8, *The Complete Works of William Shakespeare*, ed. W. J. Craig (London: Oxford University Press, 1943), 407.
42. *The Concept of the Spiritual: An Essay in First Philosophy* (Philadelphia: Temple University Press, 1988), 229.
43. Arnold Schoenberg, *Style and Idea: Selected Writings of Arnold Schoenberg*, ed. Leonard Stein (New York: St. Martin's Press, 1975), 246.

accepted much 20th-century music precisely because of its power to express unresolved discord.

**Music and Silence**. Let us consider a few particular ways in which music serves as virtual life – particularly discordant life after the Fall. We may begin with the expressiveness of musical silence. This might seem a strange beginning point for discussing the art of sonorous forms in motion, but someone has well said that music is painting with sound on a canvas of silence. As in certain styles of visual art the bare canvas contributes as eloquently as the lines and colours, so too with silences in musical painting.

The 6th-century monastic Rule of Saint Benedict includes the following instruction concerning silence:

> Let us do as the prophet says, "I have said, I will keep my ways, that I offend not with my tongue. I have been watchful over my mouth: I held my peace and humbled myself and was silent from speaking even good things." Here the prophet shows that, for the sake of silence, we are at times to abstain even from good talk. If this be so, how much more needful is it that we refrain from evil words.[44]

The Rule's quotation derives from the Latin of Psalm 39.1. The Psalm's succeeding verse is even more powerful:

> I was silent and still;
>> I held my peace to no avail;
> my distress grew worse,
>> my heart became hot within me. (Ps 39.2)

Silences in our lives can convey a gamut of significance. They can arise from a sense of personal emptiness or cosmic meaninglessness, as when Jacques Monod writes of a person's "world that is deaf to his music, just as indifferent to his hopes as it is to his sufferings or his crimes."[45] Or they can arise from a sense of life's inevitable transience, as in Eliot's *Four Quartets*, or from feelings of ambivalence and anger, as with the character in Friel's *Wonderful Tennessee*. All of these feelings can accompany musical silences, just as they accompany our lives.

Various 20th-century minimalist composers, from Anton Webern to Morton Feldman, have painted with silence as expressively as with sound. John Cage entitles his collection of musical essays *Silence*[46] and composed the notorious piano piece, *4'33"*, consisting of nothing but. Short of Cage's extreme, however, expressive uses of musical silence are nothing new. To illustrate, let us return one final time to Mozart's Piano Concerto in G.

We may recall that the second movement states its principal motto five

44. Saint Benedict, *The Rule of Saint Benedict*, tr. Cardinal Gasquet (New York: Cooper Square, 1966), 25.
45. Jacques Monod, *Chance and Necessity* (New York: Alfred A. Knopf, 1971), 173.
46. Cambridge: M.I.T. Press, 1966.

times. After each of the first four statements, the music pauses for an indefinite moment of silence, ambiguous and uncertain, charged with tension. The first of these silences leads to an orchestral continuation that seems disingenuous in its complacency. The second silence is shattered by a startling outburst of anguish from the piano. The third silence is broken by the piano's outpouring of introverted melancholy. The fourth silence ends with the piano singing serene resolution in the tenor range. Then, after all this heartrending drama, the piano resolves the motto's fifth and final statement, with no intervening silence, and McClary and I both find ourselves moved to tears, albeit for different reasons. My reason is a sense of the music's having surmounted a virtual lifetime of existential struggle.

**Music and Noise.** Certain music of the 20th century serves as virtual life through its employment of the opposite of silence, namely noise. Martha Bayles, writing criticism out of a love for popular music, bravely states the obvious:

> Just as assaultive as the lyrics and images of contemporary popular music are many of the sounds. From the shrieking clamour of thrash metal to the murky din of grunge, from the cheap, synthesised tinsel of pop ballads to the deadly pounding of computerised rhythm tracks, popular music seems terminally hostile to any sound traditionally associated with music. And herein lies frustration, because for most people the relevant comparison is not between hard rock and Mozart . . . but between popular music that abuses the ear and popular music that does not.[47]

As I write this paragraph, "grunge rock" is in the news because of the suicide of a young rock musician. Jon Pareles finds part of grunge's power in raw noise: "Grunge has a manic-depressive heritage. From punk-rock, grunge took raw noise and explosive dynamics, the manic side, while from heavy metal, it took giant power chords and a brontosaurus tread." Pareles then comments on what this noisy music seems to express:

> It is powerful music about a sense of powerlessness. Standard heavy-metal songs flaunt toughness, railing against grim destiny or trying to exorcise it through exaggeration. Punk vents anger or makes a flippant joke of it. But much of grunge turns inward, agonising over loss or confusion, feeling a bone-deep futility.[48]

Writing in 1913, long before the advent of rock music, Luigi Russolo issued a "Futurist Manifesto" declaring that the appropriate music for the 20th century is a music of noise:

> In antiquity, life was nothing but silence. Noise was really not born

---

47. *Hole In Our Soul: The Loss of Beauty and Meaning in American Popular Music* (New York: Free Press, 1994), 4.
48. "Death Sings along with Grunge," *The New York Times*, 20 April 1994.

before the 19th century, with the advent of machinery. Today noise
reigns supreme over human sensibility. . . . The Greeks, with their
musical theory mathematically determined by Pythagoras, according to which only some consonant intervals were admitted, have
limited the domain of music until now. . . . Nowadays musical art
aims at the shrillest, strangest and most dissonant amalgams of
sound. Thus we are approaching *noise-sound.*[49]

Regarded by many in his own day as merely outrageous, Russolo in fact
proved prophetic. The 20th century has brought noise into the musical
mainstream. Iannis Xenakis has composed music that he describes as ugly
sounds in interaction. His "Bohor I" is one successful realisation of his
intentions. The effect is what I imagine I might hear crawling through the
ventilation ducts of a busy Body Shop.

**Music and Chaos.** Experiences of chaos are a third of music's expressions of fallen life. Was Lejaren Hiller speaking of music or of life when
he used the phrase, "a compromise between monotony and chaos"?[50] He
was speaking of music, as it happens, but most of us know the feeling in
life as well. Xenakis and others have written what is called "stochastic
music," in which chance and probability play a part in musical composition, which is then notated for future performances. Other composers, such
as Cage, come even closer to many of life's experiences in writing "aleatory
music" or music that cannot be predicted before its actual performance –
music in which not only certain details, but some of the very parameters,
conditions, and substance are left to chance and chaos. Again music serves
as virtual life after the Fall, when the created order of Eden is delivered
over to the discordant chaos of history:

If Cain is avenged sevenfold,

truly Lamech seventy-sevenfold. (Gen 4.24)

## *Music and Life's Pilgrimage*

The sense of music as virtual life is most obvious in what is called "programme music," with explicit themes of life's pilgrimage. Examples are
"Harold in Italy" by Hector Berlioz, and "Till Eulenspiegel," "Don
Quixote," and "Ein Heldenleben" by Richard Strauss. But such explicit
evocations of life are not necessarily the most significant or the most deeply
moving. Bloch describes music as virtual life in broader terms. For him
music's "inner pilgrimage"[51] echoes the deepest hopes and fears, aspir-
ations and desperations of human experience. He writes of the sonata as

49. *The Art of Noise (Futurist Manifesto, 1913),* tr. Robert Filliou (New York:
    Something Else Press, 1967), 3-5.
50. Quoted in Pierce, *The Science of Musical Sound,* 11.
51. *Essays on the Philosophy of Music,* 123.

"that impulsive, dramatic, discontinuous excess of tension, that pure art of time and direction."[52] A fugue theme is "a character that proves steadfast and evolves in the individual parts – the incidents in its life, as it were, the currents of its world."[53] As for more programmatic music, Bloch encounters in Bach entire spiritual worlds: "Bach expresses sorrow and devotion amid tears, more readily than joy, and lingers over this in the St Matthew and St John Passions in particular, plucking sweet fruit from his gall."[54] Finally, Bloch hears in the *German Requiem* of Brahms "an awareness of death which is more genuinely present in music than anywhere else . . . a progressive groping and searching, the tracing of a path into the unknown, the awakening."[55]

Many share Bloch's sense of music as a companion in our endurance of time, though the kind of companionship varies dramatically. Performers of grunge rock seem to find music a companion in anger as life runs on to its nihilistic end. In the companionship of lighter music, popular and classical, many seem to find alternatives to life's tedium or pressures. Some, like Barth, cherish music a source of "comfort and counsel."[56] Music, it seems, is a protean companion.

Of all the struggles with this inscrutable companion that I know, I find none more honest or compelling than a 1965 performance by John Coltrane, bearing the suggestive title "Cosmos."[57] Its power rests upon Coltrane's breadth and depth as a musician. Coltrane was both formally trained and one of music's most extraordinary improvisers. His jazz is rooted in African-American experience, yet he drew from many of the world's musical traditions: improvisations on fixed modes, reminiscent of classical sitar music of India; teamwork melodies, modelled on music of central Africa; overblown harmonics, "a device common to Asian and African cultures"; and "hoarse, throaty tones, rich in partials," recollective of the "one voice chording" of Tibetan monks.[58]

As "Cosmos" begins, Coltrane's saxophone toys with a simple melodic fragment in major mode. Under it the bass and drums introduce an intent line and rhythm, not clearly related to the melody. The piano strikes a steady series of impressionistic chords. From this complex but essentially dulcet beginning, the piece launches a ten-minute trajectory through what seems like every possibility in the cosmos, rising continually in volume,

52. p.186.
53. p.186.
54. p.189.
55. pp.240-1.
56. *Church Dogmatics* 3.3, 297-8.
57. *John Coltrane featuring Pharaoh Sanders: Live in Seattle*, Impulse Records, AS-9202-2.
58. Robert Palter, "Exploring the Jazz Legacy of John Coltrane," *The New York Times*, 29 September 1974.

pitch, complexity, and passion. At its apogee the music is a chaotic pande-
monium, a tantrum of poundings, howls, and shrieks. Yet amidst the frenzy
the piano maintains its steady recital of consonant chords. Finally the tumult
subsides, the melodic fragment reappears, the music descends to a kind of
cadence, and the piano offers a final comment: two quiet, bell-like chords.

What have we heard in "Cosmos"? No two listeners are likely to agree.
What I hear is a virtual exploration of the fundamental spiritual question
of cosmos or chaos. The exploration seems unblinking in its observations,
candid about its confusions, honest with its anger, undeterrable in its
determination, and therefore entitled to its conclusions, where the final
moments suggest cosmic closure. I hear Coltrane's "Cosmos" as spiritual
pilgrimage amidst a fallen world.

Only long after I first experienced this impression directly from
Coltrane's music – after I had written the preceding paragraph, in fact –
did I begin to learn about the actual spiritual pilgrimage of Coltrane's life,
and the echoes of that pilgrimage in his music:

> Overall, I think the main thing a musician would like to do is to
> give a picture to the listener of the many wonderful things he knows
> and senses in the universe. That's what music is to me. . . . It's a
> reflection of the universe. Like having life in miniature.[59]

## Sacred Music: Evaluation and Taste

Though the Fall distorts our judgement, it does not eradicate it, and I believe
that sacramental appreciation requires us to exercise musical judgement
to the best of our abilities. Not to do so – or worse, to assume the attitude
that music allows no judgements of better or worse, of more valuable or
less valuable – seems to me equivalent to saying that music is not important. Less important, certainly, than politics, finance, athletics, or diet, where
we wrestle with evaluative judgements all the time. Let us therefore
consider a few issues of musical evaluation and taste.

I have confessed to finding spiritual value in Coltrane's "Cosmos." But
how many churches would allow jazz as part of Christian worship? Some
churches do. The Episcopal Cathedral of Saint John the Divine in New
York is reported to have a policy that "all music is sacred."[60] Alec Wyton,
former organist and master of choristers at St. John the Divine, elaborates:

59. Quoted in Eric Nisenson, *Ascension: John Coltrane and His Quest* (New
     York: St. Martin's, 1993), 122. See the discussion of the "ritual" function of
     "Cosmos" in Bill Cole, *John Coltrane* (New York: Da Capa, 1993), 178.
60. Allan Kozinn, "More Churches Are Doubling as Concert Halls," *The New
     York Times*, 7 September 1993. For an alliance of fine jazz and graceful theo-
     logical reflection I recommend *Faith in a New Key: A Conversation between
     Jazz and Christian Faith* by Bill Carter and the Presbybop Quartet (Princeton:
     Princeton Theological Seminary, 1998).

Neither the doctrine nor the practice of the church imposes
restrictions on the use of any style, from the earliest chants to rock,
pop, and jazz. A galaxy of sound makes room for a very inclusive
community. If God created everything and everyone, then everything and everyone has the right and duty to praise God with the
talents they were given.[61]

We can well imagine a performance of Coltrane's "Cosmos" in the
sanctuary of St. John the Divine. Far more typically, however, churches
are split apart, not over avant-garde jazz, but over revisions of their bland
denominational hymnals. The Second Vatican Council document
*Sacrosanctum Concilium* affirms that all true art is potentially sacred: "The
Church indeed approves all forms of true art, and admits them into divine
worship when they show appropriate qualities."[62] But what constitutes
"true art" and "appropriate qualities"?

As we saw in the Introduction, the Vatican II document asserts that
explicitly liturgical music is of greatest value for the Church: "Sacred music
increases in holiness to the degree that it is intimately linked with liturgical action."[63] The Vatican Council thus formalises a distinction between
music as art and music for liturgical use, and it makes an evaluative
judgment which Gerard Kock summarises as follows: "The tension between
the altar (liturgy) and the choir-loft (music as art) was plainly decided by
the Council in favour of the altar."[64] This distinction between music as art
and music for liturgical use, together with the tension between the two, is
traditional in western Christianity. In North American Catholicism the tension has actually given rise to two distinct and competing music journals:
*Pastoral Music*, representing the camp of the altar, and *Sacred Music*,
representing the camp of the choir-loft.[65] Miriam Therese Winter characterises the distinction in slightly different terms: an emphasis upon the
congregation's "active participation" as contrasted with an emphasis upon
"the Church's rich musical tradition."[66] She expresses a hope that in time
the church "may recognise that two streams of music emerging from Vatican II are really one, single, Spirit-inspired response arising from the people
of God":

> The capacity to create truly sacramental music that liberates, inte-
> grates, and transforms individuals and society is a God-given gift.

61. "The Episcopal Tradition," *Sacred Sound*, ed. Hoffman and Walton, 282.
62. "Constitution on the Sacred Liturgy," *The Documents of Vatican II*, 171.
63. p.171.
64. "Between the Altar and the Choir-loft: Church Music – Liturgy or Art?" in
    Collins, ed., *Music and the Experience of God*, 13.
65. Peter Jeffrey, "Chant East and West: Toward a Renewal of the Tradition," in
    Collins, ed., *Music and the Experience of God*, 22.
66. "Catholic Prophetic Sound after Vatican II," *Sacred Sound*, ed. Hoffman and
    Walton, 157.

It can come from anyone, anywhere. It belongs to no single culture,
nor does it require a particular style.[67]

In the meantime, contrasting attitudes concerning sacramental music
require continual evaluation and adjustment, which in turn require a consideration of relations between aesthetic evaluation and religious evaluation. In
his study of religious aesthetics, Frank Burch Brown not only agrees that
evaluations are possible and desirable but argues persuasively that aesthetic evaluations are essential to morality and religion: "If our analysis so
far is fundamentally sound, aesthetic taste should be understood as an
intrinsic part of morality and religion. Accordingly, bad taste would seem
to be a moral and religious liability."[68] Brown goes so far as to call bad
taste "sinful," but he is meticulous in distinguishing aesthetic judgement
from mere judgementalism. First, he writes, "evaluations involving
aesthetic taste are to some extent communal both in formation and application rather than completely private and/or universal." It follows that when

claiming aesthetic excellence for any work of art or nature, one
rationally cannot and need not claim that everyone ought to find
the same thing excellent. One is not commanding all people everywhere to take pleasure in what one finds aesthetically excellent,
but commending it to others on the basis of a conviction (subject
to modification) that some and perhaps many significant groups of
people with good taste would appreciate it to a high degree, or
would come to do so in time.[69]

Samuel Taylor Coleridge speaks of the same obligation of non-coercive
aesthetic judgement: "we *declare* an object beautiful, and feel an inward
right to *expect* that others should coincide with us. But we feel no right to
*demand* it."[70]

In a discussion useful for our purposes, Brown specifies "four major
categories of sinful taste: that of the aesthete, the philistine, the intolerant,
and the indiscriminate."[71] First, the aesthete is a person "whose chief goal
is not glorifying and enjoying God but glorying in the aesthetic delights of
creation (human or divine)."[72] The temptation here, says Brown, is "idolatry"
or misplaced devotion, of the kind that Augustine felt arising from his love of
music. Second, the opposite of the aesthete is the philistine, a person with no
aesthetic appreciation beyond what can be directly "translated into practical,
moral, or specifically religious terms."[73] Here the temptation is to limit mani-

67. p.171.
68. *Religious Aesthetics: A Theological Study of Making and Meaning* (Princeton:
    Princeton University Press, 1989), 148.
69. p.149.
70. *Biographia Literaria*, ed. J. Shawcross, 2 vols. (Oxford: Oxford University
    Press, 1907), 2:242. Coleridge's emphases.
71. p.151.
72. p.152.

festation of the Creator's grace to only "the most blatantly moral and religious art," defined according to certain narrow predilections. Third, the intolerant person "is keenly aware of aesthetic standards of appraisal, but elevates his or her own standards to the level of absolutes. . . . Intolerance is thus the aesthetic equivalent of the sin of pride. . . . It severs human ties and does violence to the freedom, integrity, and selfhood of others."[74] Coleridge, in apparent violation of his own aesthetic principles, provides an example of such intolerance in musical judgement when he writes: "The so called music of savage tribes as little deserves the name of art for the understanding, as the ear warrants it for music."[75] Fourth and finally, Brown writes that the opposite of the intolerant person is the indiscriminate, who concludes "that really there is nothing good or bad in matters of taste."[76] The result is "radical aesthetic relativism," unable to relate aesthetic experience to our moral and religious struggles with "right and wrong, righteousness and sin, wholeness and brokenness, freedom and captivity."[77]

Brown encourages us to seek aesthetic and religious judgements within the realm delimited by these four extremes. He ends his discussion, however, with an edifying reminder that as with all our human quests, we pursue our search for aesthetic taste in a fallen world:

> From a Christian perspective, the final theological reflection on sinful taste in *all* its forms should, perhaps, have to do with forgiveness. For if taste is as essential to morality and religion as we have said, then Good Taste in its highest, multifaceted form is required for human perfection. But if Good Taste at its best is as encompassing and demanding as we have also said – involving communities as well as individuals, and the discernment of goodness and holiness as well as beauty – then in taste as in other things there is always the imperfection that Christian theologians call sin. Consequently, the ultimate answer to bad taste may not be good taste but Grace.[78]

With the assistance of Brown's distinctions, and mindful of his concluding reminder, let us consider a few particulars concerning musical evaluation from a Christian point of view, first in the broad realm of our contemporary culture's music, second in the more particular realm of contemporary Christian music, and finally in relation to a general definition of sacred music. In the broad realm of music, I am inclined toward the opinion that all music has sacramental potential, but with certain specific qualifications. Helpful in this connection is Tillich's reminder that the

73. p.153.
74. p.153.
75. *Biographia Literaria*, 2:253.
76. *Religious Aesthetics*, 155.
77. p.156.
78. p.157.

religious concept of the holy includes both divine potential and demonic potential, constructive potential and destructive.[79] Tillich describes the divine dimension of the holy as that which both promises and bestows our ultimate fulfilment, that which invites and also deserves our ultimate concern, our faith. Ultimate concern for truth and justice, for example, represent faith in what Tillich calls the divine dimension of the holy.[80] If, however, we regard as holy something that is not divine but demonic, something that promises fulfilment but in fact delivers destruction, then devoting ourselves to it with ultimate concern can devour us. Such faith Tillich calls idolatrous: "The holy which is demonic, or ultimately destructive, is identical with the content of idolatrous faith."[81] Tillich's examples of idolatrous faith include ultimate devotion to one's personal success or to one's nation state.[82]

We have considered the popular music of our time known as grunge rock – ultimately concerned with human despair, suicide, and nihilism. In Tillich's language, these are profound human concerns and are thus part of the dynamics of human faith. Yet insofar as this music delivers human destruction instead of human fulfilment, it is expressive of the demonic dimension of the holy. Christians who simply dismiss or ignore such music diminish their communion with the holy. Self-destructive music expresses the concerns and needs of our fellows, and it expresses painful truths about our fallen world. For these reasons Christian people can give such music attention, learn from it, and appreciate it for the harsh realities it reveals. Yet as people called to faith in the divine dimension of the holy, people called to promote healing in a suffering world, Christians cannot rest content with self-destructive music. No one is under any compulsion to accept grunge rock as good music or pretend to like it, still less to endorse the debasing values it expresses. This would be to fall prey to what Brown calls the sin of the aesthete, valuing music apart from ethical and religious considerations, or the sin of the indiscriminate, valuing any and all music, whatever the actual merits of its conception, craft, and content.

As for the more particular realm of Christian music, one of the most distressing indications to me that I am part of a fallen world is the fact that among the music I most dislike is music that is most insistent in its claims to be Christian. Contemporary Christian music, to which growing numbers of radio stations are dedicated, is a form of pastoral music, but a particularly ideological form, it seems to me, that tries too hard to engender the feelings and convictions it harbours. It has been well said that to sing a prayer is to pray twice. In my view, however, to sing a sermon is to preach once too often. Robert Faricy says it directly: "Art at the service of an ideology,

79. *Dynamics of Faith*, 15-16.
80. p.17.
81. p.16.
82. p.11.

instrumentalised art, becomes, always, non-art."[83] In contrast, Barth praises
Mozart's music, including his "church music," for its lack of preachiness:

> Mozart's music is not, in contrast to that of Bach, a message, and
> not, in contrast to that of Beethoven, a personal confession. He
> does not reveal in his music any doctrine and certainly not himself.
> . . . Mozart does not wish to *say* anything; he just sings and sounds.
> Thus he does not force anything on the listener, does not demand
> that he make any decisions or take any positions; he simply leaves
> him free. . . . Nor does he *will* to proclaim the praise of God. He
> just does it – precisely in that humility in which he himself is, so to
> speak, only the instrument with which he allows us to hear what
> he hears: what surges at him from God's creation, what rises in
> him, and must proceed from him. . . . If I hear him rightly, in his
> church music as in all his other creations, the music is a free coun-
> terpart to that word given him.[84]

In evaluating pastoral music, we might keep in mind Faricy's important
contrast between "art at the service of 'religion' and art at the service of
God."[85] It seems to me that much contemporary Christian music is the
former, sincerely believing itself to be the latter. To make matters worse,
much of the music is also mediocre. I am not alone in these opinions. Best
is a companion critic:

> The sobering thing about so much contemporary Christian music
> and art – all types, but especially the big-scale stuff, pseudo-sym-
> phonic, classicised popular and popularised classics, oversized
> choirs and instrumental groups, or, in their absence, the ever-pres-
> ent taped accompaniment, "excellence" in absentia – the trouble
> with so much of this is that it pretends so ardently, pushing for
> something that already exists in finer form. It is gross, large-scale,
> theme park imitation – unauthentic – hence so prone toward
> kitschiness. Without possessing an inner sense of indigeneity, so
> anxious to "be like," so obsessed with overstatement and so lack-
> ing in humility and meekness, it sends out the worst signals to
> culture about the meaning of lean, disciplined, and authentic faith.[86]

Much contemporary Christian music merely skims effects off more substantial music and more profound texts. It is not surprising that the result
is at best "poorly crafted attempts to tell God how we feel,"[87] and at worst
"spiritual entertainment."[88]

83. "Art as a Charism in the Church," *Thought* 57 (1982), 96.
84. *Wolfgang Amadeus Mozart*, tr. Clarence K. Pott (Grand Rapids: Eerdmans,
      1986), 37-8. Barth's emphases
85. "Art as Charism in the Church," 94-9.
86. *Music through the Eyes of Faith*, 130.
87. Westermeyer, *Te Deum*, 318.
88. Samuel Adler, "Sacred Music in a Secular Age," *Sacred Sound*, ed. Hoffman
      and Walton, 290.

Of course there is risk in such scornful opinions as these. The danger is that as critics too close to our subject, our hearing may be distorted. Vigorous criticism always risks what Brown calls the sin of the philistine, demanding that all music translate into the "practical, moral, or specifically religious terms" that we ourselves favour, or the risk of intolerance, elevating our "own standards to the level of absolutes." Brown is right to remind us that finally not taste but grace saves us. To judge music's sacramental value is to walk the razor's edge of many adjudications in religious matters: the edge between righteous indignation and self-righteousness. One who accepts the doctrine of a fallen world does not have to be warned that we are apt to slip.

Let us complete this section by trying to answer the question "What is sacred music?" Here, as at so many places, I take Augustine as a guide. We may begin with Augustine's explanation of what makes a song a hymn:

> Hymns are praises of God with song; hymns are songs containing the praise of God. If there be praise, and it is not of God, it is not a hymn; if there be praise, and praise of God, and it is not sung, it is not a hymn. If it is to be a hymn, therefore, it must have three things: praise, and that of God, and song.[89]

We may note that Augustine does not limit his definition to liturgical music. Indeed, he does not limit his definition to songs with words. In the Introduction we encountered Augustine's commentary on Psalm 33 where he praises sheer jubilation, vocalising without words, as "singing well to God." In his commentary on Psalm 100 (Psalm 99 in the *Vulgate*) he returns to the same theme:

> One who jubilates (*iubilat*) does not speak words, but it is rather a sort of sound of joy without words, since it is the voice of a soul poured out in joy and expressing, as best it can, the feeling, though not grasping the sense. A man delighting in his joy, from some words which cannot be spoken or understood, bursts forth in a certain voice of exultation without words, so that it seems he does indeed rejoice with his own voice, but as if, because filled with too much joy, he cannot explain in words what it is in which he delights. You observe this even in those who sing improperly.[90]

With or without words, and refined or not refined, sacred music for Augustine is music in praise of God.

Our basic idea of sacramental encounter from Chapter 1 leads us further. We have said that sacramental music is any music "through which the divine is perceived to be disclosed and communicated, and through which our human response to the divine assumes some measure of shape, form, and structure."[91] By the divine we understand the origin and cause and being

89. *In psalmum* 72.1, in McKinnon, *Music in Early Christian Literature*, 158.
90. *In psalmum* 99.4, in McKinnon, *Music in Early Christian Literature*, 158.
91. McBrien, *Catholicism*, 2:732.

and life of all creation, the ultimate consonance of the world. Therefore, music that conveys glimpses of cosmic order and proportion, music that manifests trans-historical creativity, music that awakens a sense of ultimate dependence upon our Creator and co-dependence with our fellow creatures, music that evokes spiritual awe and wonder, music that confronts us with the holy in its divine dimension and – with the qualifications we have considered – in its demonic dimension as well: in all such music the sacred is present.

What music is excluded? I would say only music too vacuous to mediate sacramental depths of these kinds. Only music that discloses its entire substance to hasty exposure, music content with skimming surface effects – which, I am afraid, is quite a lot of music. Finally, what is specifically Christian sacred music? I would say that it is any music that relates us, in the midst of a fallen world, to a Christian spirit of healing and wholeness, which we shall take as our theme for the next chapter. Music that manifestly relates us to the opposite, to a spirit of deliberate hurt and divisiveness, we are bound, I think, to consider non-Christian.

## *Music and Theodicy*

Before leaving this chapter on the myth of the Fall, let us consider a final issue relating theology and music, the issue of theodicy. Put simply, theodicy is the challenge of trusting God's goodness without denying the reality of evil and, conversely, of acknowledging the reality of evil without rejecting God's goodness.

Let us begin with acknowledging the reality of evil. In an important treatise of 1558, Gioseffe Zarlino wrote about musical dissonance in language that reminds us of a traditional theological argument concerning the role of evil in the world, namely, that our experiences of evil serve to heighten our sense of the good:

> A dissonance causes the consonance that follows it to sound more agreeable. The ear then grasps and appreciates the consonance with greater pleasure, just as light is more delightful to the sight after darkness, and the taste of sweets more delicious after something bitter. We daily have the experience that after the ear is offended by a dissonance for a short time, the consonance following it becomes all the more sweet and pleasant.[92]

Zarlino then offers guidance to 16th-century composers who would make use of dissonance: "it must not be thought that these dissonances can be placed in counterpoints or compositions without rule or order, as is sometimes done, for confusion would result. Care should be taken to use them in an orderly, regular fashion, so that all may turn out well."[93] Tragically,

---

92. *Institutioni harmoniche*, in Weiss, *Music in the Western World*, 113.
93. p.113.

however, history coerces our admission that in life not all turns out well –
particularly the history of our 20th century, "one of the cruellest, most
wasteful of hope in human record"[94] This harsh truth echoes in our music.
With its wealth of resources – melodic tension, harmonic dissonance, tonal
roughness, the minor modes, atonality, and a host of others – music of our
century has proven adequate to its rueful challenge.

The glib theodicy that parallels Zarlino's discussion of dissonance and
consonance is of course not the only tradition of theology, and theologies
of our century are hardly the first to wrestle with intractable evil. The
biblical books of Lamentations, Job, Ecclesiastes, and Psalms share this
universal struggle:

Rouse yourself! Why do you sleep, O Lord?
  Awake, do not cast us off forever!
Why do you hide your face?
  Why do you forget our affliction and oppression?
For we sink down to the dust;
  our bodies cling to the ground. (Ps 44.23-4)

Nor is struggle with evil and suffering expressed in 20th-century music
alone. I think of the chill desolation of "Der Leiermann" ("The Hurdy-
Gurdy Man"), unrelieved by any glimmer of warmth, with which Schubert
concludes his cycle of twenty-four songs, *Die Winterreise* (*The Winter's
Journey*). Let us say simply that 20th-century music is unsurpassed in its
use of unresolved dissonance, as the 20th century is unsurpassed in instances of life's darkness crying for expression.

Krzysztof Penderecki's 1960 *Threnody for the Victims of Hiroshima*
remains for me the most disturbing musical example of unresolved dissonance. In the large string orchestra, tone clusters shriek and grate within
their critical bandwidths of dissonance, while pizzicatos and wooden bows
striking against wooden instruments clatter like falling debris. Glissandos
sag like melting flesh. Vicious stratospheric screeches scorch our ears, as
if in reminder of the radioactive cauldron that scorched the city of Hiroshima
and the decision to drop the bomb that sears our conscience. The *Threnody*'s
occasional steady pitches seem less fragments of melody than the wails of
sirens. In a dreadful reversal of Zarlino's principle, these rare moments of
consonance offer but paltry contrast, so that the ear "grasps and appreciates" the overall dissonance with greater horror. I hear in Penderecki's
music an aural acknowledgment of evil's reality and a deliberate rejection
of Zarlino's musical principle that all should turn out well.

The perennial question of theodicy is how we can acknowledge the
reality of evil this honestly and yet trust God's goodness? One response is
to blame the devil. The most musical of all the church's saints, Hildegard
of Bingen, makes explicit use of musical imagery to recount the story of
humanity's fall as a disruption of harmony by the "deceiver, the devil":

94. Steiner, *Real Presences*, 228.

> In Adam's voice before he fell there was the sound of every har-
> mony and the sweetness of the whole art of music. . . . But when
> his deceiver, the devil, heard that man had begun to sing through
> divine inspiration, and that he would be transformed through this
> to remembering the sweetness of the songs in the heavenly land –
> seeing the machinations of his cunning going awry, he became so
> terrified that . . . he has not ceased to trouble or destroy the
> affirmation and beauty and sweetness of divine praise and of the
> hymns of the spirit.[95]

Yet Augustine recognises that as author of the world, God must in some
profound sense be author of the world's evil:

> But then I would ask myself once more: "Who made me? Surely it
> was my God, who is not only good but Goodness itself. How, then,
> do I come to possess a will that can choose to do wrong and refuse
> to do good, thereby providing a just reason why I should be
> punished? Who put this will into me? Who sowed this seed of
> bitterness in me, when all that I am was made by my God, who is
> Sweetness itself ? If it was the devil who put it there, who made
> the devil? If he was a good angel who became a devil because of
> his own wicked will, how did he come to possess the wicked will
> which made him a devil. . .?"[96]

Augustine formulates the issue in essentially musical terms. Evil is discord, intrinsic to the world's consonance:

> In the separate parts of your creation there are some things which
> we think of as evil because they do not accord (*non conveniunt*)
> with other things. But there are other things again with which they
> are in accord (*conveniunt*), and then they are good.[97]

This imagery of discord in the midst of accord suggests a musical analogy
that avoids the glibness of theodicies paralleling Zarlino's account of
musical dissonance and consonance, the defeatism of theodicies that place
the entire weight of a fallen world on the shoulders of a depraved humanity, and the escapism of theodicies that simply blame the devil. The analogy
is between Augustine's concept of sin as discord intrinsic to cosmic
harmony and the musical phenomenon known as the Pythagorean Comma.

   In our discussion of Pythagorean intervals in Chapter 2 we glimpsed a
perplexing fact. The tidy concept of the cycle of 5ths, which generates
first the five notes of the pentatonic scale, then the seven notes of diatonic
scales, and finally the twelve notes of the chromatic scale, is in actuality
not so tidy as at first appears. If the cycle of Pythagorean 5ths were tidy,

95. *Hildegard of Bingen: An Anthology*, ed. Fiona Bowie and Oliver Davies, tr.
      Robert Carver (London: SPCK, 1990), 149.
96. *Confessions* 7.3, 136-7.
97. *Confessions* 7.13, 148-9.

the twelfth step would bring the cycle back to an F, namely, an F seven octaves above the original F where we began the cycle in our example. But this is not the case – not exactly. If all twelve steps have been exact 5ths, defined by the simple Pythagorean ratio of 2:3, the cycle does not close at that high F. It barely misses closure and wheels off into a new twelve-tone cycle of 5ths based upon a slightly higher fundamental, and so on, to infinity. The mathematical ratio between the theoretical point of exact closure and the actual cycle's point of near miss is the fraction 531441/524288.

For our purposes, let us ask three questions. First, what is the derivation of this dumbfounding fraction? Second, why did God set up the musical cosmos in this inherently discordant way? Third, how might this discrepancy pertain to our human lives in a fallen world? The first question is not so very difficult. The theoretical point of exact closure for the cycle of 5ths is F, seven octaves above the beginning F. Mathematically, it is simply the ratio of the octave, 1:2, multiplied by itself seven times, to equal $(1/2)^7$ or $1/128$. For the actual cycle of 5ths, in contrast to the theoretical, the point of near closure is twelve 5ths above the beginning F. Mathematically, it is the ratio of the 5th, 2:3, multiplied by itself twelve times, to equal $(2/3)^{12}$ or $4096/531441$. The ratio between the two, then, is $1/128$ divided by $4096/531441$, which equals $531441/524288$. The important thing is not the exact numerator and denominator of this ratio, however, but the obvious fact that this fraction is not equal to 1, as it would have to be if the cycle of twelve perfect 5ths closed to make a tonal circle of seven perfect octaves.

This fraction of discrepancy is called the Pythagorean Comma. The error of closure it represents is slightly greater than one percent, enough to bother sensitive musical ears throughout the entire seven-octave range. In contrast with the neat system of whole number ratios we examined in Chapter 2, this musical discrepancy seems to represent some fundamental flaw in the orderly structure of the musical cosmos. With the Pythagorean Comma "all simplicity has disappeared."[98] This fundamental flaw seems analogous to the presence of temptation and sin, evil and suffering, within an orderly creation pronounced by the biblical narrative to be "very good." McClain refers to the Pythagorean Comma, in fact, as "an 'original sin' . . . for which neither men nor gods are responsible."[99]

In the Augustinian doctrine of creation, however, God *is* somehow responsible. This brings us to our second question: why did God set up the musical cosmos in this inherently discordant way? In response to a similarly imponderable theological question, namely, the question of what God was doing before creation of the world, Augustine gives what I take to be the most appropriate answer:

My answer to those who ask "What was God doing before he made

98. Jeans, *Science and Music*, 166.
99. *The Myth of Invariance*, 83.

heaven and earth?" is not "He was preparing Hell for people who pry into mysteries." This frivolous retort has been made before now, so we are told, in order to evade the point of the question. But it is one thing to make fun of the questioner and another to find the answer. So I shall refrain from giving this reply. For in matters of which I am ignorant I would rather admit the fact.[100]

In relation to both the musical question of why the Pythagorean Comma and the theological question of why evil and suffering, Augustine's simple confession of ignorance seems to me our wisest response. We must simply "admit the fact." The important religious concern is not why, but rather how we shall comport ourselves in this world of God's creating. A precedent is Jesus's shift of emphasis in response to the perplexity of his disciples over the ethical paradox of a man born blind: "'Neither this man nor his parents sinned; he was born blind so that God's works might be revealed in him. We must work the works of him who sent me.'" (Jn 9.3-4).

Our third question is how the Pythagorean Comma might pertain to our human lives in a fallen world. Because of the lack of closure defined by the Pythagorean Comma, the number of actual musical tones is not five or seven or twelve but infinite. Thus the number of intervals is also infinite. Yet the octave, with its ratio of 1:2 and its near universal acceptance as a tonal identity, seems to set absolute terminal points for tonal patterning, and the generative interval of the 5th, with ratio 2:3, also seems absolute. How then, if not by means of cycling the 5th, are we to select from an infinity of tones to fill the octave's finitude? In our final chapter this question will lead us to the issue of tonal temperament. Saving details for then, let us only consider a final religious analogy.

The Pythagorean Comma means that no musical system can attain the perfection defined by its theoretical ideals and our human wishes. This imperfection is not a matter of composers who lack cleverness, instrument makers who lack craft, or performers who lack skill. It is a given and enduring complexity, pre-existing, perduring, and permeating all music. This imperfection is also a virtual image of one of Christianity's central teachings concerning human life, namely, that no person can attain the perfection defined by our ethical ideals and human hopes: "A certain ruler asked him, 'Good Teacher, what must I do to inherit eternal life?' Jesus said to him, 'Why do you call me good? No one is good but God alone'" (Lk 18.18-19). Biblical tradition offers ample precedent for Jesus's insistence that no human goodness attains to perfection. The teaching that no one is perfectly good, that everyone sins, enters the biblical story with King Solomon. In his dedicatory prayer for the first Jerusalem Temple, Solomon begins a long petition to God for his people's forgiveness with the epoch-making clause: "If they sin against you – for there is no one who

100. *Confessions* 11.12, 262.

does not sin. . ." (I Kings 8.46). That clause marks an end to traditional belief in the human possibility of moral perfectibility. Under this conviction of human fallibility the Psalmist writes:

> The LORD looks down from heaven on humankind
>> to see if there are any who are wise,
>> who seek after God.
> They have all gone astray,
>> they are all alike perverse;
> there is no one who does good,
>> no, not one. (Ps 14.2-3; also 53.2-3)

The Wisdom tradition echoes this juxtaposition of adjacent verses concerning wisdom and sin:

> Wisdom gives strength to the wise
>> more than ten rulers that are in a city.
> Surely there is no one on earth so righteous
>> as to do good without ever sinning. (Eccl 7.19-20)

Little wonder that this teaching, so deeply rooted in Judaism and expressly preserved in the sayings of Christ, becomes a leitmotif for Christianity's most ardent promulgator, the Apostle Paul. In his letter to Roman Christians, Paul quotes the Psalmist: "'There is no one who is righteous, not even one'" (Rom 3.10). Paul then repeats the message in his own words: "All have sinned and fall short of the glory of God. . ." (3.23). The author of the First Epistle of John echoes the same theme: "If we say that we have no sin, we deceive ourselves, and the truth is not in us" (1 Jn 1.8).

The Pythagorean Comma, then, is like an emblem of our world, where imperfection is unavoidable. But though both the Pythagorean Comma and human sinfulness are unavoidable, neither is irredeemable. We return to Schleiermacher's insistence that at the heart of Christian faith, sin and grace constitute an irreducible dialectic. The Pythagorean Comma is redeemable through the musical process of tempering. Human sinfulness is redeemable through the religious process of salvation. Thus we arrive at an analogy to develop in our final two chapters.

# V. Salvation: Sustaining Harmony

*Es kann in Ewigkeit kein Ton so lieblich sein*
*Als wenn des Menschen Herz mit Gott stimmt überein.*

There can in all eternity no tone so lovely be
As when the heart with God in full attunement doth agree.

## *Can Beauty Save Us?*

In Chapter 1 we encountered Weil's claim concerning the saving virtue of beauty: "A sense of beauty, although mutilated, distorted, and soiled, remains rooted in the heart of man as a powerful incentive. . . . If it were made true and pure, it would sweep all secular life in a body to the feet of God; it would make the total incarnation of the faith possible."[1] Is Weil's suggestion correct? Can beauty save us? More specifically, can the beauty of music save a fallen world? My belief is that beauty alone cannot save us. I agree with Sherrard: "Salvation through beauty – the transfiguring of things through beauty – is not an autonomous principle of art. It is a religious affirmation."[2] My religious affirmation is this: other things being equal, I believe that beauty, and in particular the beauty of music, can help to save a fallen world. But as Theodor Haecker insists, we cannot be sanguine: "In this world, nothing is apparently more helpless and powerless than beauty. In the visible order, nothing is more vulnerable, and so nothing falls more easily into the clutches of the Evil Spirit than beauty. There is no demonic truth, there is no demonic goodness, but there really does seem to be a demonic beauty."[3]

Much talk about music's saving virtues is ill defined, if not downright thoughtless, and for this reason let us begin this chapter on music's relation to Christianity's most positive claim, that our human sinfulness is redeemable, with some words of caveat. Specifically, let us begin by considering certain limitations of music in relation to goodness, truth, and beauty.

**Music and Goodness**. In relation to goodness, we may recall from Chapter 4 the biblical prophets' attacks on music in the midst of injustice. We noted Amos's attack on music amidst social injustice. Isaiah exhibits similar scorn for music in the midst of covenant betrayal:

1. *Waiting for God*, 162-3.
2. *The Sacred in Life and Art*, 20.
3. *Schönheit: Ein Versuch* (Leipzig, 1940), 78. Quoted in John Saward, *The Beauty of Holiness and the Holiness of Beauty: Art, Sanctity, and the Truth of Catholicism* (San Francisco: Ignatius Press, 1996), 36.

Ah, you . . . whose feasts consist of lyre and harp,
    tambourine and flute and wine,
but who do not regard the deeds of the LORD,
    or see the work of his hands! (Is 5.11-12)

That artistic beauty is potentially sacramental and yet can coexist with moral depravity is a distressing paradox of human experience. Weil wrestles with this paradox:

> If the beautiful is the real presence of God in matter and if contact with the beautiful is a sacrament in the full sense of the word, how is it there are so many perverted aesthetes? Nero. Is it like the hunger of those who frequent black masses for the consecrated hosts? Or is it, more probably, because these people do not devote themselves to what is genuinely beautiful, but to a bad imitation? For, just as there is art which is divine, so there is one which is demoniacal. It was no doubt the latter that Nero loved. A great deal of our art is of the devil. A person who is passionately fond of music may quite well be a perverted person – but I should find it hard to believe this of any one who thirsted for Gregorian chanting.[4]

Weil's assessment of relations between aesthetic beauty and demonic evil is sober and sobering, yet even so its final clause seems too optimistic. Liberation theologians of Latin America, for instance, have called attention to perverted collaborations between social injustices and the religious tradition of Gregorian chant. If we are honest, I believe, we are forced to accept Shakespeare's assessment of music's power for good and for ill:

Music oft hath such a charm
To make bad good, and good provoke to harm.[5]

**Music and Truth**. Both music and morality require commitment, but they require commitments of different kinds. Musical commitments are more arbitrary, we might say, whereas moral commitments are more compulsory. That is, we may involve ourselves in music or we may avoid such involvement. We cannot say the same of decisions having ethical consequences. Morality offers no rain checks. In moral life we are all auditors, performers, instrument makers, and composers, whether we choose to be or not.

What is more, we develop our moral commitments under a stronger sense of compulsory truth than is the case with our musical commitments. Grounded in certain preexisting, permeating, and perduring principles, music discloses certain given and enduring truths, yet music's principles are almost boundlessly flexible and accommodating to human creativity. Thus music can thrive under the most extreme applications – even defiance

---

4. *Gravity and Grace*, 138.
5. *Measure for Measure* 4.1.16-17, *Complete Works*, 88. See the trenchant reflections on beauty and moral truth in Richard Harries, *Art and the Beauty of God: A Christian Understanding* (London: Mowbray, 1993), 51-4.

– of its basic principles. Dissonant music can be beautiful, and atonal music can satisfy. In contrast, certain moral imperatives are less flexible and accommodating to our human preferences. "Thou shalt not bear false witness." Even as a veteran of the postmodern age, I remain enough of a Kantian to believe that human life cannot thrive if we decide to exchange that moral principle for an opposite: "Lie when you feel you must." Or "Thou shalt not kill." Surely it is empirically established that human life cannot thrive if we commit ourselves to a reverse principle: "Kill when you find it advantageous." To be sure, these given and enduring moral imperatives require our historical interpretation and application, but when we fail to acknowledge that moral truths are not boundlessly amenable to our creativity, we repeat the primordial fault of trying to be like gods, thus bringing upon ourselves anew the curses of the Fall.

I therefore have some sympathy for the distinction that Best draws between music and truth: "(1) Music is part of a divinely ordained world of relativism. (2) This particular relativism (in no way to be confused with moral relativism) stands in stark contrast, and complete subjection to, the absoluteness of truth."[6] In the end, however, it seems to me that Best draws his contrast too strongly, pressing his distinction to the point of disjunction: "Unlike truth, which is transcultural, absolute, and unchangeable, music can shift in meaning from place to place and from time to time."[7] I prefer the more conjunctive formulation we find in Plato: "The soul that has seen the most [of truth] shall enter into the birth of a man who is to be a philosopher or a lover of beauty, or one of a musical or loving nature."[8] I would simply add that Plato's formulation cannot be reversed. The most musical person is not necessarily the soul who has seen the most of truth.

**Music and Beauty**. Most music lovers will agree that music is beautiful, though by no means all music, and we have seen that music's beauty may be both amiable and terrible. Yet beauty is a concept of notorious complexity. Wittgenstein warns against the "idiotic role the word 'beautiful' plays in aesthetics."[9] Rather than abandon the concept of beauty, however, I think it better to protect this much-abused concept through attempts at clarification. We must learn to distinguish between "the beauty that saves and the beauty that enslaves."[10]

6. *Music through the Eyes of Faith*, 8.
7. p.54.
8. *Phaedrus* 248d, tr. Harold North Fowler (London: William Heinemann, 1943), 479.
9. *Culture and Value*, 52.
10. Sherrard, *The Sacred in Life and Art*, 20. See Carol Harrison's graceful comments on beauty's saving power in *Beauty and Revelation in the Thought of Saint Augustine* (Oxford, Clarendon, 1992), 271-3.

"The main species of beauty are orderly arrangement, proportion, and definiteness, " writes Aristotle, "and these are especially manifested by the mathematical sciences."[11] For all Aristotle's impatience with musical Pythagoreanism, the more cerebral approaches to music that we considered in Chapter 2 fall readily under Aristotle's definition of beauty. The more sensual, incarnational approaches to music that we considered in Chapter 3 are better described by later developments of classical tradition. Thomas Aquinas defines beauty as involving integrity or perfection (*integritas sive perfectio*), due proportion or harmony (*debita proportio sive consonantia*) and radiance (*claritas*).[12] Let us take these two triads of properties – order, proportion, and definiteness from Aristotle, and integrity, harmony, and radiance from Aquinas – as our working characterisation of beauty for this chapter's consideration of music's role in human salvation.

We cannot proceed without a further theological observation concerning music and beauty – namely, that biblical tradition exhibits a paucity of interest in creaturely beauty defined as we have just defined it. Though much biblical literature is of surpassing beauty, beauty does not appear among the Bible's cardinal virtues: justice, mercy, and humility (Mic 6.8), faith, hope, and love (1 Cor 13.13). Nor does beauty appear among Christian scripture's more extensive catalogue of derivative virtues, such as discernment, endurance, forbearance, forgiveness, humility, meekness, purity, and self-control. The Wisdom books frequently exclaim over the beauty of God's wisdom (Wis 7.29), God's holiness (Ps 29.2; 96.9), and God's presence (Ps 27.4; 50.2; 96.6). Yet even the Wisdom tradition gives attention to creaturely beauty primarily to warn against its temptations: "Charm is deceitful, and beauty is vain" (Prov 31.30). The biblical prophets, scornful of music amidst injustice and covenantal indifference, are likewise dubious about creaturely beauty more generally, as when Ezekiel cries, "Your heart was proud because of your beauty" (28.17). Isaiah opposes the fading beauty of a luxurious but unjust Israel to the abiding beauty of divine justice:

And the fading flower of its glorious beauty,
    which is on the head of those bloated with rich food,
will be like a first-ripe fig before the summer;
    whoever see it, eats it up as soon as it comes to hand.
In that day the LORD of hosts will be a garland of glory,
    and a diadem of beauty, to the remnant of his people;
and a spirit of justice to the one who sits in judgment,
    and strength to those who turn back the battle at the gate. (28.4-5)

11. *Metaphysics* 13.3 (1078b), tr. Hugh Tredennick (London: William Heinemann, 1936), 2:193.
12. *Summa Theologiae* 1a.39.8, tr. David Bourke, 60 vols. (New York: McGraw-Hill, 1963), 7:132. See the discussion of Aquinas's terms in Armand A. Maurer, *About Beauty: A Thomistic Interpretation* (Houston: Center for Thomistic Studies, 1983), 9-14.

Another passage from Isaiah, associated in Christian tradition with the figure of Christ, explicitly dissociates creaturely beauty from God's holy servant:

> He had no form or majesty that we should look at him,
>     nothing in his appearance that we should desire him.
> He was despised and rejected by others;
>     a man of suffering and acquainted with infirmity;
> and as one from whom others hide their faces
>     he was despised, and we held him of no account. (Is 53.2-3)

In considering the saving virtue of music, then, we must not forget the point from our preceding chapter, that near the heart of Christian faith is a terrible beauty of dissonance and silence. *Agape* or self-giving love, which Christian tradition identifies with God as revealed in Christ, is not identical with harmony as we usually conceive it. The way of Christ is "the way of affliction," Weil writes in a paradoxical image of harmony as dissonance:

> The cry of the Christ and the silence of the Father together make
> the supreme harmony, that harmony of which all music is but an
> imitation, that to which our harmonies, those at once the most heart-
> breaking and the most sweet, bear an infinitely far away and dim
> resemblance. The whole universe, including our own existences
> as tiny fragments of it, is only the vibration of that harmony.[13]

In Christian faith's healing vocation, the beauty of musical harmony can-not substitute for treading in Christ's way of affliction.

Yet Weil's concession to music in this passage, though small, is signifi-cant. The resemblance of our musical harmonies to Christ's way of affliction may be "infinitely far away and dim," as Weil asserts, and yet it is a resem-blance. As such, I believe, music can offer sacramental support for a life of Christian faith. For me no music is more profound in this regard than the massive processional with which Bach opens his *St. Matthew Passion*. Inconsolably minor, the music twists a chromatic path upwards, over a pedal point in the bass that reiterates the tonic note forty times, then breaks its compulsive lenten tread to ascend a scale of nearly two octaves. All the while, successive entrances of uppermost melodic voices add to the cumulative sonic weight. Infinitely far from the afflictions of Christ, yes. Nevertheless, Bach's music penetrates this listener's heart with the message of an afflicted Christ, sorely tempted, ascending Golgotha, bearing the weight of a fallen world.

## *Idol, Distraction, Offering, or Grace?*

With these opening caveats before us, let us turn to music's saving role in human experience, beginning with a brief review of the spectrum of relig-ious attitudes toward music that we have encountered so far. First, we

---

13. *Intimations of Christianity*, 9.

have seen that some reject music as an idol that attracts ultimate devotion to its own beauty at the expense of devotion to the goodness, truth, and beauty of God's holiness. Isaiah mocks the idolater who makes an idol "in human form, with human beauty, to be set up in a shrine . . . makes a god and worships it; . . . he prays to it and says, 'Save me, for you are my god!'" (44:13-17). Calvin warns of the danger that the church's sacraments themselves may become idols: "Neither ought our confidence to inhere in the sacraments, nor the glory of God be transferred to them. Rather, laying aside all things, both our faith and our confession ought to rise up to him who is the author of the sacraments and of all things."[14] As we approach music's sacramental and saving roles, these are words to take seriously. I confess that listening to a work like the 1985 *Piano and String Quartet* by Morton Feldman, who lifts up sheer sonic beauty for contemplation against a background of crystalline stillness, I know at first hand the temptation to worship music *per se*.

Second, we have seen that some reject music as a distraction. St. John of the Cross, who himself, as a composer, singer, dancer and poet, is said to have had "the soul of an artist,"[15] cautions religious novices against "consolations and sweetnesses of sense"[16] in worship as a distraction from their higher spiritual calling:

> For then the spirit, which is the higher part, is moved to pleasure and delight in God; and the sensual nature, which is the lower part, is moved to pleasure and delight of the senses, because it cannot possess and lay hold upon aught else, and it therefore lays hold upon that which comes nearest to itself, which is the impure and sensual.[17]

"It is, therefore, very fitting that they should enter into the dark night, whereof we shall speak," John says of spiritual novices, "that they may be purged from this childishness."[18] Conversely, Meister Eckhart offers a grudging recommendation of singing, but only as a diversion from doing things that are worse: "See! Praying, reading, singing, watching, fasting, and doing penance – all these virtuous practices were contrived to catch us and keep us away from strange, ungodly, things."[19]

Third, Best's recommendations of music are far from grudging. Nonetheless, he recommends music as an "offering" only, not as a sacramental

14. *Institutes of the Christian Religion* 4.14.12, 2:1287.
15. Kieran Kavanaugh, ed., *St. John of the Cross: Selected Writings* (New York: Paulist Press, 1987), 25.
16. *Dark Night of the Soul* 1.6.5, tr. E. Allison Peers (Garden City, NY: Image Books, 1959), 56.
17. *Dark Night* 1.4.2, 48.
18. *Dark Night* 1.6.6, 57.
19. "Selected Sermons," in Karen J. Campbell, *German Mystical Writers* (New York: Continuum, 1991), 107.

means of grace: "Music and worship are disconnected as to cause and effect. Music is neither an aid to worship nor a tool for producing it. It is an offering, uniquely given over to God, who is both means and end. . . . In the final analysis, music making is neither a means nor an end but an offering, therefore an act of worship."[20]

As before, my view differs somewhat from Best's. While I agree that we should guard against the abuses about which tradition so persistently warns us, I believe that we may yet accept music as a gift of God – gratuitous, abundant, and gracious. Again in this conviction I identify with Luther:

> I would certainly like to praise music with all my heart as the excell-
> ent gift of God which it is and to commend it to everyone. . . .
> [N]ext to the Word of God, music deserves the highest praise. . . .
> The Holy Ghost himself honours music as an instrument for his
> proper work. . . . After all, the gift of language combined with the
> gift of song was only given to man to let him know that he should
> praise God with both word and music, namely, by proclaiming
> through music and by providing sweet melodies with words. . . .
> But when learning is added to all this, and artistic music which
> corrects, develops, and refines the natural music, then at last it is
> possible to taste with wonder (yet not to comprehend) God's
> absolute and perfect wisdom in his wondrous work of music.[21]

Luther's final clause might serve as a précis of this book's fundamental conviction: in music we may taste with wonder, though never compre-hend, the wisdom of God.

Part of the sacramental wonder engendered by music is that it seems gratuitous. We cannot conceive of the world without the physical phenomenon of vibration. But though we may be loath to do so, we can conceive of the world without musical vibrations. Music's gratuity in the world helps account for the power of Albert Einstein's reputed response[22] when asked about the nuclear threat of human self-annihilation: "Alas, we would no longer be able to enjoy the music of Mozart."

The gift of music is not only gratuitous but abundant. If we can conceive of the world without music, we can certainly conceive of the world with-out Bach, Mozart, John Coltrane, and Joni Mitchell. Peter Kivy suggests an intriguing evolutionary account of music's possibility, namely that our human sense of sound – lying as it does between our sense of sight, which is essential to our survival, and our sense of smell, which is relatively atrophied – is just sensitive enough, but not too sensitive, for meaningful artistic creation and interpretation. "The conclusion of these observations,

---

20. *Music through the Eyes of Faith*, 9, 15.
21. "Preface to Georg Rhau's *Symphoniae jucundae* 1538," tr. Leupold, 321-4. I
    have slightly altered Leupold's translation.
22. I have been unable to document this attribution.

then, is that although the ear does, like the eye, have a strong tendency to interpret, its tendency is not to interpret sounds as representational or as natural phenomena but to interpret them as meaningful in the full linguistic sense."[23] Kivy offers a tribute to natural selection as the progenitor of music sound, in between sight and smell:

> But there, in the middle of the sandwich, is wonderful, glorious sound, the gift of an indulgent natural selection that gave our ears enough of the action to make them the fine instruments they are but not enough to make them, like the eyes, the slave of duty.[24]

I find Kivy's accounting for the possibility of music persuasive. Accounting for music's possibility, however, is by no means the same as accounting for the gratuitous abundance of Bach.

I would include both Kivy's phrase "indulgent natural selection" and my own phrase "gratuitous abundance" within the theological concept of grace, taken to mean the generous source and motive of a gift, particularly a gift sensed to flow from God, the unfathomable fountain of all. Calvin distinguishes three kinds of grace: (1) general or common (or sometimes "natural") grace; (2) special grace; and (3) saving or particular (or sometimes "special") grace. I believe that we may think of music as a gift of grace in all three senses.

By God's general or common grace[25] Calvin means the divine source of gifts to all persons alike, including our human capacities of mind and heart and will, together with the world's context in which we exercise them. Calvin includes the phenomenon of music among the gifts of God's general grace. For these natural gifts, Calvin writes, "We have nothing with which to repay God's generosity except the evidence of our gratitude."[26]

By God's "special graces"[27] Calvin means uncommon talents among humankind, such as particular gifts for virtue, learning, government, or art, including music:

> Although the invention of the lyre and of other musical instruments serves our enjoyment and our pleasures rather than our needs, it ought not on that account to be judged of no value; still less should it be condemned. Pleasure is to be condemned only when it is not combined with reverence for God and not related to the common welfare of society. But music by its nature is adapted to rouse our devotion to God and to aid the well-being of man; we need only avoid enticements to shame, and empty entertainments which

23. *Music Alone: Philosophical Reflections on the Purely Musical Experience* (Ithaca: Cornell University Press, 1990), 9.
24. pp.11-12.
25. *Institutes of the Christian Religion* 2.2.17, 1:276, 276n.
26. *Calvin: Commentaries* [on I Tim 4.1-5], tr. Joseph Haroutunian (Philadelphia: Westminster, 1958), 347.
27. *Institutes of the Christian Religion* 2.3.4, 1:293; also 2.2.17, 1:276, 276n.

keep men from better employments and are simply a waste of time.[28]
Calvin's theological dynamic of divine grace, human gratitude, and music
implies that the most proper employment of the gift of music is to give
thanks to God the giver. Luther agrees: "I would like to see all the arts,
especially music, used in the service of Him who gave and made them."[29]

Calvin thinks of God's general and special grace as active among fallen
humanity, signs of God's continuing mercy toward wayward and unrepentant creatures. God's saving or particular grace is also active among fallen
humanity. Unlike the other two kinds of grace, however, God's saving
grace in Calvin's understanding is humanity's particular way of salvation
from the dread consequences of the Fall, namely, the way of repentance,
forgiveness, and renewal of life bestowed by God through Christ. We have
just seen Calvin's view that musical talent as a gift of God's special grace
has many functions proper to human use and enjoyment. As we have seen
in our earlier survey of church attitudes towards music, however, Calvin
insists that in relation to God's saving grace, music's proper function is to
serve the divine word of salvation.

Barth took pleasure in his Calvinistic heritage of distinctions among
the various kinds of grace. Theodore Gill writes of visiting Barth and noting
the famous arrangement of his study rooms that Barth himself described
to Gill: "'There are probably very few theological study rooms in which
pictures of Calvin and Mozart are to be seen hanging next to each other
and at the same height.'" Gill reports additional comments by Barth that
are less well known: "'My special revelation,' he smiled, looking at Calvin.
'And my general revelation,' he said, as he beamed at Mozart.'"[30]

Calvin's three kinds of grace are useful distinctions, but I believe that
they cannot be contrasted absolutely or separated as Calvin sometimes
suggests, especially in distinguishing saving grace from natural and special.
Barth's distinction between Calvin and Mozart as sources of revelation is
rightfully playful, as it cannot be a dogmatic distinction. Gill seems to
suspect that Barth recognised as much: "Was he smiling because it was a
joke? Or because he knew something we didn't?" Gill makes his own
point of view quite clear: "I think that art and religion are up to exactly the
same thing: the re-presentation of primal visions."[31]

I find myself between Calvin and Gill. Art and religion, I believe, are distinct
realms of experience with significant regions of overlap. Specifically, as an out-
growth of natural acoustical phenomena, music is a gift of God's general grace.
As a sublime medium for human creativity, music is a gift of God's special
grace. And as an aid in human salvation, music is a gift of God's saving grace.

28. *Calvin: Commentaries* [on Gen 4.20], 355.
29. "Preface to the Wittenberg Hymnal," *Luther's Works*, 53:316.
30. "Barth and Mozart," *Theology Today* 43, no.3 (October 1986): 406. Here
    Barth is using "special" as synonymous with Calvin's "saving."
31. "Barth and Mozart," 406.

### *Music's Power to Heal and to Harm*

We have historical testimonies to music's saving power. The most famous is probably Beethoven's 1802 *Heiligenstadt Testament*, occasioned by the inexorable advance of his deafness:

> Such experiences almost made me despair, and I was on the point of putting an end to my life – the only thing that held me back was *my art*. For indeed it seemed to me impossible to leave this world before I had produced all the works that I felt the urge to compose; and thus I have dragged on this miserable existence – a truly miserable existence.[32]

According to Steiner, Wittgenstein "recorded that, more than once, the slow movement in Brahms's third Quartet pulled him back from the brink of suicide."[33] Sting, the popular musician of our day (Gordon Sumner), gives similar witness: "I think music is the one spiritual force in our lives that we have access to, really. There are so many other spiritual avenues that are closed off to us, and music still has that, is still important, is important for me. It saved my life. It saved my sanity."[34]

To appreciate such testimonies to music's saving power, we must appreciate what salvation means and what it does not mean. In biblical tradition, Paul writes of the Christian gospel as "the power of God for salvation to everyone who has faith" (Rom 1.16). The popular version of the Bible known as *The Living Bible* paraphrases Paul's characterisation of the gospel as follows: "It is God's powerful method of bringing all who believe it to heaven."[35] Given the widespread acceptance of this other-worldly interpretation of salvation, we must emphasise that the biblical idea of salvation is not only a method of bringing some of humankind to heaven. Biblical salvation also entails the reverse: a process of bringing something of heaven to humankind.[36]

A good first approximation to the rich biblical tradition of salvation is to understand salvation as healing, in the fundamental sense of making whole. "In Greek, the words which correspond to the English words save, salvation, Saviour, contain the sense both of soundness and of wholeness.

32. *The Letters of Beethoven*, tr. Emily Anderson (New York: W. W. Norton, 1961), Vol.3, 1352. Beethoven's emphasis.

33. *Errata: An Examined Life* (New Haven: Yale University Press, 1997), 84.

34. "Sting: A Musical Voyage," *In the Spotlight*, Educational Television Network, 15 September, 1993.

35. *The Living Bible Paraphrased*, ed. Kenneth Taylor (Wheaton, IL: Tyndale House, 1971).

36. The *New Living Translation* (1996) alters *The Living Bible*'s rendering of Romans 1.16 to reflect the Greek text and allow for a broader range of interpretation: "It is the power of God at work, saving everyone who believes." *Holy Bible: New Living Translation* (Wheaton, IL: Tyndale House, 1996).

To be saved is to attain a state in which one is sound and whole, entire."[37]
In numerous instances throughout Hebrew scripture, where ideas of heaven,
if present at all, are embryonic and indistinct, healing is used in close
association with God's saving actions toward humankind. The synonymous parallelisms that characterise Hebrew poetry are again instructive. Most
basically, healing parallels salvation:

> Heal me, O LORD, and I shall be healed;
>> save me, and I shall be saved. (Jer 17.14)

Healing also parallels God's graciousness:

> As for me, I said, "O LORD, be gracious to me;
>> heal me, for I have sinned against you. (Ps 41.4)

Healing parallels God's forgiveness:

> Bless the LORD, O my soul,
>> and do not forget all his benefits -
> who forgives all your iniquity,
>> who heals all your diseases. (Ps 103.2-3)

Healing parallels God's deliverance:

> He sent out his word and healed them,
>> and delivered them from destruction. (Ps 107.20)

New Testament writings echo these Hebrew usages. In the gospel nar-
ratives, saving is closely related to healing, and healing to making whole.
What is more, all three concepts – salvation, healing, and wholeness –
include both physical and spiritual dimensions. Christ forgives an immoral
woman and leaves her with the spiritual blessing: "Your faith has saved
(*sesoken*) you; go in peace" (Lk 7.50). Christ restores the sight of a man
who is physically blind with the charge: "Receive your sight; your faith
has saved (*sesoken*) you" (Lk 18.42). And Luke combines the physical
and spiritual dimensions of salvation in his story of Christ's healing a
leper, a foreigner, who returned to thank Christ and praise God. The story
ends with Christ's words: "Get up and go on your way; your faith has
made you well (*sesoken*)" (Lk 17.19). The King James Version reads:
"Arise, go thy way: thy faith hath made thee whole."

At basis, then, salvation is God's transformative power to heal, to make
whole. We find this sacred power in music, or at least in some music. I
said in Chapter 4 that the only music that seems to me excluded from
sacramental potentiality is music too vacuous to bear substantial meaning,
or music that deliberately hurts and divides instead of healing and making
whole. One measure of the vacuity or substance of music is its power to
transform us. Music's transformative reputation seems to be as ancient as
discussions of music itself. Plato has Socrates remark on this theme: "'And
is it not for this reason, Glaucon,' said I, 'that education in music is most
sovereign, because more than anything else rhythm and harmony find their

---

37. Sherrard, *The Sacred in Life and Art*, 3.

way to the inmost soul and take strongest hold upon it, bringing with them and imparting grace, if one is rightly trained, and otherwise the contrary?'"[38] On this point Aristotle agrees with Plato: "It is plain that music has the power of producing a certain effect on the moral character of the soul, and if it has the power to do this, it is clear that the young must be directed to music and must be educated in it."[39] Calvin's agreement with Plato concerning music's transformative power reveals his classical training that served him so well: "There is hardly anything in the world with more power to turn or bend, this way and that, the morals of men, as Plato has prudently considered. And in fact we find by experience that it has a secret and almost incredible power to move our hearts in one way or another."[40]

With the question of what kinds of transformative effects are produced by what kinds of music – the question of music's *ethos* – the ancient discussions became intense. Plato correlates the various musical modes of Greek tradition with particular effects on the soul, from intoxicating to clarifying, and from enervating to invigorating. On this basis he screens the musical modes that are suitable for educating the future guardians of the state, arriving at only two, the modes that classical Greek tradition called the Dorian and the Phrygian: "These two modes you must leave: the two which will best express the accents of courage in the face of stern necessity and misfortune, and of temperance in prosperity won by peaceful pursuits."[41] Aristotle agreed that the Dorian mode, as "more sedate and of a specially manly character," should be fundamental to education, but typically he allowed greater latitude concerning additional modes:

> For education, as has been said, the ethical class of melodies and
> of harmonies must be employed. And of that nature is the Dorian
> mode, as we have said before; but we must also accept any other
> mode that those who take part in the pursuit of philosophy and in
> musical education may recommend to us. Socrates in the *Republic*
> does not do well in allowing only the Phrygian mode along with
> the Dorian.[42]

I find that for many people today such talk of correlations between musical modes and modes of personal influence seems to fall somewhere between the quaint and the ridiculous, and many tend to dismiss the subject out of hand. But I am not so sure. Plato's kind of one-to-one correlations between musical modes and modes of thought, action, and feeling are doubtless simplistic. It does not follow, however, that there are no correlations at all. One-to-one correlations are simplistic precisely because

38. *The Republic* 401d, 1:257-9.
39. *Politics* 8.5.9 (1340b), 661.
40. "Preface" to the *Geneva Psalter*, in Strunk, *Source Readings*, 347.
41. *The Republic of Plato* 3.399c, tr. Francis MacDonald Cornford (New York: Oxford University Press, 1945), 87.
42. *Politics* 8.7.10 (1342b), 675 and 8.7.8 (1342a), 673

they trivialise a highly complex but actual phenomenon. My own experience echoes Augustine's: "I also know that there are particular modes in song and in the voice, corresponding to my various emotions and able to stimulate them because of some mysterious relationship between the two."[43] On the basis of my experiences with choir, congregation, and fellow listeners, I believe that different musical modes, even in the restricted modern sense of diatonic scales of distinctive patterns, convey distinct emotional effects. And I believe that in general terms at least we can specify certain relations between musical modes and their emotional effects upon us.

Let us consider particular examples. In preparation for Christmas a few years ago, our choir learned a new hymn, "A Stable Lamp is Lighted," with words by Richard Wilbur and music by David Hurd.[44] After a few rehearsals one of our altos asked with intensity: "What *is* it about this hymn?" Most of the choir seemed to share her curiosity. We were finding the hymn uncommonly affecting, even disturbing. Let us assume that half of this effect arose from Wilbur's haunting lyric. I believe that the other half arose from the musical mode, the Phrygian (not ancient Phrygian but modern – E to E on a keyboard's white keys). The Phrygian mode was rather novel for us. The only other hymns my church sings that make extensive use of Phrygian are the plainchant *Pange lingua*, "Sing, My Tongue, the Glorious Battle"; the great Lenten hymn, *Aus tiefer Not*, "From Deepest Woe," attributed, both tune and text, to Martin Luther; "I Heard the Voice of Jesus Say," to *The Third Tune* by Thomas Tallis; and "All Who Love and Serve Your City," to the tune *Birabus* by Peter Cutts. My choir and I find those four hymns also uncommonly affecting and disturbing. The Phrygian mode seems to engender such responses.

Our choir experienced quite a different effect from another new hymn, "Open Your Ears, O Faithful People."[45] It is in what is sometimes called the Eastern Mediterranean mode, or in Jewish tradition, the *ahavah rabbah* (Hebrew: much love), congruent with the harmonic form of the minor scale, but beginning and ending on the 5th tone instead of the tonic. Most of the choir found the hymn stirring and invigorating. One member of the congregation, on the other hand, covered her ears. The effect was in part because of novelty, as we sing no other hymns in this mode. The hymn's rhythm is also unusually vigorous. The words probably contributed little in this instance, since they are not especially notable. But much of the effect, I am convinced – whether welcomed or unwelcomed – arose directly from the vivid colourations of this chromatic mode.

A third example is personal, though I have shared my experience with a few friends whose responses generally agree with mine. The Locrian mode

43. *Confessions* 10.33, 238.
44. *The Hymnal 1982*, #104.
45. *The Hymnal 1982*, #536.

– B to B on a piano's white notes – rarely makes appearances in western harmonic music. My limited experience suggests that this mode appears but rarely in other world musics as well. Why should this be the case? The Locrian shares the minor 3rd with other minor modes, but this does not contribute to an explanation, as the world's musics richly manifest minor modes other than the Locrian. A further characteristic of the Locrian mode is probably a key to explanation. Whereas in all other modes represented in our Figure 4 the fifth tone of the scale forms a consonant 5th with the tonic tone below, and a consonant 4th with the tonic tone above, in the Locrian mode these two intervals are not the 5th and the 4th but are instead two instances of that most discordant of intervals, the tritone (B up to F, and F up to B). Be this as it may, I have heard a chant from Sikh tradition,[46] in a chromatic, symmetrical, nine-tone variant of the Locrian mode (B C E-flat E F G-flat G B-flat B), that is perhaps the most haunting, the most dolorous, the most afflictive music I have ever experienced. In this instance musical mode and vocal timbre must be largely determinative of effect, since the chant's text conveys no meaning to my western ears.

As a final example of a quite different kind, my choir and congregation sometimes sing a hymn from the renewal movement in Christian churches, "I Am the Bread of Life."[47] Some in our church love it. Unlike the modal hymns we have considered, this one never strays far from the major mode, hovers close to the tonic key, never disorients or even surprises, and is wholly accessible. Also the hymn accomplishes a certain dramatic effect by beginning low and ending high, with a total range (including descant) of two octaves – wider by a 4th than "The Star Spangled Banner." Unsupported by either harmonic strength or modal interest, however, the hymn's musical effect is in my opinion superficial and inane. I have no doubt that musical blandness and banality also exert their moulding effects upon our spirits, but in the direction of the vacuity that makes for a rarified sacramental medium.

Rhythm and melodic pattern, together with personal and cultural associations, interweave with musical modes to determine our emotional responses. Yet I am convinced that the modes themselves are ingredient to music's effects upon us. By restricting most of our hymns to the major and minor modes – indeed, to the major alone, since traditionally even most solemn hymns, such as "The Old Rugged Cross" or "Just As I Am," are in major – we impoverish our experience of worship. My denomination's hymnal is an uncommonly rich and progressive resource for worship. Yet of its seven hundred and twenty hymns, perhaps a dozen feature the Dorian mode, half a dozen the Pentatonic scale, and half that number the

46. "Sacred Music of the Sikhs," *JVC World Sounds Catalogue*, JVC, SVCD-1009, 1990.
47. *The Hymnal 1982*, #335.

Mixolydian mode. Several hymns use passing notes from the Lydian. Together with the few modal examples discussed above, and a welcome number of modal plainchant melodies from the middle ages, these constitute the few explorations beyond the major and the various minor modes. One exception proves the rule. "Christ Upon the Mountain Peak," with words by Brian Wren and music by Peter Cutts,[48] passes through the Aeolian, Phrygian, and Dorian modes to end with an "Alleluia!" written in the whole-tone scale – like the Locrian, a scale with two tritones instead of a 5th and a 4th as its pivotal intervals. It is the only use of whole-tone scale of which I am aware in Christian hymnody. At least I think it is a use of the whole-tone scale. Different editions of the hymnal have printed the notes differently, suggesting that the music copyists may have been nonplussed by this unaccustomed departure from hymnodic custom.

These various firsthand observations prevent me from simply dismissing the opening heading of the immensely influential medieval treatise by Boethius, *De institutione musica*: "Music forms a part of us through nature, and can ennoble or debase character."[49] At the very least, I would say, musical modes can distinctly brighten or darken our moods, and our moods affect our character. What is more, ancient discussions of music and moral influence are in fact less simplistic than they are sometimes made out to be. We noted earlier that the modes of ancient Greece were not the same as the medieval and modern European modes of the same names, but rather seem to have been entire musical genres, associated with specific cultural contexts and practices. In his screening of musical modes, Plato included complex cultural as well a purely musical considerations, condemning not "new songs but a new way of song": "For the modes of music are never disturbed without unsettling of the most fundamental political and social conventions."[50] Similarly, early Christian tradition shunned chromatic melodies, not as musical modes *per se*, but because of their pagan associations: "Austere and temperate songs protect against wild drunkenness; therefore we shall leave chromatic harmonies to immoderate revels and to the music of courtesans."[51] As for the uses of musical modes in education, Plato probably intended that the qualities that should give educators pause are not purely musical but associational as well, and I would agree. Surely we are wise not to introduce grunge rock into primary classrooms. The educational problems with grunge rock are not with its musical modes, however, which are mostly bluesy variations on the minor. The problems

48. *The Hymnal 1982*, #130.
49. Anicius Manlius Severinus Boethius, *Fundamentals of Music* 1.1, tr. Calvin M. Bower (New Haven: Yale University Press, 1989), 1.
50. *The Republic* 4.424b, tr. Shorey, 1:333.
51. Clement of Alexandria, *Paidagogos* 2.4, in Quasten, *Music and Worship in Pagan and Christian Antiquity*, tr. Boniface Ramsey (Washington: National Association of Pastoral Musicians, 1983), 68.

are with the desperate immaturity and social pathology of words and musical production, directly and deliberately opposed to the good of the whole. A track titled "Territorial Pissings," for example, or a refrain that screeches "Stay away!" against strident electronic distortion until voices and ears alike are raw. Or we may think of the brutal misogyny of "gangsta" rap[52] and the inciting racism of neo-Nazi songs. Music and lyrics this deliberately assaultive and abusive surely warrant the label of "demonic" as employed by Weil and Tillich.

This raises the troubling question of censorship. If we grant music's transformative power both to heal and to harm, then we must face questions concerning whether and how to regulate music, in worship, in education, and in society at large. In Chapter 4 we considered some criteria for evaluating liturgical music. Here let us devote a few thoughts to musical censorship as a broader educational and social issue.

As I write these lines the American Medical Association is recommending mandatory ratings for recorded music, based upon the content of the music's lyrics.[53] In what is agreed to be a work of Plato's old age, the *Laws*, he puts forward far more radical suggestions concerning artistic censorship, suggestions that nettle democratic nerves:

> As to the songs and the dances, this is the fashion in which they should be arranged. Among the compositions of the ancients there exist many fine old pieces of music, and likewise dances, from which we may select without scruple for the constitution we are founding such as are fitting and proper. To examine these and make the selection, we shall choose out men not under fifty years of age; and whichever of the ancient songs are approved we shall adopt, but whichever fail to reach our standard, or are altogether unsuitable, we shall either reject entirely or revise and remodel. For this purpose we shall call in the advice of poets and musicians, and make use of their poetical ability, without, however, trusting to their tastes or their wishes, except in rare instances; and by thus expounding the intentions of the lawgiver, we shall organise to his satisfaction dancing, singing, and the whole of choristry.[54]

History does not allow us to dismiss the attitudes that Plato expresses in this late dialogue as mere geriatric irascibility. The 20th century is witness to a cruel instantiation of such principles of censorship in the 1948 *Resolution on Music* issued by the Soviet Union's Central Committee of the All-Union Communist Party. The Resolution is an indictment of music composed by Sergei Prokofiev. The charge was modernism or musical

---

52. See Kelly Brown Douglas's criticism of abusive rap music, *The Black Christ* (Maryknoll, NY: Orbis, 1994), 104-5.
53. "Song Lyric Ratings Are Backed by A.M.A.," Associated Press release, 22 June 1995.
54. *Laws* 802a-c, tr. R. G. Bury (London: William Heinemann, 1942), 49-51.

"formalism." In his reply Prokofiev admits to "infection caught from contact with some Western ideas" and professes to welcome the *Resolution*, "which establishes the necessary conditions for the return to health of the whole organism of Soviet music":

> The existence of formalism in some of my works is probably explained by a certain complacency, an insufficient realisation of the fact that it is completely unwanted by our people. The Resolution has shaken to the core the social consciousness of our composers, and it has become clear what type of music is needed by our people, and the ways of the eradication of the formalist disease have also become clear.[55]

This from the composer of *Romeo and Juliet* (1936), which I regard as one of our century's surpassingly fine works of public art.

The *Resolution on Music* is all the more indefensible for the fact that between Plato and the Soviet Central Committee rises that monumental defense of free expression, Milton's *Areopagitica* of 1644. Milton's criticism of Platonic concepts of musical censorship is specific, right down to a reference to Plato's "Doric" musical mode:

> Plato . . . in the book of his laws, which no city ever yet received, fed his fancy with making many edicts to his airy burgomasters, which they who otherwise admire him wish had been rather buried. . . . If we think to regulate printing, thereby to rectify manners, we must regulate all recreations and pastimes, all that is delightful to man. No music must be heard, no song be set or sung, but what is grave and Doric. There must be licensing dancers, that no gesture, motion, or deportment be taught our youth, but what by their allowance shall be thought honest; for such Plato was provided of. It will ask more than the work of twenty licensers to examine all the lutes, the violins, and the guitars in every house; they must not be suffered to prattle as they do, but must be licensed what they may say. And who shall silence all the airs and madrigals that whisper softness in chambers? . . . The villages also must have their visitors to inquire what lectures the bagpipe and the rebec reads, even to the balladry and the gamut of every municipal fiddler.[56]

I believe that we today who regard ourselves as heirs of Milton's liberalism may at the same time agree with Plato that music is able to exert influences both healing and degrading. With some clarifying assistance from Thomas Jefferson, John Stuart Mill, Richard Rorty, the American Civil Liberties Union, and others, however, history has taught us that the kind of censorship Plato recommends is an artistic and human travesty.

55. Nicolas Slonimsky, ed., *Music Since 1900*, 4th ed. (New York: Charles Scribner's Sons, 1971). In Weiss, *Music in the Western World*, 500-2.

56. *Areopagitica and Of Education, with Autobiographical Passages from Other Prose Works*, ed. George H. Sabine (Northbrook, IL: AHM, 1951), 23-4.

Censorship is also a betrayal of the democratic principles our globe seems slowly to be learning to trust as the worst system of governance in the world except for all the others. I believe that we must therefore summon the courage and the patience to censure but not censor, to commend but not command, to pan but not ban. We must practice careful distinctions along the spectrum of authority from parental guidance, through PTA committees, school-board guidelines, public discussions, and academic debates, but stopping short of governmental legislation. We must express our musical and moral judgments, including criticism and even denunciation, be prepared to articulate our reasons, and then gird up our loins for democratic argument. *De gustibus non disputandum*, "concerning taste there is no arguing," is a misguided dictum. We argue tastes all the time, and we do well to keep our discussions open, well informed, and vigorous.

## Cosmic Harmony

To shrink from censuring – that is, from formulating and articulating judgements – is to imply that music and morality are finally not important. On the other hand, to censor – that is, to impose limits on the formulations and judgments of others – seems to distrust panentheistic faith that there is something of God everywhere, or, what is far worse, to assume that all of God is here, with me, in my authoritarian point of view. "It must be borne in mind," writes Dionysius, "that no single existing thing is entirely deprived of participation in the Beautiful, for, as the true Word says, all things are very beautiful. Holy contemplations can therefore be derived from all things."[57] Panentheistic faith entails trust that ultimately the world is a universe, and Pythagorean faith entails trust that the ultimate principle of the cosmos is consonance. From the midst of classical polytheism, Plato expresses such trust at the conclusion of *The Republic* in his myth of the harmony of the heavenly spheres:

> From the extremities was stretched the spindle of Necessity, through which all the orbits turned. . . . And the spindle turned on the knees of Necessity, and up above on each of the rims of the circles a Siren stood, borne around in its revolution and uttering one sound, one note, and from all the eight there was the concord of a single harmony.[58]

Plato's image of cosmic harmony, derived from obscure Pythagorean origins, has proven profoundly influential in western tradition.

Milton, who bitterly despised the censorship proposals in Plato's *Laws*, was nonetheless devoted to "the divine volumes of Plato,"[59] and his poetry echoes *The Republic*'s imagery of the celestial harmony of the spheres,

57. *Celestial Hierarchies*, 25-6.
58. *The Republic* 616e-617b, 1:503-5.
59. *Areopagitica and Of Education*, 91.

though Milton replaces Plato's eight celestial spheres with Dante's nine:

> then listen I
> To the celestial *Sirens* harmony,
> That sit upon the nine enfolded Sphears,
> And sing to those that hold the vital shears,
> And turn the Adamantine spindle round,
> On which the fate of gods and men is wound.[60]

In his historical survey, *The Music of the Spheres*, Jamie James presents a myriad appearances of this myth of the harmony of the spheres in western philosophy and music theory. James's tone, however, seems to combine 20th-century bemusement over an antiquated concept with a tincture of nostalgia at its passing: "The key to the universe is no longer of use to anyone, because the exquisite edifice it once unlocked has crumbled into nothingness."[61] James concludes his survey: "In pursuing the concept of the musical universe from the first notes of Western music to the latest electronic screech, we have traced its gradual passage from vitality to sterility, from substance to form."[62] In contrast to James, I believe that reports of the concept's passing are premature, that the Pythagorean myth of cosmic consonance retains substance, vitality, and saving potential. At the least, Burkert's modest assessment seems to me appropriate:

> The fascination that surrounded, and still surrounds, the name of Pythagoras does not come, basically, from specific scientific connotations, or from the rational method of mathematics, and certainly not from the success of mathematical physics. More important is the feeling that there is a kind of knowing which penetrates to the very core of the universe, which offers truth as something at once beatific and comforting, and presents the human being as cradled in a universal harmony. In the figure of Pythagoras an element of pre-scientific cosmic unity lives on into an age in which the Greeks were beginning, with their newly acquired method of rational thought, to make themselves masters of their world, to call tradition into question, and to abandon long-cherished beliefs. The price of the new knowledge and freedom was a loss in inner security; the paths of rational thought lead further and further in different directions, and into the Boundless. There the figure of the ancient Sage, who seemed still to possess the secret of unity, seemed more and more refulgent. Thus after all, there lived on, in the image of Pythagoras, the great Wizard whom even an advanced age, though it be unwilling to admit the fact, cannot entirely dismiss.[63]

60. "Arcades" 62-7, *The Poetical Works of John Milton*, 2:160.
61. *The Music of the Spheres: Music, Science, and the Natural Order of the Universe* (New York: Grove Press, 1993), xiv-xv.
62. p.241.
63. *Lore and Science in Ancient Pythagoreanism*, 482.

The western tradition of cosmic harmony, though of antique Greek origins, is important in Christian tradition as well. The myth has near parallels in biblical tradition. Psalm 19 celebrates the heavens' diurnal proclamation of their Creator's glory:

The heavens are telling the glory of God;
   and the firmament proclaims his handiwork.
Day to day pours forth speech,
   and night to night declares knowledge.
There is no speech, nor are there words;
    their voice is not heard;
yet their voice goes out through all the earth,
   and their words to the end of the world. (Ps 19.1-4)

The fifth and sixth lines of this excerpt from the Psalter ("There is no speech. . . .") are like a nudge of the rhetorical elbow to remind the reader or singer not to take the psalm's poetic images literally. Apparently not nudged sufficiently, St. Basil mocks the idea of an actual music of the spheres:

These circles, they say, carried away in a direction contrary to that of the world, and striking the aether, make sweet and harmonious sounds, unequalled by the sweetest melody. And if we ask them for the witness of the senses, what do they say? That we, accustomed to this noise from our birth, on account of hearing it always, have lost the sense of it; like men in smithies with their ears incessantly dinned. If I refuted this ingenious frivolity, the untruth of which is evident from the first word, it would seem as though I did not know the value of time, and mistrusted the intelligence of such an audience.[64]

Yet, like a host of other early Christian authors, even Basil celebrates the myth's underlying intuition of cosmic harmony:

But God, before all those things which now attract our notice existed, God, after casting about in His mind and determining to bring into being that which had no being, imagined the world such as it ought to be, and created matter in harmony with the form which He wished to give it. . . . He welded all the diverse parts of the universe by links of indissoluble attachment and established between them so perfect a fellowship and harmony that the most distant, in spite of their distance, appeared united in one universal sympathy.[65]

The earliest Christian document we possess outside the writings of the

---

64. *Hexaemeron*, "Homily 2.3" *The Treatise de Spiritu Sancto; The Nine Homilies of the Hexaemeron; and The Letters*, tr. Blomfield Jackson, A Select Library of Nicene and Post-Nicene Fathers of the Christian Church: Second Series, vol. 8, (New York: The Christian Literature Company, 1895), 66-7.
65. *Hexaemeron*, "Homily 2.2," 60.

New Testament,[66] the epistle known as 1 Clement, gives Christian expression to the concept of cosmic harmony, a gift of God's general grace and saving grace:

> The heavens move at his direction and peacefully obey him. Day and night observe the course he has appointed them, without getting in each other's way. The sun and the moon and the choirs of stars roll on harmoniously in their appointed courses at his command, and with never a deviation. By his will and without dissension or altering anything he has decreed the earth becomes fruitful at the proper seasons and brings forth abundant food for men and beasts and every living thing upon it. The unsearchable, abysmal depths and the indescribable regions of the underworld are subject to the same decrees. . . .The seasons, spring, summer, autumn, and winter, peacefully give way to each other. The winds from their different points perform their service at the proper time and without hindrance. Perennial springs, created for enjoyment and health, never fail to offer their life-giving breasts to men. The tiniest creatures come together in harmony and peace. All these things the great Creator and Master of the universe ordained to exist in peace and harmony. Thus, he showered his benefits on them all, but most abundantly on us who have taken refuge in his compassion through our Lord Jesus Christ, to whom be glory and majesty forever and ever. Amen.[67]

This early epistle then comes to the moral shared among all of these Christian celebrations of cosmic harmony. As God harmonises the cosmos, so Christians, made in God's image and redeemed by God's wisdom and word, should live "in concert":

> Take care, dear friends, that his many blessings do not turn out to be our condemnation, which will be the case if we fail to live worthily of him, to act in concert, and to do what is good and pleasing to him.[68]

Written from Rome, 1 Clement seems to amplify Paul's earlier advice to Roman Christians:

> May the God of steadfastness and encouragement grant you to live in harmony with one another, in accordance with Christ Jesus, so that together you may with one voice glorify the God and Father of our Lord Jesus Christ. (Rom 15.5-6)

66. "The Letter of the Church of Rome to the Church of Corinth, Commonly Called Clement's First Letter," *Early Christian Fathers*, ed. and tr. Cyril C. Richardson (Philadelphia: Westminster, 1953), 33.

67. pp.53-4.

68. p.54.

## *Harmony: Individual and Social*

Both cosmic harmony, then, and its moral corollary, human harmony, are concepts relating to Christian salvation. Human harmony has both an individual and a social application. In relation to the individual, Plato speaks of three capacities of human souls: a desiring or impulsive capacity, a reasoning or calculating capacity, and, mediating between the two, a tempering or spirited capacity. Apologists for Plato, eager to avoid charges of accepting a fragmenting "faculty psychology," sometimes make the point that these human capacities are inseparable, even indistinguishable. Would that it were so. Plato's observation is that our soul's capacities are separated all too easily, often coming into conflict and sometimes rending us apart: "Then, my good friend, it will never do for us to say that the soul is a harmony. . . . Harmonia, the Theban goddess, has, it seems, been [only] moderately good to us."[69] For Plato the aim of moral and spiritual education and discipline is to bring our soul's disparate capacities into greater harmony.

In passage after passage Plato conveys this opinion by use of musical imagery:

> A man must not suffer the principles in his soul to do each the
> work of some other and interfere and meddle with one another, but
> . . . having first attained to self-mastery and beautiful order within
> himself, and having harmonised these three principles, the notes
> or intervals of three terms, quite literally the lowest, the highest,
> and the mean, and all others there may be between them, and having
> linked and bound all three together and made of himself a unit,
> one man instead of many, self-controlled and in unison, he should
> then and then only turn to practice.[70]

In Plato's remark about the soul's three capacities and "all others there may be between them" we see his opinion that our soul's capacities are not only three in number, but in fact legion – as also in the gospel account of Christ's encounter with the demoniac who bears the name Legion (Mk 5; Lk 8). The soul's capacities are inseparable only in the sense that they are bound within single persons, whose moral well-being depends upon resolution of their conflicts, upon achievement of their harmony.

Plato's musical imagery goes beyond analogy. He believes that music plays an actual, healing role in harmonising the soul:

> Music too, in so far as it uses audible sound, was bestowed for the
> sake of harmony. And harmony, which has motions akin to the
> revolutions of the Soul within us, was given by the Muses to him
> who makes intelligent use of the Muses, not as an aid to irrational
> pleasure, as is now supposed, but as an auxiliary to the inner revol-

69. *Phaedo*, 94e-95a, 327-9.
70. *The Republic* 4.443d-e, 1:415.

ution of the Soul, when it has lost its harmony, to assist in restoring it to order and concord with itself. And because of the unmodulated condition, deficient in grace, which exists in most of us, Rhythm also was bestowed upon us to be our helper by the same deities and for the same ends.[71]

Of course Christians did not need Plato to teach them about divided and discordant selves in need of wholeness and harmony, about souls in need of salvation. "I do not understand my own actions," Paul writes, out of a more radical sense of divided self than Plato ever expressed: "I can will what is right, but I cannot do it. For I do not do the good I want, but the evil I do not want is what I do" (Rom 7.15, 18-19). Augustine expresses this Pauline spiritual struggle with even greater passion:

When the mind commands the mind to make an act of will, these two are one and the same and yet the order is not obeyed. Whence this monstrosity? What is the cause of it? The mind orders itself to make an act of will, and it would not give this order unless it willed to do so; yet it does not carry out its own command.[72]

But though Christians did not need Plato to learn of divided selves, and though their trust in salvation through Christ distinguished them from classical concepts of healing and wholeness, yet their writings echo Plato's musical analogies for the soul's healing. Plato writes: "I . . . should rather choose to have my lyre, or some chorus that I might provide for the public, out of tune and discordant, or to have any number of people disagreeing with me and contradicting me, than that I should have internal discord and contradiction in my own single self."[73] Saint Basil echoes: "Again, a musician would not willingly consent that his lyre should be out of tune, nor a leader of a chorus that his chorus should not sing in the strictest possible harmony, but shall each individual person be at variance with himself, and shall he exhibit a life not at all in agreement with his words?"[74]

Did early Christian authors also endorse Plato's prescription of musical experience as a means of healing our divided selves? Yes, but only explicitly spiritual music, and usually in liturgical settings. Secular music was to wait a long time for Christian baptism into the service of soteriology. Athanasius, for example, invokes the healing influence of David's music upon King Saul, but he assumes that David sang Psalms. Thus he turns this most ancient account of music therapy into a parable of the harmonizing power of psalm-singing upon the soul:

But those who sing in the manner described above – that is, with the melody of the words proceeding from the rhythm of the soul

---

71. *Timaeus* 47d-e, 109.

72. *Confessiones* 8.9, 446-8.

73. *Gorgias* 482b, tr. W. R. M. Lamb (London: William Heinemann, 1939), 381.

74. *The Letters and Address to Young Men on Reading Greek Literature*, 401.

and its harmony with the spirit – such as they sing with the tongue and sing also with the mind, not only for themselves, but also to benefit greatly those who would hear them. Hence blessed David by singing in this manner for Saul, pleased God for his own sake and removed the confusion and manic passion from Saul, and made his soul be at peace. The priests sang in this manner, summoning the souls of the people to tranquillity and to unanimity with the heavenly choir. Hence to recite the psalms with melody is not done from a desire for pleasing sound, but is a manifestation of harmony among the thoughts of the soul.[75]

Athanasius expresses the widespread Christian view that we experience salvation insofar as our souls are well ordered and whole, reattuned to the harmony of God's creation and God's will. In contrast, insofar as we remain in a state of dissonance we remain victims of the Fall. This theme too is both classical and Christian. In a traditionally inscrutable passage of *The Republic* Socrates remarks: "If one tries to express the extent of the interval between the king and the tyrant in respect of true pleasure he will find on completion of the multiplication that the king lives 729 times as happily and that the tyrant's life is more painful by the same distance." To this Socrates' companion responds: "An overwhelming and baffling calculation. . .!"[76] Overwhelming and baffling indeed, until McClain points out[77] that the ratio of the musical 5th is 3:2, that the sixth step in the cycle of 5ths reaches that most dissonant of musical intervals, the tritone, and that the numerator of the tritone's ratio is therefore $3^6 = 729$. Ever ironic, Socrates seems to be comparing the "true pleasure" of a tyrant's life to the musical dissonance of a tritone.

In a similar vein, Hildegard warns fellow Christians against the tyrant Satan, "who drew man out of the celestial harmony"[78] into the dissonance of disobedience and sin. We have seen that medieval Christians called the tritone "the devil's interval." In her characterisation of the Devil, however, Hildegard exceeds even Socrates' comparison of the tyrant to that most dissonant interval. Her morality play *Ordo virtutum* has all the characters sing their parts except the Devil, who is made to speak his lines. Thus Hildegard denies the Devil all possibility of harmony.[79] "The soul," says Hildegard, "is symphonic."[80] Her non-musical characterisation of the Devil implies a symphonic quotient of zero.

75. *Epistula ad Marcellinum* 29, in McKinnon, *Music in Early Christian Literature*, 53.
76. *The Republic* 587e, 2:397-9.
77. *The Myth of Invariance*, xi-xii.
78. *Hildegard of Bingen: An Anthology*, 149.
79. Barbara Thornton, notes to *Hildegard von Bingen: Ordo virtutum*, EMI Records, CDS 7 49249 8, 1982.
80. *Hildegard of Bingen: An Anthology*, 149.

For Clement the harmony of God's creation is uniquely manifest in the New Song of Christ, and other early Christians portray salvation as Christ's restoration of dissonance into harmony. A Gaza synagogue mosaic of the 6th century C.E. portrays David in the guise of Orpheus, soothing wild animals with the music of his lyre. Depictions of Christ as Orpheus "adorn early Christian catacombs in Rome and early Christian sarcophagi."[81] After the 3rd century these explicit associations of Christ with Orpheus disappear, but the saviour Christ as musician remains a traditional theme:

He knows how to touch the strings,
To lead from joy to joy.
With cherubim and seraphim
The soul dances in the round.
Christ is the leader of the dance.[82]

In an 11th-century illuminated manuscript of the Gospels we find a remarkable depiction of the saviour Christ that harkens to the Pythagorean tradition of musical proportions and harmonies. The depiction includes "a symbolic diagram of the music of the spheres and the perfect consonances."[83] In Chapter 2 we encountered the master musical proportion of 6:8::9:12 which incorporates, in several permutations, the ratios of the basic Pythagorean intervals: the octave (1:2), the 5th (2:3), and the 4th (3:4). We saw that classical tradition invoked this master proportion as "a device of God's contriving which breeds amazement in those who fix their gaze upon it."[84] For medieval Christians, of course, God's principal "device" is Christ upon the cross. The 11th-century Christian illuminator has brought these two sacramental strands together. Under the outstretched arms of Christ on the cross there appears the master Pythagorean proportion. In this instance the master proportion is 4:6::8:12. It incorporates the basic Pythagorean ratios, as the classical version does, but with more of its permutations expressing the ratios of the two most consonant intervals, the octave (1:2) and the 5th (2:3) – 1, 2, and 3 being also the numbers symbolic of God's unity, of Christ's two natures, divine and human, and of the Holy Trinity. The proportion's symmetry and consonance reinforce the significance of Christ's death on the cross as restoring the balance and harmony of God's creation. In his symbolism of the musical octave Augustine speaks of "how the single of our Lord and Saviour Jesus Christ corresponds to our double" which "harmonises . . . for our salvation."[85]

81. Connie Kestenbaum Green, "King David's Head from Gaza Synagogue Restored," *Biblical Archaeology Review* 20, no.2 (March/April 1994): 61.

82. Anonymous medieval verse quoted in Kathi Meyer-Baer, *Music of the Spheres and the Dance of Death: Studies in Musical Iconology* (New York: Da Capo Press, 1984), 315.

83. Meyer-Baer, *Music of the Spheres and the Dance of Death*, 83-4.

84. *Epinomis* 990e, quoted in McClain, *The Pythagorean Plato*, 8.

85. *The Trinity* 4.3.5, 134.

Turning now to Christian salvation as human harmony in its social dimension, as compared with the individual dimension we have been considering to this point, we may begin with Weil, who takes from Plato yet another image relating to proportionality. Harmonic proportion produces musical accord among disparate elements, and Plato therefore calls music "the science of love." Weil translates from Plato's *Symposium*:

> Starting with what is at first divergent, the high and the low pitch, when these are subsequently brought into proportion, harmony is produced by the art of music. For harmony is like an accord of voices, and the agreement of voices is a certain proportion . . . thus creating love and mutual accord; and music is the science of love in the domain of harmony and of rhythm.[86]

Weil relates this classical imagery of harmony and love to the domain of Christian salvation, emphasising the social dimension of salvation through the harmony or consent of love:

> To empty ourselves of our false divinity, to deny ourselves, to give up being the centre of the world in imagination, to discern that all points in the world are equally centres and that the true centre is outside the world, this is to consent to the rule of mechanical necessity in matter and of free choice at the centre of each soul. Such consent is love. The face of this love, which is turned toward thinking persons, is the love of our neighbour; the face turned toward matter is love of the order of the world, or love of the beauty of the world which is the same thing.[87]

Weil's discussion of salvation as the harmonising of contraries returns us to the ingredients of our working definition of beauty – order, proportion, and definiteness, integrity, harmony, and radiance – its dimensions now spiritually deepened and socially broadened to echo more of the beauty of holiness. To seek the kingdom of God is to seek social order that secures just proportion for individual souls, each regarded as an integral centre of freedom, all together in harmony, and all suffused with the radiance of joy – since "joy is also a manner in which beauty enters into us, even the coarsest of joys, so long as they are innocent."[88]

### Social Sharing and Immediate Experience

In relation to the social dimension of salvation as harmony, we must acknowledge that of itself music can both unite and separate. We have already considered the divisiveness arising from different musical tastes. Two further issues arise: first, separation dividing those who are music-

---

86. *Intimations of Christianity*, 107. Weil translates from Plato's *Symposium*, 186e-187d.
87. pp.159-60.
88. Weil, *Intimations of Christianity*, 102.

ally sensitive from those who are not, and second, difficulties of sharing immediate musical experiences, even among musical persons. Both of these musical issues suggest analogies in the realm of religious experience.

We say that some people are born with a musical ear and others tone-deaf. At the very least, some people seem musically responsive and others not. Freud's nephew has written of his uncle: "He despised music and considered it solely as an intrusion!"[89] Musical people often have difficulty empathising with non-musical, and vice versa, a difficulty that manifests itself in attitudes ranging from incomprehension to disdain. The New Testament gospels invoke musical unresponsiveness to make a prophetic point:

> We played the flute for you, and you did not dance;
> we wailed, and you did not weep. (Lk 7.32; also Mt 11.17)

Of unrepentant heretics Clement writes more harshly: "But if like 'deaf serpents' they do not give ear to the song which is called new, although most ancient, let them be chastised by God."[90] Harsher still, Luther's tribute to "God's wondrous work of music," which I quoted earlier in this chapter, concludes with a most unharmonious outburst: "But any who remain unaffected are unmusical indeed and are fit to hear a certain filthy poet or the music of the pigs."[91] Of course, nonmusical people may feel similar scorn for musical, especially when they overhear them gloating over their precious tonal treasures.

These separations between the musical and the nonmusical suggest certain analogies in traditional Christian theology to separations between those included in the realm of saving grace and those excluded. In the following passage replace "music" with "salvation," and, *mutatis mutandis*, we could be hearing rantings from some predestinarian preacher:

> I do not believe it to be, as the phrase goes, *meant for everybody*
> . . . a great number of people can neither feel nor understand its power. It has always seemed obvious to the impartial observer that these people were *not meant for music* and therefore *music was not meant for them.*

In fact these are rantings of Hector Berlioz.[92]

I believe that separations between the musical and the tone-deaf, as between the religious and the nonreligious, are sometimes not as radical and absolute as Berlioz or the predestinarian preacher would suggest. Education can help bridge the gap. Musical and religious aversions alike

---

89. Harry Freud, "My Uncle Sigmund" (1956) in *Freud as We Knew Him*, ed. Hendrik M. Ruitenbeek (Detroit: Wayne State University Press, 1973), 313. Quoted in Storr, *Music and the Mind*, 90.

90. *Stromata* 7.16.102, in McKinnon, *Music in Early Christian Literature*, 36.

91. "Preface to Georg Rhau's *Symphoniae jucundae* 1538," *Luther's Works*, 53:324.

92. Hector Berlioz, *The Art of Music and Other Essays*, tr. Elizabeth Csicsery-Rónay (Bloomington: Indiana University Press), 1. Berlioz's emphases.

often result from negative early experiences that can be partially rectified. Conversation can also help bridge the gap. Trained composers and theologians might do well to keep at least one ear attuned to musics and spiritualities that appeal most widely.

What is more, even a person who is tone-deaf can appreciate music's sacred silence – that is, music in its Pythagorean dimensions. The history of music offers a fascinating example. The person who made the first scientific study of the overtone series and the first calculations of tonal frequencies was Joseph Sauveur, who coined for his science the term "acoustics." Sauveur published his *Principes d'acoustique et de musique* in 1701. It became the basis for Jean-Philippe Rameau's enormously influential textbook of harmonic music, the *Traité de l'harmonie* (1722), where Rameau writes of his indebtedness to the new science of acoustics: "Notwithstanding all the experience I may have acquired in music from being associated with it for so long, I must confess that only with the aid of mathematics did my ideas become clear and did light replace a certain obscurity of which I was unaware before."[93] And yet, surprisingly, the musical mathematician Sauveur "suffered from a speech defect and is said to have had no ear for music."[94] In the religious realm we might think analogously of William James, who, though he did not regard himself as a religious person, pursued a keen interest in the study of religious experience, contributing insights into religion that still inform our theological discussions. I believe that it is time for both realms to outgrow traditional notions that people are either born to be musical or not, religious or not. Once in a radio interview I heard Irving Kolodin ask Dimitri Mitropoulos whether great conductors are born or made. The Maestro's answer was ineluctable: "*First* they must be *born*, and *then* they are *made*."

Mitropoulos's first clause still leaves us with the issue of inherently different individual sensitivities to immediate musical and religious experiences. Differing sensitivities can separate people and cause difficulties in sharing, even among people of similar musical or religious propensities. For joint participants in music there is often no difficulty. Quite the contrary. We have many examples of Christian praise for the unifying influence of congregational hymnody, for example, of which Calvin's is typical:

> It is evident that the practice of singing in church . . . is not only a
> very ancient one but also was in use among the apostles. This we
> may infer from Paul's words: "I will sing with the spirit and I will
> sing with the mind." Likewise, Paul speaks to the Colossians:
> "Teaching and admonishing one another . . . in hymns, psalms,

93. Jean-Philippe Rameau, *Treatise on Harmony*, tr. Philip Gossett (New York: Dover, 1971), xxxv.
94. C. Truesdell, "Sauveur, Joseph," *The New Grove Dictionary of Music and Musicians*, ed. Stanley Sadie (London: Macmillan, 1980), 16:524.

and spiritual songs, singing with thankfulness in your hearts to the Lord." For in the first passage he teaches that we should sing with voice and heart; in the second he commends spiritual songs, by which the godly may mutually edify one another.[95]

Yet even for musical performers sharing can be difficult. I recently enjoyed an impressive performance of Stravinsky's *Rite of Spring* by a semi-professional orchestra. I complimented one of the players, only to be told that the social costs of the intense preparations, consisting mostly of sectional rehearsals, had been so great that he had taken little pleasure in the achievement. "We played," he said, "and then we all packed up and left."

Difficulties of sharing are a frequent frustration in religious experience as well as in musical. In his study *Religious Experience*, Proudfoot minimises the need for such sharing in religious understanding: "Direct acquaintance is neither necessary nor sufficient for understanding religious experience. Such experience includes a cognitive component that can be analysed and rendered intelligible even in the absence of direct acquaintance with the experience."[96] Proudfoot argues against William James's suggestion, for example, that mystical experiences include both the mystic's cognitive judgement about the experience and "an added quality that can be called a sense of reality but cannot be analysed further." In fact, Proudfoot concludes, "nothing is added."[97] Proudfoot maintains that the original force or "authority" of a mystic's experience "is based not on direct acquaintance but on what is regarded as the best explanation of the experience."[98] In this discussion of religious experience, I believe, parallels from musical experience can help. Dismissals of the importance of "direct acquaintance" for understanding an experience seem to me unlikely to convince a person whose flesh has ever crawled in response to some passage of music. I agree with Proudfoot's observation that prior experiences and concepts are always and inevitably intertwined in our experiences, both musical and religious. But I do not share the view that direct acquaintance contributes no force or authority to religious experiences, and my view is based in part upon my analogous musical experiences of "direct acquaintance" or "added quality," which observers would need to sense in order to understand my experience fully.

A number of years ago a Hollywood movie advanced the hypothesis that Ravel's *Bolero* is the world's sexiest piece of music. A close friend asked me what I thought of this claim. Ravel himself is reported to have said of *Bolero*: "I have just written a masterpiece; unfortunately it contains

---

95. *Institutes of the Christian Religion* 3.20.32, 2:895. Calvin quotes from 1 Cor 14.15 and Col 3.16.
96. p.132.
97. p.139.
98. p.154.

no music." Recalling this, I found myself replying that *Bolero* is a master-piece, that it may be the world's most mechanical masterpiece, and that if one thinks of sex as mechanical, then perhaps *Bolero* is the world's sexiest piece of music. Apparently sensing insincerity, my friend then asked me if I cared to nominate some other piece of music for this honorific title. I mentioned Debussy's *Prélude à l'après-midi d'un faune* (*Prelude to the Afternoon of a Faun*). This was music she did not know, so we put on a CD and listened to the Montreal Symphony Orchestra perform it in the luminous acoustics of Montreal's Church of St. Eustache.

My friend was little accustomed to the diffuseness of impressionistic orchestration, and this music, which never fails to set me tingling, left her cold. I was disconsolate. My friend was a music enthusiast and completely bright in analytical capacities. But how was she ever to understand the added quality of direct musical acquaintance that comes to me yet not to her? How was I ever to convey to her the musical experience I so much wished to share? Our sense of separation was profound, though thanks to other realms of mutuality it was temporary.

I agree with Rudolph Otto's formulation of the analogy between experiences of direct acquaintance in religion and in music, in his classic of religious phenomenology, *The Idea of the Holy*:

> In ordinary fear and in moral reverence I can indicate in conceptual terms what it is that I fear or revere; injury, e.g., or ruin in the one case, heroism or strength of character in the other. But the object of *religious* awe or reverence – the *tremendum* and *augustum*, cannot be fully determined conceptually: it is non-rational, as is the beauty of a musical composition, which no less eludes complete conceptual analysis.[99]

Otto goes on to describe the value of ritual in conveying and sharing our religious experiences:

> We must have recourse to the way all other moods and feelings are transmitted, to a penetrative imaginative sympathy with what passes in the other person's mind. More of the experience lives in reverent attitude and gesture, in tone and voice and demeanour, expressing its momentousness, and in the solemn devotional assembly of a congregation at prayer, than in all the phrases and negative nomenclature which we have found to designate it.[100]

The art of religious ritual, analogous to the subtle art of *musizieren* that we considered in the Introduction, thus plays a significant role in social salvation, in healing our separations, in making us whole.

99. Tr. John W. Harvey (New York: Oxford University Press, 1958), 59. Otto's emphasis.
100. p.60.

## Temperament: Musical and Communal

We shall return to the art of communal worship in our final chapter. To conclude this chapter, let us consider a final contribution of music to our pursuit of social harmony more generally, namely, the musical art of temperament. No community of people is ever without tensions. Neither is an ensemble of instruments or voices. Yet if they are to thrive, human societies and musical ensembles need to live and work in some kind of harmony. Herein lies an analogy suggestive for communal life, I believe, an analogy with sacramental value, with power to reveal abiding verities and transmit healing grace.

Quoting from the Roman general Scipio, Augustine invokes the analogy in discussing justice:

In the case of music for strings or winds, and in vocal music, there is a certain harmony to be kept between the different parts, and if this is altered or disorganised the cultivated ear finds it intolerable; and the united efforts of dissimilar voices are blended into harmony by the exercise of restraint. In the same way a community of different classes, high, low and middle, unites, like the varying sounds of music, to form a harmony of very different parts through the exercise of rational restraint; and what is called harmony in music answers to concord in a community, and it is the best and closest bond of security in a country. And this cannot possibly exist without justice.[101]

Edwards expresses the same analogy:

The best, most beautiful, and most perfect way that we have of expressing a sweet concord of mind to each other, is by music. When I would form in my mind an idea of a society in the highest degree happy, I think of them as expressing their love, their joy, and the inward concord and harmony and spiritual beauty of their souls by sweetly singing to each other.[102]

Likewise Shakespeare presents the ideal of human government by means of a musical simile:

For government, though high and low and lower,
Put into parts, doth keep in one consent,
Congreeing in a full and natural close,
Like music.[103]

Augustine's ideal of "concord in a community," Edwards' ideal of social "concord and harmony," and Shakespeare's governmental ideal of "one consent" are of course difficult and elusive, in music and in society. Let us

---

101. *City of God* 2.21, 72. Augustine quotes from Scipio's *De republica* 2.42f.
102. Miscellany #188, *The "Miscellanies,"* 331.
103. *Henry the Fifth* 1.2.180-3, *Complete Works*, 473.

begin with music. We have seen that the cycle of 5ths, which generates the twelve notes of the chromatic scale, does not in actuality come to "a full and natural close," but misses closure by the Pythagorean Comma. For this reason, the intervals within a scale do not naturally "keep in one consent." If they are to "congree," they must undergo mutual adjustment, social accommodation. In acoustical terms this mutual accommodation is known as musical temperament. Murray Campbell and Clive Greated state the problem succinctly:

> The fact that it is impossible to derive a scale in which all the ratios are correct according to the harmonic series is a fundamental problem which has been tackled over the ages in many diverse ways by musicians, philosophers and mathematicians alike. . . . It is impossible to devise a fixed scale in which all the perfect fifths and major and minor thirds are true.[104]

The "true" intervals referred to here are intervals defined by their simple Pythagorean ratios of whole numbers listed in Figure 2. Because a scale consisting of none except true intervals is impossible, music beyond the most rudimentary melodies requires the adjusting of intervals. This process combines science and art, "for we must orient ourselves by the few 'pure' intervals which we can hear accurately and then slightly deform them – we call it 'tempering' – to ensure cyclic agreement."[105]

The different ways of tempering musical scales are legion, and none of them is simple. What is called "Pythagorean temperament" derives eleven notes of the chromatic scale from the cycle of 5ths using pure 5ths only, leaving the entire discrepancy engendered by the Pythagorean Comma to fall between steps eleven and twelve in the cycle, producing a final 5th that is disturbingly out of tune. One might think this satisfactory, requiring only that improvisers and composers avoid that final, dissonant 5th. The problem is that while all the 5ths except one are in tune, most of the major and minor 3rds are as badly out of tune as the final 5th. For fifteen centuries, Christianity was more or less satisfied with Pythagorean tuning. Since the church forbade harmonic 3rds and chromatic music, the inevitable dissonances did not arise. For many melodic patterns, and for the Church's earliest harmonies involving only 5ths and 4ths, Pythagorean tuning was adequate.

This totalitarianism of the pure 5th could not last, however. Further developments in harmony, particularly with the introduction of organs and other keyboard instruments, demanded more thoroughgoing tonal tempering than the Pythagorean. The ancient system called "just intonation" is built upon a combination of some pure 5ths and some pure 3rds, yielding some triads – chords consisting of 5ths with a 3rd in the middle – in perfect tune but others decidedly out of tune. The temperament behind Bach's

104. *The Musician's Guide to Acoustics* (New York: Schirmer, 1987), 172, 174.
105. McClain, *The Pythagorean Plato*, 5.

*The Well-Tempered Clavier* is thought to have been a more subtle system known as "1/6 comma meantone temperament." This temperament deforms all 5ths and 3rds in such a way as to allow use of all musical keys "without running into total disaster."[106] Yet since the deformations are not the same for all intervals of any one kind – one 5th remains rather rogue, for example, and a handful of major and minor 3rds are even more so – different harmonic keys retain different colourations. In the forty-eight preludes and fugues of *The Well-Tempered Clavier*, it seems that Bach was not only showing off the possibility of playing in all keys but also exhibiting the colouration peculiar to each key. He did it once in the twenty-four preludes and fugues of Book I, with one prelude and fugue for each of the twelve keys of the chromatic scale, in major and in minor. Then in Book II he did it all again. *The Well-Tempered Clavier* is thus a celebration of a harmonic universe, complex and full of tensions, not pure and not perfect, yet through the prudent and mutual accommodations of tonal temperament, not only redeemable but bounteous and joyful.

In most harmonic music of our day "equal temperament" reigns supreme. All its 5ths and 3rds are deformed. The 5ths are slightly compressed, and all by a common amount. The major 3rds are all expanded by a common amount, but an amount proportionally greater than the deformation of the 5ths – enough to disturb sensitive musical ears. The minor 3rds are all compressed by a common amount, proportionally greater still. The result is that all harmonic keys sound equally good – or equally bad, depending upon the acuity of one's discernment. In an inevitable trade off, what equal temperament gains in democracy it loses in variety. So it is with our social communities, where equal access comes at the expense of individual distinction and multicultural diversity challenges social concord.

In Chapter 2 we considered certain of Rorty's ideas concerning foundations of knowledge. Rorty deserves a brief revisit in the context of our present discussion of musical analogies for possible social communities. In *Philosophy and the Mirror of Nature*, Rorty opposes "the assumption that all contributions to a given discourse are commensurable." He characterises his philosophy as "largely a struggle against this assumption" and defines the crucial term: "By 'commensurable' I mean able to be brought under a set of rules which will tell us how rational agreement can be reached on what would settle the issue on every point where statements seem to conflict."[107] Rorty sides with those pragmatic philosophers who are sceptical "about the whole project of universal commensuration."[108] In *Contingency, Irony, and Society*, where Rorty applies his philosophical views to society more broadly, he argues for "the contingency of community," since "in the ironist view I have been offering, there is no such

106. Hall, *Musical Acoustics*, 456.
107. p.316.
108. p.368.

thing as a 'natural' order of justification for beliefs or desires."[109]I have commented on the fact that musical experiences and musical imagery are virtually absent from Rorty's discussions. This is unfortunate, I believe, for music has a great deal to suggest in relation to Rorty's issues of communal conflict and commensurability.

At the very heart of music lies a fundamental problem arising from incommensurability, namely, the incommensurability of 3rds, 5ths, and octaves. That musical problem is resolved by various methods of tempering scales to achieve workable commensuration. This art of musical temperament – the discovery of rational rules leading to tonal agreement – serves as an important metaphor for social commensurability in Plato's *Republic*. Plato perceives justice as a fundamental social problem arising from incommensurabilities among the various constituents of a community, namely, the different social classes, and he believes that social commensuration is possible by rational adjustments analogous to those of musical temperament. What are these rational adjustments as they apply to societies? First, Plato makes the point that justice is served only if each person seeks no more than what is due. In this connection he has Socrates invoke an amusing comparison to a musician's illogical attempt to "outdo" the tuning of a fellow instrumentalist: "Do you think then, my friend, that any musician in the tuning of a lyre would want to overreach another musician in the tightening and relaxing of the strings or would claim and think fit to exceed or outdo him?"[110] In a just society, Plato argues, attempting to "outdo" others in securing what is due is correspondingly illogical.

Second, Plato has Socrates make the further point that a society thrives best where each individual person moderates demands for justice (*dikaiosune*) defined as "what is due" with a sense of temperance or soberness (*sophrosune*) that includes awareness of the greater good of the community. In the passage most crucial for our discussion, Socrates likens this social temperance to a kind of musical temperament, operative throughout the community's range of constituencies:

> "Do you see then," said I, "that our intuition was not a bad one just now that discerned a likeness between temperance and a kind of harmony?" "Why so?" "Because its operation is unlike that of courage and wisdom, which residing in separate parts respectively made the city, the one wise and the other brave. That is not the way of temperance, but it extends literally throughout the entire gamut, bringing about the unison in the same chant of the strongest, the weakest and the intermediate.[111]

109. p.83.
110. *Republic* 349e-350a, 91.
111. *Republic* 431e-432a, 1:363, altering Shorey's translation "soberness" to "temperance."

Plato's phrase translated here as "throughout the entire gamut" is in Greek *dia pason*. The English translation is precise, for just as "gamut" is a term in English for all the tones of a musical scale, so also, as we saw in Chapter 2, is the Greek term *diapason*. Allan Bloom's translation renders Plato's phrase as "from top to bottom of the entire scale," and Bloom notes: "The Greek sentence has a double sense: (a) stretching through every member of the whole city; (b) stretching through every note in the scale."[112] Plato's wordplay thus clinches his analogy between the mutual adjustments necessary for a justly tempered musical scale and the mutual adjustments necessary for a just and temperate social order.

Indeed, Plato extends the concept of temperament throughout the entire cosmos. We have seen that in Plato's myth of the harmony of the spheres, which concludes the *Republic*, the eight heavenly spheres rotate about Necessity's spindle, while the eight attendant Sirens sing their notes in "the concord of a single harmony." Plato continues his description:

> And there were other three who sat round about at equal intervals, each one on her throne, the Fates, daughters of Necessity, clad in white vestments with filleted heads, Lachesis, and Clotho, and Atropos, who sang in unison with the music of the Sirens, Lachesis singing the things that were, Clotho the things that are, and Atropos the things that are to be. And Clotho with the touch of her right hand helped to turn the outer circumference of the spindle, pausing from time to time. Atropos with her left hand in like manner helped to turn the inner circles, and Lachesis alternately with either hand lent a hand to each.[113]

What are these daughters of Necessity doing, lending their hands, helping to turn the circles, and pausing from time to time? It appears that they are tempering the music of the spheres. If so, what scheme of cosmic temperament are they using? Plato tells us that they are seated "at equal intervals." Thus McClain speculates: "Plato's *Republic* embodies a treatise on equal temperament . . . exactly two thousand years ahead of time."[114]

Rorty, asserting his ironist's view that "there is no such thing as a 'natural' order of justification for beliefs or desires," is sceptical about "the whole project of universal commensuration." For Plato, in contrast, the natural cosmos is commensurated throughout in equal temperament. These are profoundly different alternatives. Yet I believe that these two alternatives are themselves more nearly commensurate than their advocates are typically ready to admit. At the least each has something to teach and something to learn. On the side of Rorty, two points. First, we must recall

112. *The Republic of Plato*, tr. Allan Bloom (New York: Basic Books, 1968), 110, 456.
113. *Republic* 617c-d, 2:505.
114. *The Pythagorean Plato*, 5.

that equal temperament, though democratic, is theoretically imperfect. In this sense, the metaphor of temperament is more appropriate to Rorty's idea of pragmatic compromise than to any Pythagorean ideal of theoretical perfection. Second, we must recall that Plato wishes to put severe limits on the social application of musical temperament. One reason for Plato's utopian wish to allow only the Dorian and Phrygian modes in education was that this limitation to only two musical modes would minimise the difficulties of musical temperament and modulation: "These two modes you must leave. . . . Our songs and airs, then, will not need instruments of large compass capable of modulation into all the modes."[115] Here again I believe that Plato's dictatorial tendencies need a generous infusion of Rorty's liberal insistence on democratic pluralism.

The highest ideal for social commensuration, however, as for musical, might be neither equal temperament, as with Plato, nor abandonment of the entire concept of commensuration, as with Rorty. Rather, the highest social ideal might be a multiplicity of temperaments. Yehudi Menuhin offers traditional music of India as a case in point:

> In music the difference between East and West begins even before actual performance, for the Indian method of tuning instruments is not at all like ours. Their sense of the meaning of a particular scale varies from ours. . . . An Indian listening to a Western orchestra for the first time might well consider the tuning-up to be the most promising and interesting part of the performance, for Indian musicians spend half an hour or more tuning up. Their accuracy of pitch is in fact inseparable from their inspiration. The audience enjoys the preparation just as much, feeling that it is already sharing in the process of what is to follow, and in its turn the music emerges imperceptibly out of the process of tuning. The perfect fifth supports the sympathetic strings tuned to the particular scale or note sequence called a raga. The Indian raga lies somewhere between a scale and a melody. There are hundreds of ragas, each designed for a partic-ular time of day and night, thus uniting performer and listener to nature and time in a unique way.[116]

Analogously, the most just and temperate society might be a society in which myriad patterns of mutual adjustment, not merely an authoritarian few, are practised and enjoyed. This procedure, in the language of Menuhin's description, unites "performer and listener to nature and time" – not to time only, as Rorty's philosophy of contingency would have it, and not to nature only, as Pythagorean schemes of eternal proportions might seem to insist. Yet whatever its particular temperament, the Indian raga is founded upon the natural Pythagorean fifth – pre-existing, pervading, and

115. *Republic* 399c, tr. Cornford, 87,
116. *The Music of Man*, 50-1.

perduring – sounding in the performers' sympathetic strings.

Augustine states our analogy between tempered music and a temperate society: "The concord of different sounds, controlled in due proportion, suggests the unity of a well-ordered city."[117] Temperaments, both musical and social, are multifarious commensurations among the members of a community, involving both human creativity and natural order interacting in the interest of communal ends. These commensurations are complex and difficult, but they are possible. Just how complex and multifarious can musical temperaments be and still actually contribute to communal commensuration? Consider J. Murray Barbour's description of the many different temperaments simultaneously at play in a symphony orchestra:

> The pedals of the harp are constructed to produce the semitones of equal temperament; therefore, once the harp is put in tune with itself, it, and it alone of all the instruments, will be in equal temperament. The violins show a tendency toward the Pythagorean tuning, both because of the way they are strung and because of the players' tendency to play sharps higher than enharmonic flats. Furthermore, in a high register both the violins and the flutes are likely to play somewhat sharp for the sake of brilliance. . . . [T]he brass instruments, making use of a more extended portion of the harmonic series than the woodwinds, have a natural inclination toward just intonation in certain keys. The result is "a very great lack of precision," with heterogeneous sounds that are a mixture of "just, Pythagorean, tempered, or simply false." Of course the ears of the audience, trained for years to endure such cacophony, actually are pleased by what seems to be a good performance.[118]

A symphony orchestra thus offers an analogy for society as a vastly complex togetherness of diversity.

What is the score from which we play? By necessity we play from the score of coexistence on a single planet. Wisdom might lead us to play from a score of thriving together. "I listen to the third movement of his [Mozart's] 40th symphony and am immediately convinced by the demonstration of a specific, eminently tenable social order that sounds in the fugal polyphony, where a number of different voices cause the whole to flourish in their very own flourishing."[119]

Communitarian traditions, especially Platonic, are often criticised for

117. *City of God* 17.14, 744.

118. *Tuning and Temperament: A Historical Survey* (New York: Da Capo, 1972), 199-200. Barbour's quotations are from J. P. L. Anglas, *Précis d'acoustique physique, musical, physiologique* (Paris, 1910), 206.

119. Smith, *The Concept of the Spiritual*, 229. See the historical survey of various orchestral metaphors by John Spitzer, "Metaphors of the Orchestra – The Orchestra as a Metaphor," *The Musical Quarterly* 80:2 (Summer 1996), 234-64.

their implicit authoritarianism, for "oppressive preoccupation with oneness."[120] Iris Marion Young discusses this problem:

> The ideal of community . . . privileges unity over difference, immed-
> iacy over mediation, sympathy over recognition of the limits of one's
> understanding of others from their point of view. Community is an
> understandable dream, expressing a desire for selves that are transpar-
> ent to one another, relationships of mutual identification, social close-
> ness and comfort. The dream is understandable, but politically prob-
> lematic. . . . Deconstruction . . .shows that a desire for unity or whole-
> ness in discourse generates borders, dichotomies, and exclusions.[121]

As her alternative, Young recommends "a politics of difference," a "political
vision of inexhaustible heterogeneity."[122] I believe, however, that musical
analogy can aid us in endorsing communitarian ideals without condoning
the totalitarian tendencies of Platonic tradition. Ivan Nagel calls musical
ensemble the "least totalitarian of totalities,"[123] and James McClendon
suggests an illustration in the music of Charles Ives:

> His music would have a unity, not one achieved through an orderly
> progression of key changes and back home again by the book, but
> through a rugged plurality mightily heaped together so that its unity
> reflected nothing smaller than the grand plural unity of the cosmos.
> In such unity "disharmonies" were overcome not by filtering them
> out but by enclosing them in a whole perhaps not fully or finally seen.[124]

In resisting the totalitarian tendencies of idealist and utopian philoso-
phies of community, Theodore Adorno sought what he called a "redemption of transcendence" that would support societies of "distinctness without domination," where community is "a togetherness of diversity."[125]
Certain representatives of Christian tradition have also sought such a
redemption of transcendence, and musical analogy has served their means
of discourse. A remarkable example comes from Dionysius. He teaches
that to be filled with the harmony and beauty of God's holiness is not to
lose the integrity of one's own individual distinctness, but rather to gain it.
God's holiness, Dionysius writes,

120. Krister Stendahl, "Alumni/ae Day 1993," *Harvard Divinity Bulletin* 22, no.4
     (1993): 4.
121. "The Ideal of Community and the Politics of Difference," in *Feminism/
     Postmodernism*, ed. Linda J. Nicholson (New York: Routledge, 1990), 300-1.
122. p.301.
123. *Autonomy and Mercy: Reflections on Mozart's Operas*, tr. Marion Faber and
     Ivan Nagel (Cambridge: Harvard University Press, 1991), 34.
124. James Wm. McClendon, Jr., *Biography as Theology: How Life Stories Can
     Remake Today's Theology*, 2nd ed. (Philadelphia: Trinity Press, 1990), 145.
125. Wayne Whitson Floyd, 'Transcendence in the Light of Redemption: Adorno
     and the Legacy of Rosenzweig and Benjamin," *Journal of the American Acad-
     emy of Religion* 61 (Fall 1993): 547-8.

lovingly reveals Itself by illuminations corresponding to each separate creature's powers, and thus draws upwards holy minds into
such contemplation, participation and resemblance of Itself as they
can attain. . . . And It is called the Universal Cause since all things
came into being through Its bounty, whence all being springs; and
It is called Wise and Fair because all things which keep their own
nature uncorrupted are full of all Divine harmony and holy
Beauty.[126]

Calling the three persons of the Trinity "the Creative Originals," Dionysius
declares that as God is unique and beautiful, so also God's creatures, made
in God's image, are unique and beautiful, each in its own way:

For there is no exact similitude between the creatures and the
Creative Originals; for the creatures possess only such images of
the Creative Originals as are possible to them, while the Originals
Themselves transcend and exceed the creatures by the very nature
of Their own Originality.[127]

Finally, Dionysius envisions God's creatures in a community of distinctness without domination, harmonised by a common yearning, each for the
beauty appropriate to itself:

From this Beautiful all things possess their existence, each kind
being beautiful in its own manner, and the Beautiful causes the
harmonies and sympathies and communities of all things. And by
the Beautiful all things are united together and the Beautiful is the
beginning of all things, as being the Creative Cause which moves
the world and holds all things in existence by their yearning for
their own Beauty.[128]

In this chapter we have taken salvation to mean healing leading to wholeness, both individual and communal. In his mystical vision of "harmonies
and sympathies and communities of all things," Dionysius portrays
salvation as a uniting of all creatures in distinctness without domination,
harmonised by common yearning for beauty appropriate to each. Such
images of tempered harmony, I believe, can help to save a fallen world.

126. *The Divine Names*, 1.2, 1.4, 54, 56-7.
127. 2.8, 75.
128. 4.7, 96.

# VI. Final Bliss: Surpassing Language

*Geh hin, wo du nicht kannst: sieh, wo du siehest nicht;*
*Hör, wo nichts shallt und klingt; so bist du, wo Gott spricht.*

Go where thou canst not go: see where thou canst not see;
Hear where naught resounds and rings; then where God speaks,
    thou'lt be.

## *Hope for Harmony*

In his essay "Music at Night," Aldous Huxley reflects on musical bliss
and mystical bliss as he listens to the *Benedictus* of Beethoven's *Missa
Solemnis*:

> There is, at least there sometimes seems to be, a certain blessedness
> lying at the heart of things, a mysterious blessedness, of whose
> existence occasional accidents or providences (for me, this night
> is one of them) make us obscurely, or it may be intensely, but always
> fleetingly, alas, always only for a few brief moments aware. In the
> *Benedictus* Beethoven gives expression to this awareness of
> blessedness. His music is the equivalent of this Mediterranean night,
> or rather of the blessedness at the heart of the night, of the blessed-
> ness as it would be if it could be sifted clear of irrelevance and
> accident, refined and separated out into its quintessential purity.[1]

Huxley then speaks of the impossibility of conveying his sense of bliss "in
his own words," or in any words:

> "Our own words" are inadequate even to express the meaning of
> other words; how much more inadequate, when it is a matter of
> rendering meanings which have their original expression in terms
> of music. . . . We cannot isolate the truth contained in a piece of
> music; for it is a beauty-truth and inseparable from its partner. The
> best we can do is to indicate in the most general terms the nature
> of the musical beauty-truth under consideration and to refer curious
> truth-seekers to the original. Thus, the introduction to the
> *Benedictus* in the *Missa Solemnis* is a statement about the blessed-
> ness that is at the heart of things. But this is about as far as our
> "own words" will take us. . . .If we want to know, we must listen.[2]

Huxley's reflections suggest our themes for this final chapter: experiences
of mystical blessedness, the inadequacy of words to express these experi-

---

1. *Music at Night and Other Essays* (Freeport, NY: Books for Libraries Press,
    1970), 41.
2. pp.43, 47.

ences, and the wealth of relations between mystical and musical experiences of bliss.

Traditions of classical Greece present the transcendent aim of human experience as a harmony of goodness, truth, and beauty. Can such a transcendent aim be achieved? Yes, though only in utopian images generated by great imaginations, in fleeting moments of dazzling philosophical insight, or in a few lives of rarest spiritual discipline and depth. For most classical seekers, the harmony of goodness, truth, and beauty remains a hope, a hope for spiritual immortality that will liberate our souls from the limitations of temporal and physical embodiment. Certain great mystics of Christian tradition, such as Dionysius, retain and develop this classical theme of hope for eternal bliss.

Christianity's roots in biblical tradition draw from a different ideal of blessedness. The difference between Greek and biblical religious traditions is similar to that between the Pythagorean and Incarnational sacramental traditions we considered in Chapters 2 and 3. Biblical images of blessedness imply not liberation from embodiment but rather embodiment's fulfilment. Biblical hopes centre not in the soul's immortality but rather in the semi-immortality of incarnation and resurrection of the body. According to New Testament images, we are not pre-existing immortal souls, as Plato taught, but unique historical persons, body and spirit, conceived at a point in space and a moment in time, and exerting indelible effects upon consequent space and time. In the traditional language of Christian liturgy, we are everlasting. At a minimum – and I suspect that others will join me in affirming that this minimum is necessary and possibly sufficient for Christian commitment – we may understand this to mean that our unique, mortal lives may embody eternal values and have everlasting consequences. Our lives may manifest virtue, and thus we participate in eternal goodness, truth, and beauty. At the point of death, we commit our completed lives and the fulfilment of their consequences to God. Throughout death's everlasting rest, consequences of our lives are actual, significant, indelible. Thus our embodied personal lives have a discrete beginning, develop through a lifetime of spiritual struggle and growth, and endure in never ending significance. The significance may not appear great, but Mother Teresa redeems our perspective with her teaching that we can do small things with great love: "To God there is nothing small. The moment we give it to God, it becomes infinite."[3]

The traditional Mass for the Dead prays God's grace upon the deceased:

Absolve, O Lord, the souls of all the faithful departed from every bond of sin. And by thy helping grace, may they be able to escape the avenging judgement, and enjoy the bliss of everlasting light.[4]

3. Ann and Jeanette Petrie, Producers, *Mother Teresa*, (Burlingame, CA: Petrie Productions, 1986).
4. *The Missal for Sundays and Principal Feasts of the Year* (Tournhout, Belgium: Brepols Catholic Press, 1934), 369.

This tradition envisions the everlasting light of blessedness as shining most brightly upon lives that incarnate the communion of human faithfulness and divine grace, lives that embody the biblical ideal of salvation as an espousal of justice and peace:

> Surely his salvation is at hand for those who fear him,
>> that his glory may dwell in our land.
> Steadfast love and faithfulness will meet;
>> righteousness and peace will kiss each other. (Ps 85.9-10)

This biblical ideal expresses an eschatology, not of escape from time, as in classical traditions, but rather of temporal fulfilment. It envisions historical passage from harmony lost to harmony restored. For Christian faith, the historical symphony of which Eve and Adam constitute the prelude begins its fulfiling movement with the story of Mary and Christ. "For Eve had conceived all weeping in pain," writes Hildegard; "but in Mary joy resounded with the music of the lyre, with the harmony of song."[5] Communion between God and humankind in Eden, disrupted by the discord of languages at Babel (Gen 11.9), commences restoration in the mystical communication between God's Spirit and humankind in the concord of ecstatic tongues at Pentecost (Acts 2.4). Eden's tree of life, guarded by the flaming sword of the cherubim (Gen 3.22), appears again beyond the flames of the Apocalypse (Rev 22.2), as the New Jerusalem descends to earth in consequence and in fulfilment of Christ's prayer: "Thy kingdom come on earth as in heaven."

Both classical tradition and biblical tradition often express their concepts of final bliss in terms of hope and mystery, as contrasted with certainty and dogma. In Plato's *Phaedo*, for example, at the conclusion of his lengthy portrayal of souls "released from this earthly prison" and living "henceforth altogether without the body," Socrates explains that all he has said about existence after death constitutes a great "hope," and he cautions his companions against presumptions of certainty:

> Now it would not be fitting for a man of sense to maintain that all this is just as I have described it, but that this or something like it is true concerning our souls and their abodes, since the soul is shown to be immortal, I think he may properly and worthily venture to believe; for the venture is well worth while.[6]

Thus Socratic faith ventures through life and into death in hope of the moral soul's immortal worth. Similarly, Paul speaks of resurrection of the body as the central "hope" (Acts 23.6) and "mystery" (1 Cor 15.51) of Christian faith, rebuffing the question of how exactly a resurrected body

5. *Ad Vitam S. Ruperti Epilogus 1*, quoted in Barbara Newman, *Sister of Wisdom: St. Hildegard's Theology of the Feminine* (Berkeley: University of California Press, 1987), 179.
6. *Phaedo* 114d, 391.

is to be understood: "But someone will ask, 'How are the dead raised? With what kind of body do they come?' Fool!" (1 Cor 15.35-6). Metaphorical language then carries Paul to a concluding simile: "As was the man of dust, so are those who are of the dust; and as is the man of heaven, so are those who are of heaven" (1 Cor 15.48). Our resurrection body is the image within us of Jesus Christ, the first citizen of heaven.

## *Varieties of Mystical Experience*

These traditions of hope and mystery, classical and biblical, combine in Christianity to constitute a rich spiritual resource, but it is a resource that suffers neglect. In search of spiritual sustenance, particularly the sustenance offered by mystical immediacy, many persons are turning from Christian tradition to religious traditions of Asia. Slowly and steadily, resulting infusions of spiritual life are enriching Christianity. At the same time, Christian seekers often overlook or undervalue the mystical riches to be discovered within their own tradition. Many are too quick in rejecting glib declarations of Christian certainty that eclipse more profound experiences of religious mystery, too ready in abandoning facile expressions of Christian dogmatism that obscure fuller confessions of religious hope. I believe that in a reappreciation of Christian traditions of mystical experience, music can play a sacramental role, a role even more significant than the role of verbal language.

In such a reappreciation we face two beginning challenges. Mystical experiences are reported in so many varieties that our first challenge is to develop some fundamental distinctions that will aid us in exploring their bewildering complexity. Musical experiences can help to clarify these fundamental distinctions. Second, mystical experiences are notoriously difficult to communicate. We shall consider this second subject, the communication of mysticism, in our next section. In this section let us develop four orienting distinctions among the varieties of mystical experience. These distinctions will suggest a few decisions as to the scope of our discussion of Christian mysticism. We can scarcely presume to consider everything that is of mystical significance, and some basic delimitations will also help dispel the common notion that *mysticism* and *mystification* are synonymous terms.

**Outwardly and Inwardly Oriented Mysticisms.** Robert M. Gimello draws a useful distinction between mystical experiences oriented outwardly and mystical experiences oriented inwardly. Outwardly oriented experiences encounter transcendent reality infinitely greater than oneself. Though a person may prepare for such encounter through spiritual exercises, religious ceremonies, pilgrimages to sacred locations, and the like, such mystical encounters are usually felt to befall a person. "Such an encounter is usually said to be gratuitous, in the sense that those subject to it are not them-selves responsible for its occurrence, and it is typically described as both overwhelming and self-authenticating."[7] In contrast, inwardly oriented mystical experiences attain a supernal state of mind and spirit. "Such an attainment is usually held . . . to be the result of the subject's own efforts in following a certain contemplative discipline or method."[8] Outwardly oriented experiences are more characteristic of the western covenantal religious traditions of Judaism, Christianity, and Islam, while inwardly oriented experiences are more common in the eastern religious traditions of Hinduism, Buddhism, and Taoism.[9]

Attention to the kinds of music associated with these two varieties of mystical experience can help us compare them. For example, plainchant in Christian worship is notable for humbling worshippers before the sacred transcendence to whom their chanted prayers are offered. Traditional Christian descriptions do not portray plainchant as a means of spiritual attainment. In contrast, many practices of meditation with Asian roots utilise chanting as a technique for inward quieting and centering, without partic-ular reference to transcendence.

I agree with Gimello that these two varieties of mystical experience "differ markedly," though not with his further suggestion that the two experiences are "primary," neither reducible to the other.[10] As we shall see, a search of either western or eastern religious traditions will disclose elements of both varieties of mysticism, outward-oriented and inward-oriented, often interpenetrating. What is more, this study presupposes a theology of panentheism, which I have characterised as acknowledging both transcendent immanence and immanent transcendence, formulas which render outward and inward orientation inseparable. Of the two basic varieties of mystical experience, however, outward orientation is by far the more common in the Augustinian religious traditions that inform this study. In what follows I shall concentrate on outwardly oriented mystical experiences: encounters with transcendence infinitely greater than ourselves. I have already spoken in Chapter 3 of such en-counter in musical terms, in relation to my oceanic feeling of "indis-soluble bond" upon listening to the second movement of Brahms's Fourth Symphony.

---

7. "Mysticism and Meditation," in *Mysticism and Philosophical Analysis*, ed. Steven T. Katz (New York: Oxford University Press, 1978), 172. Gimello is following Ninian Smart, *Reasons and Faiths: An Investigation of Religious Discourse, Christian and Non-Christian* (London: Routledge and Kegan Paul, 1958).
8. p.172.
9. p.171.
10. p.171.

**Meanings of Transcendence.** This concentration on outwardly oriented encounter with transcendence brings us to the question of what we mean by transcendence. Brown distinguishes four meanings. The first is what he calls "negative transcendence," a transcendence so totally beyond us that we experience it "chiefly as a kind of Holy Void," or as "Infinite Difference, Hiddenness, and Darkness."[11] Dionysius expresses this sense of negative transcendence with great power when he speaks of God as a numinous Hiddenness, invisible, beyond even the experience of Moses, who

> presses forward to the topmost pinnacle of the Divine Ascent. Nevertheless he meets not with God Himself, yet he beholds – not Him indeed (for He is invisible) – but the place wherein He dwells. And this I take to signify that the divinest and the highest of the things perceived by the eyes of the body or the mind are but the symbolic language of things subordinate to Him who Himself transcendeth them all.[12]

We find inward and outward mystical orientations combining here in Dionysius's characterisation of the inward mind's passive stillness as the mystical soul plunges outward into "the Darkness of Unknowing":

> He renounces all the apprehensions of his understanding and is enwrapped in that which is wholly intangible and invisible, belonging wholly to Him that is beyond all things and to none else (whether himself or another), and being through the passive stillness of all his reasoning powers united by his highest faculty to Him that is wholly Unknowable, of whom thus by a rejection of all knowledge he possesses a knowledge that exceeds his understanding.[13]

How do we respond to this experience of negative transcendence? Dionysius answers, as he must, with a paradox, and, as often helps, with a musical image: "We may offer Him that transcends all things the praises of a transcendent hymnody, which we shall do by denying or removing all things that are."[14] We may well wonder how such a "transcendent hymnody" might sound. I like Brown's suggestion of "numbingly repetitive chants" or "music that borders on silence or chaos, as in passages of Penderecki's *Magnificat* (1974) and *Requiem* (1987)."[15]

The second meaning of transcendence is what Brown calls "radical transcendence," a transcendence infinite yet communicative.[16] "Christians in the Reformed line (mainly Calvinist) are among those in whose experience

---

11. *Religious Aesthetics*, 117-18.
12. *The Mystical Theology*, 193-4.
13. p.194.
14. p.195.
15. *Religious Aesthetics*, 118.
16. p.119.

radical transcendence predominates."[17] In Chapter 5 we considered Calvin's sense of God's grace, disclosing transcendence that we are unable to attain by our own powers or through our common experiences. Gracious divine disclosure distinguishes Brown's second meaning of transcendence. Brown rightly discerns the central role of music, as a temporal art, in theologies of radical transcendence, where suppression of the more static visual arts is typically severe: "Traditionally the one sensuous art that the Reformed tradition employs extensively is . . . aural and thus intangible – namely music, the physical medium of which conveniently self-destructs rather than remaining as a potential distraction and temptation."[18] We have seen that the music of Calvinist worship exists to serve the text of God's word, not to serve as a means of human display or an object of human devotion.

Brown calls a third meaning of transcendence "proximate transcendence," namely, transcendence disclosed through human experiences of God's presence and grace. This is the meaning fostered by the sacramental traditions of Roman Catholicism, Eastern Orthodoxy, and Anglo-Catholicism or Episcopalianism, as well as by the Evangelical Christianity of Black Free church and Pentecostal congregations.[19] Proximate transcendence is intrinsic to the Pythagorean and Incarnational sacramental traditions we have considered, which teach that both intellectual and sensible experiences can disclose transcendence. From my grounding in these traditions I have asserted that all music has sacred potential, provided only that it is not destructive of wholeness or too superficial to manifest dimensions of depth.

Finally, Brown speaks of "transcendent immanentalism" or "sacramentalism pushed to the limit," for which "the whole world . . . is the sacrament" and transcendence resides "within the ordinary."[20] In this fourth meaning of transcendence, depth becomes equivalent to length and breadth, and it is fitting that Brown suggests as a musical expression of transcendent immanentalism the *Missa Gaia* of Paul Winter and his ensemble, which I find musically rather shallow, although I admire wholeheartedly its intention of "blending Franciscan piety with a renewed sense of the earth as itself holy."[21]

Unlike the contrast between outwardly and inwardly oriented mysticisms, where I chose the former as more characteristic of Augustinian traditions, the different meanings of transcendence that Brown outlines are all present in those traditions, and all four will make appearances in our discussion of mysticism, language, and music. I trust it is clear, however, that the third meaning, proximate or sacramental transcendence, most nearly touches the heart of this study.

17. p.120.
18. p.121.
19. p.123.
20. p.129.
21. pp.129-30.

**Communion with Transcendence.** In his classic *Music and Trance*, Rouget distinguishes two different kinds of mystical communion with transcendence: trance and ecstasy. Rouget describes trance as a state of transport into or possession by the transcendent that involves personal dissociation, loss of a sense of self. As a consequence, trance "is characterised by total amnesia,"[22] and first person accounts of trance are therefore lacking. In contrast, ecstasy is a sense of personal communion with or filling by the transcendent, where ecstatic loss of self is not through dissociation but through a sense of personal enlargement or completion. Unlike trance, ecstasy "is a keenly memorable experience which one can recall and ponder over at leisure."[23] Thus we have an abundance of first person accounts of ecstatic experience, albeit in paradoxical, indirect, cryptic, or metaphorical language. Rouget further observes that trance "is always associated with a greater or lesser degree of sensory overstimulation – noises, music, smells, agitation," and usually occurs in a social setting. In contrast, he asserts that ecstasy "is more often tied to sensorial deprivation – silence, fasting, darkness," and usually occurs in "silence, immobility, and solitude."[24]

Having made these initial distinctions between mystical trance and mystical ecstasy, Rouget then devotes his analysis exclusively to the experience of trance. Our concentration here will be the complement. Ecstatic experience is intrinsic to the Augustinian traditions at the core of this study, whereas trance is exceptional. Even Teresa of Avila, for example, whose mystical experiences were intense in the extreme, reports not ultimate loss of self but rather final self-fulfilment. We shall depart from Rouget's study in another, more substantial, way as well. His discussion acknowledges that the traditions of trance and ecstasy are not mutually exclusive but are rather "opposite poles of a continuum."[25] Yet when he comes to the roles of music in these traditions, Rouget draws a distinction that is absolute. Trance experiences, he writes, are "associated most of the time with music."[26] For ecstatic experiences, however, he claims the contrary:

> Whereas trance, as we shall see throughout this book, is very frequently and very closely associated with music, ecstasy, as it has just been defined, never makes use of it at all. There is an inherent incompatibility between the practice of ecstasy and music. This is, after all, only logical. Excluding certain deliberately contrived experiences, immobility, silence, and sensorial deprivation are incompatible with music.[27]

22. *Music and Trance*, 9.
23. p.9.
24. pp.7-10.
25. p.11.
26. p.xvii.
27. p.12.

I believe that this puts the matter too simply. Huxley's awareness of blessedness, which opened this chapter, may represent mysticism in a mild form, yet clearly it is a mild form of ecstasy, not of trance, and Huxley relates his ecstatic awareness directly to Beethoven's *Benedictus*. What is more, music may have many relations to ecstatic experiences other than that of direct inducement or causation, to which Rouget limits his attention. Whereas Rouget asserts an inherent incompatibility between ecstasy and music, I am interested in exploring inherent compatibilities between the two.

Nevertheless, Rouget's analysis helps me better understand why for me certain kinds of music, though potentially sacramental, fail to convey much transcendence. Mystical experiences that matter most to me are of the ecstatic sort, religious experiences that enlarge and fulfil. They are memorable, and subsequent reflections on them clarify understanding and heighten sensibility. For me such experiences usually relate to music that is perfect or classic, in the particular senses I have defined: music in which I would change nothing, or music that rewards repeated exposure with new disclosure. In contrast, much music seems to me to associate more readily with trance than with ecstasy. I am thinking of the religious music of a charismatic kind known as "renewal music," for example, high on psychological energy but confined in spiritual compass, or of a good deal of rock music, suspending time with repetitiousness and filling space with decibels but, for me, fulfilling few needs of the spirit. Such music offers transitory dissociation, temporary escape, but I do not find it memorable. Lacking depth for intellectual clarification or substance for sensible enrichment, it does not sustain reflection or revisit memory.

By way of analogy, the difference I am trying to describe, while never absolute, is rather like the difference between intoxication and genuine euphoria, taking the latter in its etymological sense, "bearer of the good." No one has described this difference more perceptively than Thomas De Quincy in his extraordinary 1821 apology for the euphoric effects of opium, as contrasted with the intoxicating effects of alcohol:

> But the main distinction lies in this, that whereas wine disorders the mental faculties, opium, on the contrary (if taken in a proper manner), introduces amongst them the most exquisite order, legislation, harmony. Wine robs a man of his self-possession: opium greatly invigorates it. Wine unsettles and clouds the judgement, and gives a preternatural brightness, and a vivid exaltation to the contempts and the admirations, the loves and hatreds, of the drinker: opium, on the contrary, communicates serenity and equipoise to all the faculties, active or passive: and with respect to the temper and moral feelings in general, it gives simply that sort of vital warmth which is approved by the judgement, and which would probably always accompany a bodily constitution of primeval or antediluvial health.

"This is the doctrine of the true church on the subject of opium," De Quincy concludes "of which church I acknowledge myself to be the only member – the alpha and the omega."[28]

De Quincy may seem an eccentric, if not blasphemous, source for analogy between religious and musical experiences. For a more orthodox source, I recommend the classic treatise by Jonathan Edwards, *Religious Affections*,[29] in which Edwards distinguishes between "genuine" and "counterfeit" religious experiences largely upon the basis of the substance and permanence of their contributions to a person's Christlike character. Edwards' analysis, incidentally, is the best basis I know for religious evaluation of drug-induced experiences. Yet I stand by De Quincy. We need not join De Quincy's "true church" or follow his claims all the way back to the "primeval or antediluvial" wholeness of Eden to accept the usefulness of a distinction between music or religion that intoxicates and music or religion that genuinely bears the good. De Quincy goes on, of course, to warn of opium's fated and fatal misuse. Mystical and musical ecstasies are subject to misuse also. The difference is that misuse of mystical and musical ecstasy, unlike the misuse of opium of which De Quincy gravely warns, is not inevitable.

Let us summarise the results of our first three orienting distinctions concerning mystical experiences, and then proceed to a fourth and final one. The mystical experiences most typical of Augustinian heritage, and therefore the kinds of experience to which we shall relate the analysis that is to follow, include the following qualities: a sense of intimate communion with transcendent reality infinitely greater than ourselves; a range of sensibilities concerning the nature of transcendent reality, from astounding hiddenness, through radical yet communicative divinity, to proximate or immanent holiness; an ecstatic sense of spiritual completion, as contrasted with the spiritual intoxication of trance; and awareness of profound intellectual and emotional enlargement and fulfilment.

**Mysticisms of Knowledge and of Love.** The idea of mystical enlargement and fulfilment invites a final distinction to guide our explorations. It is the contrast between mysticism that emphasises intellectual experience and mysticism that emphasises emotional experience. Classical traditions contrast the way of the god Apollo with the way of the god Dionysius, associating the philosophical, Apollonian way with the Dorian musical mode, and the Dionysian way, "violently exciting and emotional,"[30] with the Phrygian. We have encountered this contrast between intellect and

28. *Confessions of an English Opium Eater* (Middlesex: Penguin Books, 1971), 73-5.
29. *A Treatise concerning Religious Affections*, ed. John E. Smith (New Haven: Yale University Press, 1959).
30. Aristotle, *Politics* 8.7.8 (1342a), 673.

emotion in the different outlooks of the Pythagorean and Incarnational sacramental traditions of Christianity. We find a similar contrast between two recurrent types of Christian mysticism: mysticism of being, and mysticism of love.

Such Christian mystics as Dionysius and Eckhart represent the first type, mysticism of being. "As Eckhart puts it, we possess at the very core of our being a silent sanctuary where the divine word is eternally spoken, the divine being fully present. Here we are already at one with God. In order to experience this oneness, however, it is necessary first to withdraw one's attention from outward things. . . . For this reason, Eckhart places 'disinterest' (*Abgeschiedenheit*) at the summit of the hierarchy of contemplative virtues."[31] In contrast, such Christian mystics as Heinrich Suso and Mechthild of Magdeburg represent the second recurrent type, mysticism of love. "At the summit of the hierarchy of contemplative virtues, one finds not disinterest, but ardent longing. Mechthild of Magdeburg . . . speaks not only of the soul's longing to return to God, but also of God's burning desire for the soul."[32]

Platonic tradition has considered the Apollonian spiritual tradition and its associated Dorian mode superior to the Dionysian spiritual tradition and its Phrygian mode. Similarly, and in part because of direct indebtedness to this Platonic tradition, western Christian theology has tended to tip the balance between what Edwards calls intellect and love – *logos* and *agape* – in favour of intellect. For example, this tendency is expressed in the *filioque* clause that the western church gradually adopted as part of the Nicene Creed. In the 4th- century text of the Nicene Creed, its third section commences: "And [we believe] in the Holy Spirit, the Lord and life-giver, Who proceeds from the Father. . . ."[33] Between the 5th and 10th centuries, however, western churches gradually adopted the supplementary clause that to this day separates western Christianity from eastern: "Who proceeds from the Father *and the Son* (*filioque*). . . ." This *filioque* clause derives from certain verses of the New Testament gospels that seem to subordinate God's Spirit to Christ, God's Son, God's Word. "When the Advocate comes," says Christ, "whom I will send to you from the Father, the Spirit of truth who comes from the Father, he will testify on my behalf" (Jn 15:26).

The tiny *filioque* clause makes a significant difference. God's Spirit is commonly, though by no means exclusively, identified with love (Gal 5.22) and freedom (2 Cor 3.17). God's Spirit is said to blow where it listeth (Jn 3.8). In contrast, God's Word is commonly portrayed as the principle of divine order, instruction, and discipline. "But as for what was sown on good soil," says Christ in the parable of the sower of seeds, "this is the one who hears the word (*logos*) and understands

31. Carol Zaleski, "Foreword," in Campbell, *German Mystical Writers*, xi.
32. p.xi.
33. Leith, *Creeds of the Churches*, 33.

it" (Mt 13.23). Or again: "The word (*logos*) that I have spoken will serve as judge. . ." (Jn 12.48). Edwards contrasts Word and Spirit along these lines: "As the Son of God is spoken of as the wisdom, understanding, and *Logos* of God . . . so the Spirit of God is spoken of as the love of God."[34] In these terms, to subordinate Spirit to Word, as the *filioque* clause does, can invite a tip of the balance of worship toward understanding and away from love.

In discussing contrasting spiritual orientations and the musical modes with which they are associated, Aristotle, as is typical of him, recommends "that we ought to pursue the mean between extremes."[35] For the Episcopal tradition of worship in which I am a practitioner, however, I believe that the best advice is somewhat different. My tradition needs not an Aristotelian mean between the extremes but rather a redress of balance, a more equal honouring of both Word and Spirit.

**Musical Illustrations.** Domination of worship by the Word – by the principle of order, instruction, and discipline – can foster the abstraction and formalism that drive many spirited people from the religious traditions of their upbringing. How may worship, particularly the formalised worship of Episcopal tradition, accord more honour to Spirit? A variety of simple means might help, all consonant with traditional rubrics: more spontaneous congregational contributions to prayers of adoration and thanksgiving; more individual petitions in prayers of intercession and confession; freer exchanges of the Peace, with congregational embracing; fuller participation by children, as children, and more natural interactions between younger people and older; inclusion of liturgical dance in religious services. Most of all, for me, more varied and more spirited music. "What the word has made clear," Schleiermacher writes, "music must make alive."[36]

To consider but one small realm of possibilities, I opened this book with a reference to the inspiriting effect of the Maryland Gospel Choir upon the dense logocentrism of a professional conference on the study of religion, and in Chapter 4 we considered the possibility of jazz in worship. We live in a time when the inspiriting riches of spirituals and gospel music are accessible to Christian congregations of every persuasion. Traditional spirituals, such as "Every Time I Feel the Spirit," have long been available in arrangements by William L. Dawson[37] and others. Composed spirituals, such as Mark Hayes's "Walking in the Spirit,"[38] are also within the

34. *Treatise on Grace*, 59.
35. *Politics* 8.7.10-11 (1342b), 675.
36. *Weihnachtsfeier*, Critical Edition, ed. Hermann Mulert (Leipzig: Verlag der Dürr'schen Buchhandlung, 1908), 22
37. Music Press, Tuskegee Institute (Park Ridge, IL: Neil A. Kjos, 1973).
38. Chapel Hill: Hinshaw Music, 1989.

capacities of most choirs and many congregations. Nor are inspiriting effects limited to music that addresses the theme of God's Spirit explicitly. Rhonda Sandberg's "The Solid Rock"[39] is an admirable case in point. In its traditional Protestant setting, the hymn that Sandberg has newly arranged, "On Christ the Solid Rock I Stand," is musically as bland and blank as any hymn one might name or imagine. Its harmonic inspiration is limited to the three primary chords of the major mode, and the rhythmic pattern of its phrases remains unchanged through seven hapless repetitions. (Even "Happy Birthday to You" has one small rhythmic variation to mitigate its monotony.) Sandberg takes this unfortunate, jiggy hymn and converts it to a broad gospel waltz – expansive, varied, and mounting chromatically to a spirited climax. Her arrangement is true to gospel tradition, full of spirit, and notated for universal accessibility.

I am suggesting that such musical infusions can contribute toward a redress of balance between Word and Spirit in worship, can even introduce a tincture of ecstasy. Churches willing to "test the spirits" (1 Jn 4.1) need not fear such innovations. The earliest Christian disciples at Pentecost appeared drunk (Acts 2.13), but Peter, his discernment guided by his religious tradition, rose to the challenge of distinguishing between intoxication and the genuine euphoria of God's spirit.

## *Beyond Verbal Language*

"It is ... wrong to reproach the mystics, as has been done sometimes, because they use love's language," writes Weil. "It is theirs by right. Others only borrow it."[40] But what is love's rightful language? What is the rightful language of mystical spirit? The disciples at Pentecost spoke verbal languages, but in the form of ecstatic "tongues." The testimony of both mystics and students of mysticism seems almost universal: ordinary verbal language is inadequate to convey mystical experiences. In the face of this inadequacy, some mystics appeal to musical analogies: "This should be known: it is one thing to hear for oneself a sweet lute, sweetly played, and quite another ing merely to hear about it."[41] In this section we shall consider the difficulty of expressing mystical experiences in verbal languages. In the next we shall consider significant relations between mystical language and musical experiences.

Job's reaction to his mystical encounter with God out of the whirlwind is paradigmatic:

39. Fort Lauderdale: Aberdeen Music, 1990.
40. *Waiting for God*, 172.
41. Heinrich Suso, *Little Book of Eternal Wisdom*, tr. James M. Clark, in Campbell, *German Mystical Writers*, 148.

See, I am of small account; what shall I answer you?
I lay my hand on my mouth.
I have spoken once, and I will not answer;
    twice, but will proceed no further. (Job 40.4-5)

Paradigmatic, that is, with one qualification. Laying his hand on his mouth, Job actually falls silent. Many other mystics confess their inability to speak of their experience and then persist in trying to do so. "O secrets of God!" writes Saint Teresa. "I would never tire of trying to explain them if I thought I could in some way manage to do so; thus I will say a thousand foolish things in order that I might at times succeed and that we might give great praise to the Lord."[42] These verbalising mystics confirm the validity of Schleiermacher's observation concerning a profound religious need for communication:

> Persons want witnesses and participants for that which enters their senses and stirs their feelings. How are they supposed to keep to themselves precisely those influences of the universe that appear to them greatest and most irresistible? How are they to wish to hold within themselves precisely that which most powerfully forces them out of themselves, and which impresses them with nothing so strongly as with this: that they cannot know themselves from themselves alone. On the contrary, if a religious insight has become clear to them, or a pious feeling has penetrated their soul, their first endeavour is to direct others to that object as well, and to communicate the vibrations of their heart and mind to them wherever possible. And if, compelled by their nature, religious persons necessarily speak, this same nature also creates their listeners.[43]

Jonathan Edwards provides an instance, as wonderful as any I know, of a mystic's need and attempt to communicate the ineffable:

> I walked abroad alone, in a solitary place in my father's pasture, for contemplation. And as I was walking there, and looking up on the sky and clouds, there came into my mind so sweet a sense of the glorious *majesty* and *grace* of God, that I know not how to express. I seemed to see them both in a sweet conjunction; majesty and meekness joined together; it was a sweet and gentle, and holy majesty; and also a majestic meekness; an awful sweetness; a high, and great, and holy gentleness.[44]

---

42. "The Interior Castle" 5.1.4, *The Collected Works of St. Teresa of Avila*, tr. Kieran Kavanaugh and Otilio Rodriguez, 2 vols. (Washington, DC: Institute of Carmelite Studies, 1976), 2:337.

43. *Reden über die Religion*, ed. G. Ch. Bernhard Pünjer (Braunschweig: C. A. Schwetschke und Sohn, 1879), 181-2.

44. "Personal Narrative," *Selected Writings of Jonathan Edwards*, ed. Harold P. Simonson (New York: Frederick Ungar, 1970), 31. Edwards' emphases.

Edwards' passage is filled with the paradoxical juxtaposition of opposites so characteristic of mystical authors, not least his verbal disclaimer (". . . that I know not how to express") followed by verbal eloquence ("I seemed to see. . .").

Anglo-American philosophers seem finally to be emerging from a widespread tendency to reduce all our significant mental experience to linguistic experience, and from the corollary assumption that if experience cannot be verbalised it has no claim to rational legitimacy. This linguistic reductionism has stemmed in part from assertions made by Wittgenstein in his early treatise of 1921, *Tractatus Logico-Philosophicus*: "*The limits of my language* mean the limits of my world."[45] The first in importance to emerge from this constricting view of language was Wittgenstein himself. The closing pages of his *Tractatus* and his later writings broaden the notion of language remarkably, to include not merely verbalising but what Wittgenstein in later writings calls entire forms of life: "To imagine a language means to imagine a form of life."[46] Wittgenstein poses the rhetorical question, "But how many kinds of sentence are there?", and answers:

> There are *countless* kinds: countless different kinds of use of what we call "symbols," "words," "sentences." And this multiplicity is not something fixed, given once for all; but new types of language, new language-games, as we may say, come into existence, and others become obsolete and get forgotten.[47]

Wittgenstein's illustrative list of language-games includes various kinds of verbal speech and writing, but also "play-acting," "guessing riddles," "asking, thinking, cursing, greeting, praying," and "singing catches." Among language-games Wittgenstein thus includes expressions of religion and of music – which Stravinsky appropriately calls "le Jeu de Notes" ("the Game of Notes").[48] Wittgenstein concludes his listing with an explicit repudiation of the narrowly verbal view of language that he had suggested in his earlier *Tractatus*:

> It is interesting to compare the multiplicity of the tools in language and of the ways they are used, the multiplicity of kinds of word and sentence, with what logicians have said about the structure of language. (Including the author of the *Tractatus Logico-Philosophicus*.)[49]

Summarizing Wittgenstein's vision, Steiner writes: "The categories of felt being to which only silence (or music) gives access, are neither fictitious

45. *Tractatus Logico-Philosophicus* 5.6 (London: Routledge and Kegan Paul, 1922), 149. Wittgenstein's emphasis.
46. *Philosophical Investigations*, tr. G. E. M. Anscombe, 3d ed. (New York: Macmillan, 1958) 19, 8.
47. *Philosophical Investigations* 23. Wittgenstein's emphasis.
48. Quoted in Bernstein, *The Unanswered Question*, 129.
49. *Philosophical Investigations* 23, 12.

nor trivial. On the contrary. They are, indeed, the most important, life-transforming categories conceivable."[50]

Unfortunately, Wittgenstein's redefinition of his own earliest views concerning verbal language was insufficient to stem their influence. Writing in 1963, Wilfrid Sellars described his strand of linguistic philosophy, "psychological nominalism," as a philosophy "according to which *all* awareness of *sorts, resemblances, facts,* etc., in short, all awareness of abstract entities – indeed, all awareness even of particulars – is a linguistic affair. According to it, not even the awareness of such sorts, resemblances, and facts as pertain to so-called immediate experience is presupposed by the process of acquiring the use of a language."[51] Rorty quotes this passage from Sellars with approval,[52] and develops his own linguistic philosophy accordingly:

> For it is essential to my view that we have no pre-linguistic consciousness to which language needs to be adequate, no deep sense of how things are which it is the duty of philosophers to spell out in language. What is described as such a consciousness is simply a disposition to use the language of our ancestors, to worship the corpses of their metaphors.[53]

We may weigh Rorty's view against the almost universal testimony of persons who have sensed mystical experience precisely as what Rorty calls "a deep sense of how things are," which they often feel a duty to spell out in language, but for which they find verbal language finally inadequate. I have no doubt that whatever mystical awareness we experience is inextricably related to our verbal language. To reduce mystical experience to "simply a disposition to use the language of our ancestors," however, seems to ignore the claim of mystics to find traditional language inadequate to express what Schleiermacher calls the "greatest and most irresistible" influence of the universe that "enters their senses and stirs their feelings." It is for this reason that mystics often supplement their attempts at verbal communication with other communicative forms of life – play-acting, guessing riddles, asking, thinking, cursing, praying, and singing catches – compelled by a need to communicate the sympathetic vibrations of their hearts and minds in resonance with the universe.

Musicians also have a deep sense of how things are that verbal language cannot express. Reporting his good-natured frustration in this regard while interviewing the young Russian pianist Evgeny Kissin, Andrew Solomon draws a parallel between musical prodigies and religious saints:

50. *Real Presences*, 103.
51. *Science, Perception and Reality* (London: Routledge and Kegan Paul, 1963), 160. Sellars' emphases.
52. *Philosophy and the Mirror of Nature*, 182.
53. *Contingency, Irony, and Solidarity*, 21.

Watching Kissin perform, one sees a man who seems, literally, possessed by his music. Though Kissin can speak of music with intellectual clarity, he can no more verbalise how he has arrived at his way of playing the piano than the leopard can explain how he got his spots. "How do you choose your encores?" I asked him. . . . "They come to me," he said. "How do you judge an audience?" "I feel something in the air." "How do you decide when you are ready for a piece?" "This is always very clear to me." "How do you decide which concerts to attend?" "I attend the ones I'm interested in." It must have been like this to interview the early saints.[54]

## *Music and Transcendence*

"Not conceptual speech," writes James in his classic discussion of mysticism, "but music rather, is the element through which we are best spoken to by mystical truth."[55] We have distinguished four varieties of transcendence. Let us first consider music in relation to the latter three of those varieties, what Brown calls radical, proximate, and immanent transcendence. Then we shall consider music in relation to that most paradoxical variety of the species, negative transcendence.

**Intimacy.** We have taken as our fundamental characterisation of mystical experience a sense of intimate communion with reality infinitely greater than ourselves. Music's first relation to such religious experience is an analogous sense of intimacy. Whereas vision entails interactions between our eyes and outer objects on which we focus, our organs of hearing, the middle and inner ear, are palpably more inward, their sensitivity is more omnidirectional, and their selectivity is less delineating. Thus our hearing conveys immediacy and immersion. Indeed, the sense of intimacy is even nearer. Our inner ear perceives sound not only by means of the outer ear but also directly from vibrations within our skull, and we feel sound, especially low frequency vibrations such as those of drums, bass instruments, and large organ pipes, in our chest and abdomen. As mystical religious experience conveys immediacy and immersion in cosmic rhythm, dissonance, and harmony, music conveys immediacy and immersion in their sonic equivalents.

**Penetration.** Our sense of musical intimacy can be insistent and coercive, and the same is true of experiences of mystical intimacy. When cars with throbbing subwoofers pass by, I often feel bodily discomfort. Reporting

54. "Questions of Genius," *The New Yorker* (August 26 and September 2, 1996): 114.
55. *Varieties of Religious Experience* (New York: New American Library, 1958), 322.

that it "was possible to hear the pop festival on the Isle of Wight from three kilometres away," Alain Roux comments that there was "no resisting it except by flight."[56] Expressing a mystical sense of God's presence, the Psalmist presents an analogous sense of inescapability:

Where can I go from your spirit?
Or where can I flee from your presence?
If I ascend to heaven, you are there;
if I make my bed in Sheol, you are there.
If I take the wings of the morning
and settle at the farthest limits of the sea,
even there your hand shall lead me,
and your right hand shall hold me fast. (Ps 139.7-10)

Nor does music have to be at the cataclysmic dynamic levels of a heavy metal band to generate experiences of acoustical aggression. When Plato wrote that "more than anything else rhythm and harmony find their way to the inmost soul and take strongest hold upon it,"[57] he might have added, "whether we like it or not." We are able to avoid sights by closing our eyelids, but not being equipped with earlids, we cannot so simply avert sounds. Sound penetrates us as light cannot. Again the Psalmist expresses the mystical analogy of God's penetrating omnipresence:

If I say, "Surely the darkness shall cover me,
and the light around me become night,"
even the darkness is not dark to you. (Ps 139.11-12)

Augustine gives a notable account of the power of sound to penetrate our bodies, coerce our wills, and dictate to our sight. He relates that his young friend Alypius, as a newcomer to Rome, was appalled by gladiatorial shows: "At first he detested these displays and refused to attend them." Companions nevertheless dragged Alypius to the arena, where the sounds of "this cruel and bloodthirsty sport" rendered him vulnerable to "an extraordinary craving":

They found seats as best they could and Alypius shut his eyes tightly, determined to have nothing to do with these atrocities. If only he had closed his ears as well! For an incident in the fight drew a great roar from the crowd, and this thrilled him so deeply that he could not contain his curiosity. Whatever had caused the uproar, he was confident that, if he saw it, he would find it repulsive and remain master of himself. So he opened his eyes, and his soul was stabbed with a wound more deadly than any which the gladiator, whom he was so anxious to see, had received in his body. He fell, and fell more pitifully than the man whose fall had drawn that roar of excitement from the crowd. The din had pierced his

56. Quoted in Rouget, *Music and Trance*, 120.
57. *Republic* 401d, 1:257-9.

ears and forced him to open his eyes, laying his soul open to receive
the wound which struck it down.[58]

Shakespeare more than once invokes music's penetrating, violative
capacity:

With sweetest touches pierce your mistress' ear,
And draw her home with music.[59]

One whom the music of his own vain tongue
Doth ravish like enchanting harmony.[60]

Jeremiah is less delicate than Shakespeare in describing divine violation
of his soul:

O LORD, you have enticed me,
and I was enticed;
you have overpowered me,
	and you have prevailed. (Jer 20.2)

This mystical language of violation makes the utterances of Berlioz concerning music seem a bit less extreme than when we encountered them in
an earlier context: "My arteries beat violently. Tears, which normally her-
ald the end of the paroxysm, occasionally betoken an intermediate stage
soon to be surpassed. When this happens, my muscles contract spasmod-
ically, a trembling overtakes my limbs and a numbness my hands and feet,
while the nerves of sight and hearing are partially paralysed; I can no
longer see, I can barely hear, I become dizzy and fall into a half-faint."[61]

For all their extremity, these mystical and musical experiences nonetheless fall within our definition of ecstasy, not trance. Hildegard is explicit
on this point: "For everything I had written in my earlier visions and came
to know later I saw under heavenly mysteries while my body was fully
awake and while I was in my right mind. I saw it with the inner eye of my
spirit and grasped it with my inner ear. In this connection I was never in a
condition similar to sleep, nor was I ever in a state of spiritual rapture."[62]
Teresa refers to her mystical ecstasies as "raptures," but she likewise
describes them as memorable, not amnestic, experiences. Indeed, in defend-
ing her raptures against various suspicions – both her own suspicions and
those of her ecclesiastical superiors – Teresa appeals to memorableness as
one criterion of a vision's genuine spiritual value: "Is it true that it is

58. *Confessions* 6.8, 122. I am grateful to Margaret Miles who cites this passage
    in "Vision: The Eye of the Body and the Eye of the Mind in Saint Augustine's
    *De trinitate* and *Confessions*," *The Journal of Religion* 63 (April 1983), 128.
59. *Merchant of Venice* 5.1.67-8, *Complete Works*, 214.
60. *Love's Labour's Lost* 1.1.165-6, *Complete Works*, 145.
61. *The Art of Music and Other Essays*, 4.
62. *The Book of Divine Works*, tr. Robert Cunningham, in Campbell, *German
    Mystical Writers*, 5.

forgotten afterward? That majesty and beauty remain, so impressed that they are unforgettable."[63]

**Fulfilment.** We should not leave this part of our survey with the impression that violation and pain are the final word in ecstatic experiences of mystical communion with the divine. Teresa reports visions imbued with pain, yet imparting spiritual heightening, intellectual enlargement, and emotional fulfilment: "You can't exaggerate or describe the way in which God wounds the soul and the extreme pain this wound produces, for it causes the soul to forget itself. Yet this pain is so delightful that there is no other pleasure in life that gives greater happiness."[64] The person who experiences the highest degree of mystical ecstasy, writes Teresa's protégé John of the Cross, "is only able to say that he is satisfied, tranquil and contented and that he is conscious of the presence of God, and that, as it seems to him, all is going well with him; but he cannot describe the state of his soul, nor can he say anything about it save in general terms like these."[65]

## *Silence or Succour?*

As we have seen in the quotation from Berlioz, the highest degree of musical enjoyment can elicit descriptions analogous to these mystics' words concerning religious communion with God. But does music bear any relation to the first variety of transcendence that Brown characterises, negative transcendence, with its corresponding mystical sense of God's hiddenness or absence? Often silence, not music, accompanies a sense of God's ultimate and unutterable mystery:

> But the LORD is in his holy temple;
>> let all the earth keep silence before him! (Hab 2.20)

> Be still, and know that I am God! (Ps 46.10).

From the perspective of a mysticism of love, Teresa expresses the religious instinct implicit in these biblical verses: "Every way in which the Lord helps the soul here, and all He teaches it, takes place with such quiet and so noiselessly that, seemingly to me, the work resembles the building of Solomon's temple where no sound was heard. So in this temple of God, in this His dwelling place, He alone and the soul rejoice together in the deepest silence."[66] Writing in the 4th century, Gregory of Nyssa expresses the same

---

63. "The Book of Her Life" 28.9, *The Collected Works of St. Teresa of Avila*, tr. Kieran Kavanaugh and Otilio Rodriguez, 2 vols. (Washington, DC: Institute of Carmelite Studies, 1976), 1:185.
64. "The Book of Her Life" 29.10, 1:192.
65. *Dark Night,* 2.17.5, 161.
66. "The Interior Castle" 7.3.11, *The Collected Works of St. Teresa of Avila*, 2:441-2. For Teresa's reference to Solomon's temple see 1 Kings 6.7.

instinct from the complementary perspective of a mysticism of knowledge: "For there is no way of comprehending the indefinable as it is by a scheme of words. For the Divine is too noble and too lofty to be indicated by a name: and we have learned to honour by silence that which transcends reason and thought."[67] In Chapter 4 we considered the musical role of silence, but only in its relation to sound. Teresa and Gregory associate God's transcendence with a silence more profound, as if forcing us to confront a theological equivalent to the question, "What is the sound of a black hole?"

Eckhart's emphasis on "the central silence"[68] of mystical contemplation is even more severe than Gregory's. He takes a verse from the book of Wisdom:

> For when quiet silence kept all things, and the night was in the midst of her course, your Almighty Word leapt down from heaven from your royal throne, as a fierce conqueror into the land of destruction. (Wis 18.14-15)

In his commentary on this verse Eckhart empties mystical contemplation of every sensible medium: "According to this, you should know that at the Son's coming into the mind it is necessary that every medium be still. The nature of a medium shrinks from the union that the soul desires with and in God."[69]

Though perhaps the most influential of all German mystics, Eckhart was accused of heresy. He died during the course of his Papal hearings, but twenty-eight of his sentences were posthumously condemned. One suspicion directed against Eckhart was that in so vigorously rejecting any role for material media in the soul's communion with God, he opposed the central tenet of Christian faith: the Incarnation, the Word made flesh in Christ. More particularly, many of Eckhart's sentences appear to oppose our argument here concerning the sacramental nature of music: "Therefore the soul in which this birth is to happen must have purity and nobility of life, and be unitary and self-contained; it must not be dissipated in the multiplicity of things, through the five senses."[70]

In fairness to Eckhart, however, and not merely for the sake of this book's argument, we must note that Eckhart intends his ascetic severity only for those who are perfected or proficient in mystical contemplation, not for spiritual novices:

> I repeat, as I have said before, that this exposition and this activity are for those good and perfect persons only, who have so absorbed the essence of virtue that virtue emanates from them without their trying to make it do so, and in whom the useful life and noble teachings of our Lord Jesus Christ are alive. Such persons know

---

67. *Contra Eunomium*, quoted in Otto, *The Idea of the Holy*, 185-6.
68. "Selected Sermons," *German Mystical Writers*, 95.
69. "Commentary on the Book of Wisdom," *Meister Eckhart: Teacher and Preacher*, ed. Bernard McGinn (New York: Paulist Press, 1986), 173.
70. "Selected Sermons," *German Mystical Writers*, 94.

that the best life and the loftiest is to be silent and to let God speak
and act through one.[71]

Two things follow from Eckhart's qualification of his severe teachings
concerning silence. First, the culmination of his kind of ascetic contemplation is not self-emptying but rather the filling and fulfiling of our emptied
selves by God's Spirit, who acts through us. For all its emphasis upon
inward quieting, Eckhart's mysticism is nonetheless oriented outwardly to
God, and Eckhart teaches that God's Spirit within us is made manifest in
an outward life of spiritual, social, and physical service to others:

> We ought to to stop amusing ourselves with such raptures for the
> sake of that better love, and to accomplish through loving service
> what men most need, spiritually, socially, or physically. As I have
> often said, if a person were in such a rapturous state as St. Paul
> once entered, and he knew of a sick man who wanted a cup of
> soup, it would be far better to withdraw from the rapture for love's
> sake and serve him who is in need.[72]

If the self-emptying or "disinterest" of Eckhart's ascetic experience of
negative transcendence is genuine, it makes room in the soul for a spirit of
loving service. Mysticisms of contemplation and mysticisms of love are
not as distinct as we might suppose. Second, Eckhart acknowledges that
only "an angel knows itself and God without a medium."[73] Mortals are not
angels, and most mortals are not saints either. Traditions tend to preserve dramatic and exotic accounts of mystical experiences, experiences that most of
us can scarcely comprehend, still less emulate. This tendency is understandable but unfortunate if it leads us to think of mystical experience in dramatic
and exotic terms only. If we supplement the dramatic accounts from Teresa of
Avila, for example, with the modest accounts from Teresa of Lisieux and Teresa
of Calcutta, we may come to understand that countless lives of service have
been motivated by experiences of mystical communion with God that are far
from exotic. Most mortals are not proficient contemplatives but rather spiritual seekers who require sacramental media for the revelation of transcendence. We who are neither saints nor angels may take comfort from the irony
of Eckhart's comment on his text from *Wisdom* concerning silence, "This is
what the church *sings*,"[74] and from the eucharistic imagery of John of the Cross:

> Silent music,
> Sounding solitude,
> The supper that refreshes, and deepens love.[75]

71. pp.96-7.
72. "The Talks of Instruction," *German Mystical Writers*, 79. Eckhart's reference
to St. Paul might relate to Acts 9.3ff, 22.6ff, 26.12ff, or 2 Cor 12.2.
73. "Sermon 71," *Meister Eckhart: Teacher and Preacher*, 324.
74. "The Commentary on the Book of Wisdom," *Meister Eckhart: Teacher and
Preacher*, 173. My emphasis.
75. *The Spiritual Canticle* 15, *St. John of the Cross: Selected Writings*, 223.

Our thesis is that music has sacramental potential. We find that even these ascetic mystics of negative transcendence acknowledge such sacramental potential, and the need for such sacramental succour, for most of us.

## *Music and the Numinous*

Let us turn, therefore, to music's value in the explicitly sacramental medium of worship. Mystics who emphasise God's negative transcendence may serve as our beginning point by reminding us that worship is in part acknowledgement of transcendent mystery. We may recall that the Latin *sacramentum* translates the Greek *mysterion*. Sacramental worship should acknowledge holy mystery that transcends our schemes of knowledge and morality. To speak of this holy transcendence, Otto coined the word we have used in earlier contexts, "numinous," from the Latin *numen*, relating to the majesty of divinity. Otto augments this term with the phrase *mysterium tremendum et fascinans*, "mystery tremendous and fascinating."[76] By *mysterium* Otto means to convey the paradoxical sense that God is wholly other than ourselves yet wholly related to us. He quotes Augustine:

> "What is that which gleams through me and smites my heart without wounding it? I am both a-shudder and a-glow. A-shudder, in so far as I am unlike it, a-glow in so far as I am like it."[77]

By *tremendum* Otto connotes Augustine's shudder, a quelling sense of God's inconceivable majesty. By *fascinans* he connotes Augustine's glowing sense of irresistible curiosity and attraction. A sense of the numinous bestows "a beatitude beyond compare," Otto writes, yet it is a sense of bliss that we "can neither proclaim in speech nor conceive in thought, but may know only by a direct and living experience":

> It is a bliss which embraces all those blessings that are indicated or suggested in positive fashion by any "doctrine of salvation," and it quickens all of them through and through; but these do not exhaust it. Rather by its all-pervading, penetrating glow it makes of these very blessings more than the intellect can conceive in them or affirm of them. It gives the peace that passes understanding, and of which the tongue can only stammer brokenly. Only from afar, by metaphors and analogies, do we come to apprehend what it is in itself, and even so our notion is but inadequate and confused.[78]

As numinous metaphors and analogies are essential to worship, Otto observes, so worship has a natural affinity with music: "The object of religious awe or reverence – the *tremendum* and *augustum* – cannot be fully determined conceptually: it is non-rational, as is the beauty of a

---

76. *The Idea of the Holy*, Chapters 2-6.
77. *The Idea of the Holy*, 28n, quoting Augustine's *Confessions* 11.9.
78. pp.33-4.

musical composition, which no less eludes complete conceptual analysis."[79]
Otto quotes an Isaac Watts hymn text that "expresses the numinous feeling more adequately than many texts that are more familiar":

Eternal Power, whose high abode
Becomes the grandeur of a God,
Infinite length beyond the bounds
Where stars revolve their little rounds:

Thee while the first Archangel sings,
He hides his face beneath his wings;
And ranks of shining ones around
Fall worshipping and spread the ground.

Lord, what shall earth and ashes do?
We would adore our Maker too:
From Sin and dust to Thee we cry
The Great, the Holy, and the High!

Earth from afar has heard thy fame
And we have learned to lisp Thy name;
But oh the glories of Thy mind
Leave all our soaring thoughts behind.

God is in Heaven, and men below;
Be short our tunes, our words be few;
A sacred reverence checks our songs,
And praise sits silent on our tongues.[80]

As for examples of text and music in combination, I sense the numinous in Olivier Messiaen's communion anthem, *O sacrum convivium* (*O Sacred Feast*).[81] The luminous colours of its chromaticism are darkened by dissonant 2nds and diminished chords (two tritones superimposed), and its pentatonic simplicity and stillness alternate with ravishing impressionistic sensuality. Finally, however, even in Messiaen's anthem I sense more of *mysterium fascinans* than of *mysterium tremendum*. For musical expressions of *mysterium tremendum et fascinans*, I am most thoroughly ravished by some of Messiaen's compositions for organ, and then, I confess, I have to go beyond the texts and music of the church. I find numinous mystery, terror, and fascination conjoined and expressed most powerfully in Stravinsky's *Rite of Spring*, particularly in the four bars (68-71) Stravinsky labels "The Kiss of the Earth." Amidst stupendous orchestral

79. p.59.
80. pp.221-2.
81. Paris: Durand, 1937.

tumult in the surrounding passages, three of the four measures introduce a sudden, ghostly hush, ambivalent as to major or minor. They are punctuated by three taut heartbeats, one heartbeat skipped, and then a fourth. Stravinsky himself describes the passage: "A Procession arrives. It is the Saint, the Sage, the Pontifex, the oldest of the clan. All are seized with terror. The Sage gives a benediction to the Earth, stretched flat, his arms and legs stretched out, becoming one with the soil."[82] In the fourth hushed bar, the benediction comes as a pianissimo chord for strings. For me it is the most numinous chord in music. Its structure seems straightforward enough: nine of the twelve chromatic pitches distributed over four octaves framed by a low C and high D, including string harmonics. Yet even in memory it chills my spine. Stravinsky calls his *Rite* a "work of faith,"[83] and I agree. "The Kiss of the Earth" is a preternatural moment, a moment of mystery, tremendous and fascinating, a moment of profound worship.

## *A Sacramental Vessel*

Of course worship is more than acknowledgement of the numinous. Let us return again to our working idea of sacramental encounter from Chapter 1: "The word *sacramental* . . . applies to any finite reality through which the divine is perceived to be disclosed and communicated, and through which our human response to the divine assumes some measure of shape, form, and structure." The second half of our definition will particularly serve us here. Worship is our "human response to the divine." It includes the quieting of our souls, praise and thanksgiving to God, confession of sin and confirmation of forgiveness, communal edification, and social sharing. For all of these components of worship, music may serve as a sacramental vessel providing "shape, form, and structure."

**Quieting.** Music serves as a quieting component of worship. When Dionysius speaks of the "passive stillness" imparted by "transcendent hymnody,"[84] his image conveys both metaphorical and actual meanings. Music can promote a stillness replete with the receptivity prerequisite to sensitive worship. It seems paradoxical that music, the art of sonorous forms in motion, can induce stillness. Yet it is true. The opening of Part 3 of Ravel's *Daphnis and Chloe* (bars 155ff) contains a flux of notes in flutes, clarinets, and harp as highly concentrated as any measures in orchestral music, yet in combination with the broader movement of legato strings the affect is languor. Or to take an example from sacred music, the

---

82. In an interview in the *Boston Evening Transcript*, February 12, 1916, tr. Edward Burlingame Hill. In Weiss, *Music in the Western World*, 440.
83. p.441.
84. *The Mystical Theology*, 194-5.84.

concluding movement of Gabriel Fauré's *Requiem*, "In Paradisum," is a *mobile perpetuum*, yet its perpetual motion echoes the cosmic harmony that "moves the sun and other stars,"[85] and the effect is sempiternal rest.

Eckhart's younger contemporary Johannes Tauler speaks in an Advent sermon of the conjunction of stillness and music. Like Eckhart, he refers to the church's Advent practice of singing the verses from The Wisdom of Solomon concerning silence:

> What is truly needful is the creation of inner stillness and peace, a retreat protecting us from our senses, a refuge of tranquillity and inward repose. This will be the subject of next Sunday's Mass when we sing the Entrance Hymn: "While all things were in quiet silence, and the night was in the midst of its course, Your almighty Word, O Lord, came down from Heaven, out of Your royal throne."[86]

For my own choir and congregation, I sense that the Advent hymn "Let All Mortal Flesh Keep Silence"[87] serves as a similar vessel of stillness. "A melancholy air," writes Edwards, "doth really help religious thoughts; because the mind is not fit for such high, refined, and exalted contemplations, except it be first reduced to the utmost calmness."[88]

**Preparing.** Music can prepare for worship in other ways. The early Christian monastic Evagrius Ponticus writes of psalmody's preparatory value: "Pray with moderation and calm, and chant psalms with understanding and proper measure, and you will be raised on high like a young eagle. Psalmody lays the passions to rest and causes the stirrings of the body to be stilled; prayer prepares the mind to perform its proper activity."[89]

**Abasing.** We have considered the humility intrinsic to plainchant. In 1325, Pope John XXII issued a papal decree commending plainchant for its abasing role, its "modest risings and temperate descents," as contrasted with more virtuosic musical styles brought in from abroad by the Crusaders.[90] To consider another example, perhaps the most nearly universal element throughout Christian worship is the Lord's Prayer: "Our Father, who art in heaven, hallowed be thy name. . . ." Most musical settings I have encountered seem too self-important for the prayer's emphasis upon God's holiness, God's kingdom, God's will, as contrasted with our human needs and our mortal susceptibilities to temptation and evil. Of all the musical settings I know, only one seems both appropriate to the prayer's

85. Dante, *The Divine Comedy,* "Paradise", 33.145, 347

86. "Selected Sermons," tr. Maria Shrady, *German Mystical Writers*, 178.

87. *The Hymnal 1982*, #324.

88. Miscellany "w", *The "Miscellanies,"* 175.

89. *De oratione* 82-3, in McKinnon, *Music in Early Christian Literature*, 59.

90. Alexander L. Ringer, *Encyclopedia of Religion*, s.v. "Religious Music in the West."

tone and conducive to the humility the prayer expresses. It is the austere *Pater Noster* by Stravinsky,[91] beautiful in the severity of its conviction. Liturgical music by the "mystical minimalists" – composers such as Arvo Pärt and John Tavener – has introduced the tone of worshipful abasement into concert halls, and this music is now making its way into our churches as well. For accomplished choirs, Pärt's *Berliner Messe*[92] might offer a good point of entry, and any choir with a good organ and organist can worship with the humble "Kyrie" from Erik Satie's mystical *Messe des Pauvres*.[93]

**Attracting.** Music's most effective contribution to worship may be its power to attract. Amidst my struggles with religious faith during college years, only the music of a wonderful chapel choir kept me from sleeping in on Sundays. In time I was accepted into the choir, and my first real attraction to Christian doctrines, like my first real attraction to the Latin and German languages, came by way of the anthems we sang. Little did I realise that some sixteen centuries earlier Basil of Caesarea had given a precise theological accounting for my youthful behaviour:

> What did the Holy Spirit do when he saw that the human race was not led easily to virtue, and that due to our penchant for pleasure we gave little heed to an upright life? He mixed sweetness of melody with doctrine so that inadvertently we should absorb the benefit of the words through gentleness and ease of hearing, just as clever physicians frequently smear the cup with honey when giving the fastidious some rather bitter medicine to drink. Thus he contrived for us these harmonious psalm tunes, so that those who are children in actual age as well as those who are young in behaviour, while appearing only to sing, would in reality be training their souls.[94]

**Constituting.** Music serves to structure, shape, and constitute the worship to which it attracts. In the Introduction I described how music in the National Cathedral in Washington articulated pattern and structure for worship. Here I am thinking of music's power to constitute worship in a profounder sense as well. The essence of music is to inhabit time and permeate space. Music can therefore engender and sanctify the very context of ritual by filling a

91. New York: Boosey and Hawkes, 1949.
92. Vienna: Universal Editions, 1990.
93. Paris: Editions Salabert, 1920.
94. *Homilia in psalmum* 1, in McKinnon, *Music in Early Christian Literature*, 65. For exactly the same insight expressed by Basil's contemporary John Chrysostom, see Chrysostom's *Exposition of Psalm XLI*, in Strunk, *Source Readings in Music History*, 67.

period of time and flooding a tract of place with sacred sounds and texts. Even the Grand Ballroom of a barren convention hotel is susceptible to transformation by music's sacramental energy. Hans-Georg Gadamer speaks of time and space thus constituted and consecrated as neither empty nor filled, but rather "fulfiled."[95]

**Proclaiming.** Within the sacred periods and places it helps to create, music also proclaims sacred messages. We have seen that Calvin was especially concerned that sacred music serve sacred texts, specifically the texts of the biblical Psalter. Luther took a somewhat broader view. He believed that music should range more widely, including texts from elsewhere in biblical scripture, as well as original hymn lyrics composed to proclaim the Christian gospel. Luther sought out young poets to write hymn texts for this purpose, and he wrote them himself. He also composed hymn tunes, believing, as we glimpsed in Chapter 5, that music speaks of God in its own language: "Next to the Word of God, music deserves the highest praise."

**Celebrating.** Music deserves high praise because it offers high praise, the praise of celebration. I have held that music may offer praise with or without texts. Because I believe in music's intrinsic capability for religious praise, I feel that when hymns proclaim their texts with too great an insistence they become unnecessarily preachy, whereupon, as we considered in Chapter 4, ideology tends to undermine art. For this reason, I prefer a hymn such as "God of Grace and God of Glory,"[96] where a lyric of religious and ethical substance combines with music (*Cwm Rhondda*) that sings its own language of celebration, to a hymn such as "God, Who Stretched the Spangled Heavens,"[97] where the message is similar and of similar worth, but so dense with descriptive, conceptual, and instructive proclamation as to render its melody ("Holy Manna" from *The Southern Harmony*) breathless. This is by no means to marginalise the value of hymn texts, but rather to recommend full partnership wherever music and text are combined and to recall that the chief end of religion, in the language of the Calvinist catechism, is not didacticism but "to glorify God and enjoy God forever." We might note parenthetically that the most didactic of Christ's texts concerning human sin and divine forgiveness, the parable of the prodigal son, climaxes as the reconciled father and son "celebrate" with "music and dancing" (Lk 15.24-5).

95. *The Relevance of the Beautiful and Other Essays*, tr. Nicholas Walker (Cambridge: Cambridge University Press, 1986), 41.
96. *The Hymnal 1982*, #594.
97. *The Hymnal 1982*, #580.

## *Music and Final Bliss*

One thing music does not usually do in Episcopal worship. Music does not directly induce ecstatic experience or trance. The ecstasy of worship in Pentecostal traditions has precedent in biblical scripture, it is true. Elisha calls for music to induce prophetic insight: "'But get me a musician.' And then, while the musician was playing, the power of the LORD came on him" (2 Kings 3.14-15). Yet in biblical tradition, Elisha's experience is an exception proving the rule that music is usually not employed to induce ecstasy. From the history of Judaism, Hoffman reports that only "individual theorists, like Abraham Abulafia (1240-1291) combined musical instruction with the liturgical recitation of the letters in the divine name, in order to induce ecstatic trance."[98]

In this respect the Jewish and Christian mainstreams differ from many other traditions. Ellen Koskoff describes a Korean tradition of female shamans: "Trance is induced by performance on various musical instruments, including a double-headed, hour-glass drum, flute, gong, one-stringed fiddle, and a large wand upon which are fastened five to nine jingle bells."[99] Alf Hiltebeitel describes a strand of the Hindu tradition of aesthetic appreciation known as *rasa* which "reached its peak in the person of the Bengali saint Caitanya . . . whose ecstatic dancing and singing enabled him to experience the love of Radha and Krsna."[100] A similar tradition is very much alive today in Islamic *qawwali*, practiced in western settings by Nusrat Fateh Ali Khan, whose singing induces sacred trance in himself and in those of his audience who are attuned to such experience. Jean During calls this musically-induced mystical experience "clair-audition," an auditory equivalent to clairvoyance: "One never knows whether it is the music which creates the ecstasy or whether it is the ecstasy which liberates the power of the sounds."[101]

Within the traditions of Christianity to which this study has appealed, the ecstatic experiences nearest to musically induced mysticism might seem to be those of Hildegard. Yet even she describes her visions as inexplicably induced by God and independent of stimulation from her physical senses: "I do not hear them with my outward ears, nor do I perceive them

---

98. "Musical Traditions and Tensions in the American Synagogue," in *Music and the Experience of God*, ed. Collins, 30. Hoffmann cites Moshe Idel, *The Mystical Experience in Abraham Abulafia* (Albany, NY, 1988), 53-71.

99. "Both In and Between: Women's Musical Roles in Ritual Life," in *Music and the Experience of God*, ed. Collins, 89.

100. *The Encyclopedia of Religion*, s.v. "Hinduism."

101. "Revelation and Spiritual Audition in Islam," *The World of Music/Le Monde de la Musique/Die Welt der Musik: Journal of the International Institute for Comparative Music Studies and Documentation (Berlin) in association with the International Music Council (UNESCO)* 26, no.3 (1984): 75-6.

by the thoughts of my own heart or by any combination of my five senses, but in my soul alone, while my outward eyes are open. So I have never fallen prey to ecstasy in the visions, but I see them wide awake, day and night."[102] Hildegard's visions are not musically induced but rather musically experienced and musically expressed: "Then I saw the lucent sky, in which I heard different kinds of music, marvellously embodying all the meanings I had heard before. I heard the praises of the joyous citizens of Heaven, steadfastly persevering in the ways of Truth; and laments calling people back to those praises and joys; and the exhortations of the virtues."[103]

For non-Pentecostal Christians, this deficit in musically induced mysticism is significant, but we may put the deficit in perspective. This study has sought to appreciate traditions of Christian spirituality, much neglected, in which music plays numerous sacramental roles other than inducement of ecstasy: propaedeutic, preparatory, constitutive, expressive, analogical, anagogical, metaphorical, celebrative. In these traditions the music we sing and play is not assumed to be the very language of the angels or of God. Rather, our music only echoes a more transcendent harmony:

> The hymns thy people raise,
>> the psalms and anthems strong,
> hint at the glorious praise
>> of thy eternal song.[104]

In much Christian mythology, heaven resounds with music, but with a heavenly dialect of that universal language, a dialect we are able to comprehend but faintly. The portrayal of final blessedness that concludes the New Testament likens the voices of heaven to music:

> And I heard a voice from heaven like the sound of many waters and like the sound of loud thunder; the voice I heard was like the sound of harpists playing on their harps, and they sing a new song before the throne.

Yet the new song is in heavenly dialect, for we are told that "no one could learn that song" except those "who have been redeemed from the earth" (Rev 14.3). In similar spirit Edwards writes of heavenly music as transcending all that we mortals know of harmony:

> When we think of the sweet harmony of the parts of the corporeal world it fills us with such astonishment that the soul is ready to break. Yet take all that infinite variety of sweet proportions, harmonious motions, and delightful correspondences . . . and they are all but shadows of excellency."[105]

---

102. "Epistle to Guibert of Gembloux," quoted by Barbara J. Newman, "Introduction," *Scivias*, 18.
103. *Scivias* 3.13, 525.
104. Edward Grubb, "Our God, to Whom We Turn," *The Hymnal 1982*, #681.
105. Miscellany #42, *The "Miscellanies,"* 224.

To me 'tis probable that the glorified saints, after they have again received their bodies, will have ways of expressing the concord of their minds by some other emanations than sounds, of which we cannot conceive, that will be vastly more proportionate, harmonious and delightful than the nature of sounds is capable of; and the music they will make, will be in a medium capable of modulations in an infinitely more nice, exact and fine proportion than our gross air, and with organs as much more adapted to such proportions.[106]

Let us conclude our study with Dante's matchless development of this theme of heavenly music beyond our earthly conceiving. In the "Inferno" of *The Divine Comedy* there is no music. Dante employs a few musical images, but their context is the dismal and cacophonous reality of unending life apart from God's light and love:

And as the cranes go chanting their harsh lay,
>     Across the sky in long procession trailing,
>     So I beheld some shadows borne my way,
Driven on the blast and uttering wail on wailing.[107]

Toward the close of "Purgatory" Dante reaches the Earthly Paradise, representing the innocence of Eden, now emptied of people by the Fall, and silent except for the singing of birds:

>                          but still
>     The little birds the topmost twigs among
>     Spared not to practise all their tiny skill;
> Rather they welcomed with rejoicing song
>     The dawn-wind to the leaves, which constantly
>     To their sweet chant the burden bore along.[108]

To his amazement, Dante encounters a single, musical figure:

>     A lady all alone, who wandered there
>         Singing and plucking flower on floweret gay,
>         With which her path was painted everywhere.[109]

Dante invites the singer to draw near, in order that he might understand her song:

>     "Advance," said I, "if it seem good to thee,
>     So near the river that, when thou dost sing,
>     The words thou singest may be clear to me."[110]

As Dante and the singing lady are still in the Earthly Paradise, not yet in the Heavenly, Dante is able to comprehend the music she sings to him:

---

106. Miscellany #188, *The "Miscellanies,"* 331.
107. 5.46-9, tr. Dorothy Sayers, 98.
108. 28.13-18, 289.
109. 28.40-2, 290.
110. 28.46-8, 290.

And of my prayer she gave me full content,

    Coming so close that I could well divine

    Not only the sweet sounds but what they meant.[111]

Dante then drinks the waters of Lethe, therewith losing his memory of sin, followed by the waters of Eunoë, therewith regaining his memory, but freed from guilt, in order that he may savour the grace that allows him entrance into the Heavenly Paradise. Thus he departs Purgatory, "Pure and prepared to leap up to the stars."[112]

In "Paradise" Dante hears music repeatedly, but now it is heavenly music, beyond his mortal comprehension:

Such were those fiery carols – they who seek

    To hear them must find wings to reach that goal,

    Or wait for tidings till the dumb shall speak.[113]

The harmony of this heavenly music is the harmony of God's very Word and Wisdom, known fully only in heaven as the love that moves the heavenly spheres and harmonises the cosmos:

E'en so I saw it move, the glorious wheel,

    And voice with voice harmonious change and chime

    Sweetness unknown, there only knowable,

Where ever-present joy knows naught of time.[114]

The sweet harmony of this heavenly music, paradoxically including the painful dissonance of Christ's cross, surpasses meanings conveyed by mortal language, yet bears meaning in itself and attracts the listener:

As harp and viol, with strings of various pitch

    Twangling attuned, in dulcet harmony

    Speak to the ear by sounds which have no speech,

So from the light which there appeared to me

    Swelled in the cross a song, obscure to sense,

    Which yet entranced me with its melody;

For some high song of praise I knew it, since

    "Arise" and "conquer" caught my ear, although

    I heard it not with full intelligence.[115]

Arriving in the only sphere of paradise where music does *not* resound, Dante inquires concerning the significance of music's absence:

And say why in the region of this wheel

    No strains of heavenly symphony arise

    As through the other spheres devoutly peal?[116]

111. 28.58-60, 290.
112. 33.145, 335.
113. 10.73-5, 137.
114. 10.145-8, 139.
115. 14.118-26, 181.
116. 21.58-60, 242.

He learns that he has reached the domain of saints who while on earth attained such proficiency in spiritual contemplation as Eckhart describes. Their mystical intuitions of divine harmony have transcended the sacramental medium of music of the kind perceptible to Dante's ears:

> Thou hast but mortal ears. . . ,
> . . . hence we forbear to sing.[117]

Finally, paradise rejoices over Dante's salvation with the singing of the *Te Deum*, though again in heaven's immortal dialect:

> When I had done, the Court of Heaven rang
> With the *Te Deum*, through the circles chiming
> In melody as never mortal sang.[118]

What, we might wonder, are the differences between the earthly and heavenly dialects of music? How could we know? But with Christian tradition as our guide, we may surmise that one difference must consist in comprehensiveness. Our music offers acoustical delight, and in that delight we enjoy intimations of heavenly harmony. Surely heaven's harmony transcends acoustics, embracing moral, social, and cosmic harmony as well. To mistake our musical harmony for God's universal harmony is to commit the synechdocal fallacy: mistaking part for whole, expression for what is expressed, sacramental medium for sacred reality. Our theme has been the sacred in music, not music's sacredness.

For fallen humanity, harmony as comprehensive as God's love is not a matter of enjoyment and delight but of duty and aspiration. Salvation, we have said, is wholeness. *The Book of Common Prayer* has us pray for the particular wholeness of duty and delight:

> For the sake of your Son Jesus Christ,
> have mercy on us and forgive us;
> that we may delight in your will,
> and walk in your ways,
> to the glory of your Name.[119]

"Holiness," says Mother Teresa, "consists in doing God's will joyfully."[120]

Dante's salvation in the Heavenly Paradise is precisely the doing of God's will joyfully, the harmony of delighting in God's will and walking in God's ways, the wholeness of duty and delight. Even for the great Dante, however, in the presence of true holiness, art finally fails and love alone prevails:

117. 21.61-2, 243.
118. 24.112-14, 268.
119. "Confession of Sin," 360.
120. Petrie and Petrie, *Mother Teresa*.

Thither my own wings could not carry me,
    But that a flash my understanding clove,
    Whence its desire came to it suddenly.
High phantasy lost power and here broke off;
    Yet, as a wheel moves smoothly, free from jars,
    My will and my desire were turned by love,
The love that moves the sun and the other stars.[121]

121. 33.139-45, 347.

# Codetta

In a famous passage, sometimes cited carelessly, Barth addresses a tribute to Mozart, in the care of heaven:

> How things stand with music there, where you now find yourself, I have only a faint premonition. The hunch I cherish in this regard I once formulated in this way: I am not absolutely sure whether the angels, when they are engaged in the praise of God, play just Bach; I am sure, however, that when they are among themselves they play Mozart, and that then, indeed, the dear God also listens to them with special pleasure. Well, the contrast may be false. And besides, you know about this better than I do. I mention it only to intimate figuratively to you what I mean. And so, truly yours, Karl Barth.[1]

If we would honour the sacred in music, yet avoid the idolatry of worshipping music, or worshipping Mozart, we must follow Barth's example. Barth characterises his image of final bliss as only a fanciful hunch, a figurative premonition. This theological modesty readies us to worship a harmony that transcends our sacramental music, the holy consonance of God's logic and God's love.

---

1. "Dankbrief an Mozart," *Wolfgang Amadeus Mozart* (Basel: Evangelischer Verlag AG. Zollikon, 1956), 13.

# BIBLIOGRAPHY

Abbot, Walter M., ed., "Constitution on the Sacred Liturgy." *The Documents of Vatican II*. Translated by Joseph Gallagher New York: Herder and Herder, 1966.

Adler, Samuel. "Sacred Music in a Secular Age." In *Sacred Sound and Social Change: Liturgical Music in Jewish and Christian Experience*. Edited by Lawrence A. Hoffman and Janet R. Walton. Notre Dame: University of Notre Dame Press, 1992.

Aquinas, Thomas. *Summa Theologiae*. Translated by David Bourke. 60 vols. New York: McGraw-Hill, 1963.

Aristotle. *Metaphysics*. Translated by Hugh Tredennick. London: William Heinemann, 1936.

    *Nichomachean Ethics*. Translated by H. Rackham. London: William Heinemann, 1956.

    *Politics*. Translated by H. Rackham. London: William Heinemann, 1950.

Athanasius, Saint. *Against the Heathen*. Edited by Archibald Robertson. A Select Library of Nicene and Post-Nicene Fathers of the Christian Church: Second Series, vol. 4. Edited by Philip Schaff and Henry Wace. Grand Rapids: William B. Eerdmans, 1957.

Augustine. *Concerning the City of God against the Pagans*. Translated by Henry Bettenson. New York: Penguin, 1984.

    *Confessiones*. Edited by W. H. D. Rouse. 2 vols. London: William Heinemann, 1968.

    *Confessions*. Translated by R. S. Pine-Coffin. Harmondsworth: Penguin, 1961.

    *On Christian Doctrine*. Translated by D. W. Robertson, Jr. Indianapolis: Bobbs-Merrill, 1958.

    *On Music*. Translated by Robert C. Taliaferro. In *Fathers of the Church*. Edited by Roy Joseph Deferrari. New York: Christian Heritage, 1947.

    *On Free Choice of the Will*. Translated by Anna S. Benjamin and L. H. Hackstaff. Indianapolis: Bobbs-Merrill, 1964.

    *The Literal Meaning of Genesis*. Translated by John Hammond Taylor. New York: Newman, 1982.

    *The Trinity*. Translated by Stephen McKenna. In *Fathers of the Church*. Edited by Roy Joseph Deferrari. Washington: Catholic University of America Press, 1963.

Balthasar, Hans Urs von. *The Glory of the Lord: A Theological Aesthetics*. Vol. 4. *The Realm of Metaphysics in Antiquity*. Translated by Brian McNeil et al. San Francisco: Ignatius Press, 1989.

    *Prayer*. Translated by A. V. Littledale. New York: Sheed and Ward, 1961.

Barbour, J. Murray. *Tuning and Temperament: A Historical Survey*. New York: Da Capo, 1972.

Barrow, John D. *Pi in the Sky: Counting, Thinking, and Being*. Oxford: Clarendon, 1992.

Barth, Karl. *Church Dogmatics*. Edited by G. W. Bromiley and T. F. Torrance. Edinburgh: T. & T. Clark, 1960.

    *The Epistle to the Romans*. 6th ed. Translated by Edwyn C. Hoskyns. London:

Oxford University Press, 1933.

"Dankbrief an Mozart." *Wolfgang Amadeus Mozart*. Basel: Evangelischer Verlag AG. Zollikon, 1956.

*Wolfgang Amadeus Mozart*. Translated by Clarence K. Pott. Grand Rapids: William B. Eerdmans, 1986.

Basil the Great, Saint. *The Treatise de Spiritu Sancto; The Nine Homilies of the Hexameron; and The Letters*. Translated by Blomfield Jackson. A Select Library of Nicene and Post-Nicene Fathers of the Christian Church: Second Series, vol. 8. Edited by Philip Schaff and Henry Wace. New York: The Christian Literature Company, 1895.

Bayles, Martha. *Hole In Our Soul: The Loss of Beauty and Meaning in American Popular Music*. New York: Free Press, 1994.

Benedict, Saint. *The Rule of St. Benedict*. Translated by Cardinal Gasquet. New York: Cooper Square, 1966.

Bernstein, Leonard. *The Unanswered Question: Six Talks at Harvard*. Cambridge: Harvard University Press, 1976.

Blackwell, Albert. "The Antagonistic Correspondence of 1801 between Chaplain Sack and His Protégé Schleiermacher." *Harvard Theological Review* 74, no. 1 (1981): 101-21.

"The Role of Music in Schleiermacher's Writings." *Internationaler Schleiermacher-Kongreß 1984*, edited by Kurt-Victor Selge. Vol. 1. *Schleiermacher-Archiv*, edited by Herman Fischer et al. Berlin: Walter de Gruyter, 1985.

Bloch, Ernst. *Essays on the Philosophy of Music*. Translated by Peter Palmer. Cambridge: Cambridge University Press, 1985.

Boethius, Anicius Manlius Severinus. *Fundamentals of Music*. Translated by Calvin M. Bower. New Haven: Yale University Press, 1989.

Bonaventure, Saint. *The Soul's Journey into God; The Tree of Life; The Life of St. Francis*. Translated by Ewert Cousins. New York: Paulist Press, 1978.

*The Book of Common Prayer*. New York: The Church Hymnal Corporation, 1977.

Brown, Frank Burch. *Religious Aesthetics: A Theological Study of Making and Meaning*. Princeton: Princeton University Press, 1989.

Burkert, Walter. *Lore and Science in Ancient Pythagoreanism*. Translated by Edwin L. Minar, Jr. Cambridge: Harvard University Press, 1972.

Butler, Janet Wydom, and Paul G. Daston. "Musical Consonance as Musical Preference: A Cross-Cultural Study." *The Journal of General Psychology* 79 (1968): 129-42.

Cage, John. *Silence*. Cambridge: M.I.T. Press, 1966.

Calvin, John. *Calvin: Commentaries*. Translated by Joseph Haroutunian. Philadelphia: Westminster, 1958.

*Commentary on the Book of Psalms*. 5 vols. Translated by James Anderson. Edinburgh: Calvin Translation Society, 1845.

*Commentary on the Book of Psalms*. 6 vols. Translated by James Anderson. Grand Rapids: Baker Book House, n.d.

*Institutes of the Christian Religion*. Translated by Ford Lewis Battles. Philadelphia: Westminster, 1960.

Campbell, Karen J. *German Mystical Writers*. New York: Continuum, 1991.

Campbell, Murray and Clive Greated. *The Musician's Guide to Acoustics*. New York: Schirmer, 1987.

Carter, Bill. *Faith in a New Key: A Conversation between Jazz and Christian Faith.* Princeton: Princeton Theological Seminary, 1998.

Cassiodorus, Flavius Magnus Aurelius. *Explanation of the Psalms.* 3 vols. Translated by P. G. Walsh. New York: Paulist Press, 1990.

Clement of Alexandria. *The Exhortation to the Greeks.* Translated by G. W. Butterworth. London: William Heinemann, 1953.

Cole, Bill. *John Coltrane.* New York: Da Capo, 1993.

Coleman, Earle J. *Creativity and Spirituality: Bonds between Art and Religion.* Albany: State University of New York Press, 1998.

Coleridge, Samuel Taylor. *Biographia Literaria.* Edited by J. Shawcross. 2 vols. Oxford: Oxford University Press, 1907.

Collins, Mary, David Power and Mellonne Burnim, eds. *Music and the Experience of God.* Edinburgh: T. & T. Clark, 1989.

Coltrane, John. "Cosmos." *John Coltrane featuring Pharaoh Sanders: Live in Seattle.* Impulse Records, AS-9202-2, 1971.

*Love Supreme.* Wotre Music, France, 860106 WM 321, 1965.

Cone, James. "Black Spirituals: A Theological Interpretation." In *Music and the Experience of God,* edited by Mary Collins, et al. Edinburgh: T. & T. Clark, 1989.

Cooke, Deryck. *The Language of Music.* London: Oxford University Press, 1959.

Cornford, F. M. "Mysticism and Science in the Pythagorean Tradition." In *The Pre-Socratics,* edited by Alexander P. D. Mourelatos. Garden City, NY: Anchor Books, 1974.

Crosby, Sumner McKnight. *The Royal Abbey of Saint-Denis.* New Haven: Yale University Press, 1987.

Dante. *The Divine Comedy.* Translated by Dorothy L. Sayers and Barbara Reynolds. New York: Penguin, 1962.

Dawson, William L. "Every Time I Feel the Spirit." Music Press, Tuskegee Institute. Park Ridge, IL: Neil A. Kjos, 1973.

Day, Thomas. *Why Catholics Can't Sing: The Culture of Catholicism and the Triumph of Bad Taste.* New York: Crossroad, 1990.

De Quincy, Thomas. *Confessions of an English Opium Eater.* Middlesex: Penguin, 1971.

Dionysius the Pseudo-Areopagite. *The Divine Names and the Mystical Theology.* Translated by C. E. Rolt. London: SPCK, 1940.

*The Mystical Theology and the Celestial Hierarchies.* 2nd ed. Surrey: The Shrine of Wisdom, 1965.

Dixon, John. *Nature and Grace in Art.* Chapel Hill: University of North Carolina Press, 1964.

Douglas, Kelly Brown, *The Black Christ.* Maryknoll, NY: Orbis, 1994.

Dryden, John. *The Poems of John Dryden.* Edited by James Kinsley. 4 vols. Oxford: Clarendon, 1958.

Dun, Tan. *Symphony 1997.* Sony CD SK 63368, 1997.

During, Jean. "Revelation and Spiritual Audition in Islam." *The World of Music/ Le Monde de la Musique/Die Welt der Musik: Journal of the International Institute for Comparative Music Studies and Documentation (Berlin) in Association with the International Music Council (UNESCO)* 24, no. 3 (1982): 68-94.

Eckhart, Meister. "Commentary on the Book of Wisdom." *Meister Eckhart: Teacher and Preacher.* Edited by Bernard McGinn. New York: Paulist Press, 1986.

"Selected Sermons." In *German Mystical Writers*, by Karen J. Campbell. New York: Continuum, 1991.

"The Talks of Instruction." In *German Mystical Writers*, by Karen J. Campbell. New York: Continuum, 1991.

Edwards, Jonathan. *The "Miscellanies (Entry Nos. a-z, aa-zz, 1-500)."* Edited by Thomas A. Schafer. New Haven: Yale University Press, 1994.

*The Nature of True Virtue.* Ann Arbor: University of Michigan Press, 1960.

"Notes on the Mind." *Jonathan Edwards: Representative Selections.* Edited by Clarence H. Faust and Thomas H. Johnson. Rev. ed. New York: Hill and Wang, 1962.

"Personal Narrative." *Selected Writings of Jonathan Edwards.* Edited by Harold P. Simonson. New York: Frederick Ungar, 1970.

*The Philosophy of Jonathan Edwards from His Private Notebooks.* Edited by Harvey G. Townsend. Eugene, OR: University of Oregon Press, 1955.

*A Treatise concerning Religious Affections.* Edited by John E. Smith. New Haven: Yale University Press, 1959.

*Treatise on Grace and Other Posthumous Writings including Observations on the Trinity.* Edited by Paul Helm. Cambridge: James Clarke, 1971.

Eliade, Mircea, ed. *The Encyclopedia of Religion.* New York: Macmillan, 1987.

Eliot, T. S. *T. S. Eliot: Collected Poems 1909-1962.* New York: Harcourt Brace Jovanovich, 1984.

Faricy, Robert. "Art as a Charism in the Church." *Thought* 57 (1982): 94-9.

Fassler, Margot, and Peter Jeffery. "Christian Liturgical Music from the Bible to the Renaissance." In *Sacred Sound and Social Change: Liturgical Music in Jewish and Christian Experience.* Edited by Lawrence A. Hoffman and Janet R. Walton. Notre Dame: University of Notre Dame Press, 1992.

Faulkner, Quentin. *Wiser than Despair: The Evolution of Ideas in the Relationship of Music and the Christian Church.* Westport, CN: Greenwood Press, 1996.

Floyd, Wayne Whitson. "Transcendence in the Light of Redemption: Adorno and the Legacy of Rosenzweig and Benjamin." *Journal of the American Academy of Religion* 61 (Fall 1993): 539-51.

Freud, Harry. "My Uncle Sigmund." In *Freud as We Knew Him*, edited by Hendrik M. Ruitenbeek. Detroit: Wayne State University Press, 1973.

Freud, Sigmund. *Civilization and Its Discontents.* Translated by James Strachey. New York: W. W. Norton, 1961.

Friel, Brian. *Wonderful Tennessee.* Loughcrew, Ireland: Gallery, 1993.

Gadamer, Hans-Georg. *The Relevance of the Beautiful and Other Essays.* Translated by Nicholas Walker. Cambridge: Cambridge University Press, 1986.

Gill, Theodore. "Barth and Mozart." *Theology Today* 43, no.3 (October 1986): 403-11.

Gimello, Robert M. "Mysticism and Meditation." In *Mysticism and Philosophical Analysis*, edited by Steven T. Katz. New York: Oxford University Press, 1978.

Green, Connie Kestenbaum. "King David's Head from Gaza Synagogue Restored." *Biblical Archaeology Review* 20, no. 2 (March/April 1994): 58-63, 94.

Hall, Donald. *Musical Acoustics: An Introduction.* Belmont, CA: Wadsworth, 1980.

Hammond, N. G. L. and H. H. Scullard, eds. "Music." *The Oxford Classical Dictionary.* 2nd ed. Oxford: Clarendon, 1970.

Han, Kuo-huang and Lindy Li Mark. "Evolution and Revolution in Chinese Music." In *Musics of Many Cultures*, edited by Elizabeth May. Berkeley: University of California Press, 1980.

Hanslick, Eduard. *Vom Musikalisch-Schönen*. 16th ed. Wiesbaden: Breitkopf and Härtel, 1966.

Harries, Richard. *Art and the Beauty of God: A Christian Understanding*. London: Mowbray, 1993.

Hayes, Mark. "Walking in the Spirit." Chapel Hill: Hinshaw Music, 1989.

Hildegard of Bingen. *The Book of Divine Works*. Translated by Robert Cunningham. In *German Mystical Writers*, by Karen J. Campbell. New York: Continuum, 1991.

*Hildegard of Bingen: An Anthology*. Edited by Fiona Bowie and Oliver Davies. Translated by Robert Carver. London: SPCK, 1990.

Hindemith, Paul. *A Composer's World: Horizons and Limitations*. Cambridge: Harvard University Press, 1952.

Hocking, William Ernest. *The Meaning of Immortality in Human Experience*. Rev. ed. Westport, CN: Greenwood, 1957.

Hoffman, Lawrence A. "Musical Traditions and Tensions in the American Synagogue." In *Music and the Experience of God*, edited by Mary Collins et al. Edinburgh: T. & T. Clark, 1989.

Holt, Jim. "Roll Over, Pythagoras." *The New Yorker*, June 5, 1995.

Huxley, Aldous. "Music at Night." *Music at Night and Other Essays*. Freeport, NY: Books for Libraries, 1970.

*The Hymnal 1982*. New York: The Church Hymnal Corporation, 1985.

Irwin, Joyce. *Neither Voice nor Heart Alone: German Lutheran Theology of Music in the Age of the Baroque*. New York: Peter Lang, 1993.

James, Jamie. *The Music of the Spheres: Music, Science, and the Natural Order of the Universe*. New York: Grove, 1993.

James, William. *Varieties of Religious Experience*. New York: New American Library, 1958.

Jeans, James. *Science and Music*. New York: Macmillan, 1937.

Jeffrey, Peter. "Chant East and West: Toward a Renewal of the Tradition." In *Music and the Experience of God*, edited by Mary Collins et al. Edinburgh: T. & T. Clark, 1989.

Johannes Scotus Erigena (John the Scot). "*De divisione naturae*." Translated by Anselm Hughes. In *The New Oxford History of Music*. London: Oxford, 1954.

*Periphyseon: On the Division of Nature*. Translated by Myra L. Uhlfelder, summaries by Jean A. Potter. Indianapolis: Bobbs-Merrill, 1976.

*Periphyseon (De Divisione Naturea). Liber Tertius*. Edited by I. P. Sheldon-Williams. Dublin: The Dublin Institute for Advanced Studies, 1981.

John of the Cross, Saint. *Dark Night of the Soul*. Translated by E. Allison Peers. Garden City, NY: Image Books, 1959.

Jones, Ivor H. *Music: A Joy for Ever*. London: Epworth, 1989.

Kandinsky, Vasilii. "On the Spiritual in Art." In *The Life of Vasilii Kandinsky in Russian Art: A Study of "On the Spiritual in Art,"* translated by John E. Bowlt. Newtonville, MA: Oriental Research Partners, 1980.

Kahn, Charles H. "Pythagorean Philosophy before Plato." In *The Pre-Socratics*, edited by Alexander P. D. Mourelatos. Garden City, NY: Anchor Books, 1974.

Kant, Immanuel. *Critique of Judgment*. Translated by J. H. Bernard. New York: Hafner, 1951.

Kavanaugh, Kieran, ed. *St. John of the Cross: Selected Writings*. New York: Paulist Press, 1987.

Kierkegaard, Søren. *The Immediate Erotic Stages Or The Musical-Erotic. Either/ Or, Part I*. Translated by Howard V. Hong and Edna H. Hong. Princeton: Princeton University Press, 1987.

Kircher, Athanasius. *Musurgia Universalis*. Edited by Ulf Scharlau. Hildesheim: Georg Olms, 1970.

Kirk, G. S., J. E. Raven, and M. Schofield. *The Pre-Socratic Philosophers*. 2nd ed. Cambridge: Cambridge University Press, 1983.

Kittel, Gerhard, ed. *Theological Dictionary of the New Testament*. Translated by Geoffrey W. Bromiley. 10 vols. Grand Rapids: William B. Eerdmans, 1965.

Kivy, Peter. *Music Alone: Philosophical Reflections on the Purely Musical Experience*. Ithaca: Cornell University Press, 1990.

Kock, Gerard. "Between the Altar and the Choir-loft: Church Music – Liturgy or Art?" In *Music and the Experience of God*, edited by Mary Collins et al. Edinburgh: T. & T. Clark, 1989.

Koskoff, Ellen. "Both In and Between: Women's Musical Roles in Ritual Life." In *Music and the Experience of God*, edited by Mary Collins et al. Edinburgh: T. & T. Clark, 1989.

Kozinn, Allan. "A Challenge for a Cellist: More Notes per Octave." *The New York Times*, 14 March 1998.

 "More Churches Are Doubling as Concert Halls." *The New York Times*, 7 September 1993.

Küng, Hans. *On Being a Christian*. Translated by Edward Quinn. Garden City, NY: Doubleday, 1984.

Leith, John H., ed. *Creeds of the Churches*. Garden City, NY: Anchor, 1963.

Leppert, Richard and Susan McClary, eds. *Music and Society: The Politics of Composition, Performance and Reception*. Cambridge: Cambridge University Press, 1987.

"The Letter of the Church of Rome to the Church of Corinth, Commonly Called Clement's First Letter." *Early Christian Fathers*. Edited and translated by Cyril C. Richardson. Philadelphia: Westminster, 1953.

Levarie, Siegmund and Ernst Levy. *Tone: A Study in Musical Acoustics*. 2nd ed. Kent, OH: Kent State University Press, 1980.

Ligeti, György. *Ligeti*. Deutsche Grammophon, CD423 244-2, 1988.

*The Living Bible Paraphrased*. Edited by Kenneth Taylor. Wheaton, IL: Tyndale House, 1971.

Luther, Martin. "Preface to Georg Rhau's *Symphonie jucundae* 1538." Translated by Ulrich S. Leupold. In *Luther's Works*, edited by Jaraslov Pelikan. Philadelphia: Fortress, 1965.

Maconie, Robin. *The Concept of Music*. New York: Oxford University Press, 1990

Malm, William P. *Music Cultures of the Pacific, the Near East, and Asia*. 2nd ed. Englewood Cliffs, NJ: Prentice-Hall, 1977.

Maurer, Armand A. *About Beauty: A Thomistic Interpretation*. Houston: Center for Thomistic Studies, 1983.

May, Elizabeth, ed. *Musics of Many Cultures*. Berkeley: University of California Press, 1980.

McAllester, David P. "Some Thoughts on 'Universals' in World Music."

*Ethnomusicology* 15, No.3 (September 1971): 379-80.

McBrien, Richard P. *Catholicism*. 2 vols. Minneapolis: Winston, 1980.

McClain, Ernest G. *The Myth of Invariance: The Origin of the Gods, Mathe-matics and Music from the Rig Veda to Plato*. New York: Nicolas Hays, 1976.

*The Pythagorean Plato: Prelude to the Song Itself*. Stony Brook, NY: Nicolas Hays, 1978.

McClary, Susan. "Afterword." In Jacques Attali, *Noise: The Political Economy of Music* (Minneapolis: University of Minnesota Press, 1985), 149-58.

"The Blasphemy of Talking Politics during Bach Year." In *Music and Society: The Politics of Composition, Performance and Reception*. Cambridge: Cambridge University Press, 1987.

"A Musical Dialectic from the Enlightenment: Mozart's *Piano Concerto in G Major, K. 453*." *Cultural Critique* 4 (Fall 1986): 129-69.

McClendon, James Wm., Jr. *Biography as Theology: How Life Stories Can Remake Today's Theology*. 2nd ed. Philadelphia: Trinity Press, 1990.

McKinnon, James W. *Music in Early Christian Literature*. Cambridge: Cambridge University Press, 1987.

Mechthild of Magdeburg. *The Flowing Light of the Godhead*. Translated by Lucy Menzies. In *German Mystical Writers*, by Karen J. Campbell. New York: Continuum, 1991.

Menuhin, Yehudi and Curtis W. Davis. *The Music of Man*. Toronto: Methuen, 1979.

Messiaen, Olivier. "O sacrum convivium." Paris: Durand, 1937.

Meyer, Leonard. *Emotion and Meaning in Music*. Chicago: University of Chicago Press, 1956.

Meyer-Baer, Kathi. *Music of the Spheres and the Dance of Death: Studies in Musical Iconology*. New York: Da Capo, 1984.

Miles, Margaret. "Vision: The Eye of the Body and the Eye of the Mind in Saint Augustine's *De trinitate* and *Confessions*." *The Journal of Religion* 63 (April 1983): 125-42.

Milton, John. *Areopagitica and Of Education, with Autobiographical Passages from Other Prose Works*. Edited by George H. Sabine. Northbrook, IL: AHM, 1951.

*The Poetical Works of John Milton*. Edited by Helen Darbishire. 2 vols. Oxford: Clarendon, 1952-5.

*The Missal for Sundays and Principal Feasts of the Year*. Turnhout, Belgium: Brepols' Catholic Press, 1934.

Mitchell, Joni. *Joni Mitchell*. Reprise Records. 6293, 1968

*Clouds*. Reprise Records. 6341, 1969.

Monod, Jacques. *Chance and Necessity*. New York: Alfred A. Knopf, 1971.

Nagel, Ivan. *Autonomy and Mercy: Reflections on Mozart's Operas*. Translated by Marion Faber and Ivan Nagel. Cambridge: Harvard University Press, 1991.

Nettl, Bruno. "Ethnomusicology: Definitions, Directions, and Problems." In *Musics of Many Cultures*, edited by Elizabeth May. Berkeley: University of California Press, 1980.

*The Study of Ethnomusicology*. Chicago: University of Illinois Press, 1983.

Newman, Barbara. *Sister of Wisdom: St. Hildegard's Theology of the Feminine*. Berkeley: University of California Press, 1987.

Nisenson, Eric. *Ascension: John Coltrane and His Quest*. New York: St. Martin's, 1993.

Otto, Rudolf. *The Idea of the Holy*. Translated by John W. Harvey. New York: Oxford University Press, 1958.

Ovid. *Metamorphoses*. Translated by Mary M. Innes. Harmondsworth: Penguin, 1955.

Palter, Robert. "Exploring the Jazz Legacy of John Coltrane." *The New York Times*, 29 September 1974.

Panofsky, Erwin, ed. *Abbot Suger on the Abbey Church of St.-Denis and Its Art Treasures*. 2nd ed. Princeton: Princeton University Press, 1979.

Pareles, Jon. "Death Sings along with Grunge." *The New York Times*, 20 April 1994.

Pärt, Arvo. *Berliner Messe*. Vienna: Universal Editions, 1990.

Petrie, Ann and Jeanette, producers. *Mother Teresa*. Burlingame, CA: Petrie Productions, 1986.

Pierce, John R. *The Science of Musical Sound*. New York: Scientific American Books, 1983.

Plaistow, Stephen. Program notes to *Ligeti*. Deutsche Grammaphon CD 423 244-2, 1988.

Plank, Steven. *"The Way to Heavens Doore": An Introduction to Liturgical Process and Musical Style*. Metuchen, NJ: Scarecrow Press, 1994.

Plato. *Gorgias*. Translated by W. R. M. Lamb. London: William Heinemann, 1939.
    *Laws*. Translated by R. G. Bury. London: William Heinemann, 1942.
    *Phaedo*. Translated by Harold North Fowler. London: William Heinemann, 1943.
    *Phaedrus*. Translated by Harold North Fowler. London: William Heinemann, 1943.
    *Republic*. Translated by Paul Shorey. London: William Heinemann, 1969.
    *The Republic of Plato*. Translated by Allan Bloom. New York: Basic Books, 1968.
    *The Republic of Plato*. Translated by Francis MacDonald Cornford. New York: Oxford University Press, 1945.
    *Timaeus*. Translated by R. G. Bury. London: William Heinemann, 1942.

Plotinus. *Enneads*. Translated by A. H. Armstrong. London: William Heinemann, 1966.

Plutarch. *Plutarch's Moralia*. Translated by Benedict Einarson and Phillip H. DeLacy. London: William Heinemann, 1967.

Proudfoot, Wayne. *Religious Experience*. Berkeley: University of California Press, 1985.

Quasten, Johannes. *Music and Worship in Pagan and Christian Antiquity*. Translated by Boniface Ramsey. Washington: National Association of Pastoral Musicians, 1983.

Reagon, Bernice Johnson, *We'll Understand It Better By and By: Pioneering African American Gospel Composers*. Washington: Smithsonian Institution, 1992.

Rorty, Richard. *Contingency, Irony, and Solidarity*. Cambridge: Cambridge University Press, 1989.
    *Philosophy and the Mirror of Nature*. Princeton: Princeton University Press, 1979.

Rothstein, Edward. *Emblems of Mind: The Inner Life of Music and Mathematics*. New York: Times Books, 1995.

Rouget, Gilbert. *Music and Trance: A Theory of the Relations between Music and Possession*. Translated by Brunhilde Biebuyck. Chicago: University of Chicago Press, 1985.

Routley, Erik. *The Church and Music*. London: Gerald Duckworth, 1950.

Russolo, Luigi. *The Art of Noise (Futurist Manifesto, 1913)*. Translated by Robert Filliou. New York: Something Else Press, 1967.

Sacks, Oliver. *The Man Who Mistook His Wife for a Hat and Other Clinical Tales*. New York: Summit Books, 1985.

"Sacred Music of the Sikhs," *JVC World Sounds Catalogue*, JVC, SVCD-1009, 1990.

Sandberg, Rhonda. "The Solid Rock." Fort Lauderdale: Aberdeen Music, 1990.

Satie, Erik. *Messe des Pauvres*. Paris: Editions Salabert, 1920.

Saward, John. *The Beauty of Holiness and the Holiness of Beauty: Art, Sanctity, and the Truth of Catholicism*. San Francisco: Ignatius Press, 1996.

Schaff, Philip. *Theological Propaedeutic: A General Introduction to the Study of Theology, Exegetical, Historical, Systematic, and Practical, Including Encyclopaedia, Methodology, and Bibliography*. New York: Charles Scribner's Sons, 1893.

Schleiermacher, Friedrich. *The Christian Faith*. Translated by H. R. Mackintosh and J. S. Stewart. Edinburgh: T. & T. Clark, 1928.

*On Freedom*. Translated by Albert Blackwell. Lewiston, NY: Edwin Mellen, 1992.

*On Religion: Speeches to Its Cultured Despisers*. Translated by John Oman. New York: Harper Torchbooks, 1958.

*On Religion: Speeches to Its Cultured Despisers*. Translated by Richard Crouter. Cambridge: Cambridge University Press, 1988.

*"Rede am Sarge Zelters."* In *"Vergessene Dokumente aus dem musikalischen Leben Schleiermachers,"* edited by Walther Sattler. *Zeitschrift für Musikwissenschaft* 7 (October 1924-September 1925): 535-44.

*Reden über die Religion*. Edited by G. Ch. Bernhard Pünjer. Braunschweig: C. A. Schwetschke und Sohn, 1879.

*Weichnachtsfeier*. Critical edition. Edited by Hermann Mulert. Leipzig: Verlag der Dürr'schen Buchhandlung, 1908.

Schneider, Marius. "On Gregorian Chant and the Human Voice." *The World of Music/Le Monde de la Musique/Die Welt der Musik: Journal of the International Institute for Comparative Music Studies and Documentation (Berlin) in Association with the International Music Council (UNESCO)* 24, no. 3 (1982): 3-22.

Schoenberg, Arnold. *Style and Idea*. Edited by Leonard Stein. New York: St. Martin's, 1975.

Sellars, Wilfrid. *Science, Perception and Reality*. London: Routledge and Kegan Paul, 1963.

Shakespeare, William. *The Complete Works of William Shakespeare*. Edited by W. J. Craig. London: Oxford University Press, 1943.

Shakespeare, William, and John Fletcher. *The Two Noble Kinsmen*. Edited by Eugene M. Waith. Oxford: Clarendon Press, 1989.

Sherrard, Philip. *The Sacred in Life and Art*. Ipswich: Golgonooza Press, 1990.

Sherry, Patrick. *Spirit and Beauty: An Introduction to Theological Aesthetics*. Oxford: Clarendon, 1992.

Silesius, Angelus. (Johannes Scheffler.) *Angelus Silesius: Sämtliche Poetische Werke*. Edited by Hans Ludwig Held. 3 vols. München: Carl Hanser, 1949.

Sloboda, John A. *The Musical Mind: The Cognitive Psychology of Music*. Oxford:

Clarendon, 1986.

Smart, Ninian. *Reasons and Faiths: An Investigation of Religious Discourse, Christian and Non-Christian*. London: Routledge and Kegan Paul, 1958.

Smith, Steven G. *The Concept of the Spiritual: An Essay in First Philosophy*. Philadelphia: Temple University Press, 1988

So, Jenny F. "Bells of Bronze Age China." *Archaeology* 47 (January/February 1994): 42-51.

Söhngen, Oskar. "Music and Theology: A Systematic Approach." *Sacred Sound: Music in Religious Thought and Practice*. Edited by Joyce Irwin. Chico, CA: Scholars Press, 1983.

Solomon, Andrew. "Questions of Genius." *The New Yorker* (August 26 and September 2, 1996): 112-16, 118-20, 122-3.

Solomon, Maynard. *Mozart: A Life*. New York: HarperCollins, 1995.

"Song Lyric Ratings Are Backed by A.M.A." Associated Press Release, June 22, 1995.

Spencer, Jon Michael. *Sing a New Song: Liberating Black Hymnody*. Minneapolis: Fortress, 1995.

Spitzer, John. "Metaphors of the Orchestra – The Orchestra as a Metaphor." *The Musical Quarterly* 80, Number 2 (Summer 1996): 234-264.

Steiner, George. *Errata: An Examined Life*. New Haven: Yale University Press, 1997.

   *No Passion Spent: Essays 1978-1995*. New Haven: Yale University Press, 1996.

   *Real Presences*. Chicago: University of Chicago Press, 1989.

Stendahl, Krister. "Alumni/ae Day 1993." *Harvard Divinity Bulletin* 22, no. 4, 1993.

"Sting: A Musical Voyage." *In the Spotlight*. Educational Television Network, September 15, 1993.

Storr, Anthony. *Music and the Mind*. New York: The Free Press, 1992.

Stravinsky, Igor. "Pater Noster." New York: Boosey and Hawkes, 1949.

Strunk, Oliver. *Source Readings in Music History*. New York: W. W. Norton, 1950.

Suso, Heinrich. *Little Book of Eternal Wisdom*. Translated by James M. Clark. In *German Mystical Writers*, by Karen J. Campbell. New York: Continuum, 1991.

Tauler, Johannes. "Selected Sermons." Translated by Maria Shrady. In *German Mystical Writers*, by Karen J. Campbell. New York: Continuum, 1991.

Teresa of Avila, Saint. *The Collected Works of St. Teresa of Avila*. 2 vols. Translated by Kieran Kavanaugh and Otilio Rodriguez. Washington, DC: Institute of Carmelite Studies, 1976.

Thornton, Barbara. Notes to *Hildegard von Bingen: Ordo virtutum*. EMI Records, CD S7 49249 8, 1982.

Tillich, Paul. *Dynamics of Faith*. New York: Harper Torchbooks, 1957.

   *The Protestant Era*. Translated by James Luther Adams. Abridged ed. Chicago: The University of Chicago Press, 1957.

   *Systematic Theology*. 3 vols. Chicago: University of Chicago Press, 1951-63.

Tommasini, Anthony. "A Bit Off Key and Proud of It." *The New York Times*, 22 May 1997.

Tracy, David. *The Analogical Imagination: Christian Theology and the Culture of Pluralism*. New York: Crossroad, 1981.

Truesdell, C. "Sauveur, Joseph." In *The New Grove Dictionary of Music and*

*Musicians*, edited by Stanley Sadie. London: Macmillan, 1980.

von Falkenhausen, Lothar. "The Sound of Bronze Age Music." *Archaeology* 47 (January/February 1994): 47.

Walhout, Donald. "Augustine on the Transcendent in Music." *Philosophy and Theology* 3, no. 3 (Spring 1989): 283-92.

Weil, Simone. *Gravity and Grace.* Translated by Emma Craufurd. London: Ark Paperbacks, 1987.

    *Intimations of Christianity among the Ancient Greeks.* Translated by Elisabeth Chase Geissbuhler. London: Routledge and Kegan Paul, 1957.

    *The Notebooks of Simone Weil.* 2 vols. Translated by Arthur Wills. London: Routledge and Kegan Paul, 1956.

    *Waiting for God.* Translated by Emma Craufurd. New York: Putnam, 1951.

Weiss, Piero and Richard Taruskin. *Music in the Western World: A History in Documents.* New York: Schirmer, 1984.

Welch, Gillian. *Hell among the Yearlings.* Almo Sounds. AMSD-80021, 1998.

Werner, Eric. *The Sacred Bridge: The Interdependence of Liturgy and Music and Synagogue and Church during the First Millennium.* New York: Columbia University Press, 1959.

Westermeyer, Paul. *Te Deum: The Church and Music.* Minneapolis: Fortress Press, 1998.

Winter, Miriam Therese. "Catholic Prophetic Sound after Vatican II." In *Sacred Sound and Social Change: Liturgical Music in Jewish and Christian Experience.* Edited by Lawrence A. Hoffman and Janet R. Walton. Notre Dame: University of Notre Dame Press, 1992.

Wittgenstein, Ludwig. *Culture and Value.* Edited by G. H. von Wright. Translated by Peter Winch. Chicago: University of Chicago Press, 1980.

    *Philosophical Investigations.* Translated by G. E. M. Anscombe. 3rd ed. New York: Macmillan, 1958.

    *Tractatus Logic-Philosophicus.* London: Routledge and Kegan Paul, 1922.

Wyton, Alec. "The Episcopal Tradition." In *Sacred Sound and Social Change: Liturgical Music in Jewish and Christian Experience.* Edited by Lawrence A. Hoffman and Janet R. Walton. Notre Dame: University of Notre Dame Press, 1992.

Yeats, William Butler. *The Collected Poems of W. B. Yeats.* New York: Macmillan, 1938.

Young, Iris Marion. "The Ideal of Community and the Politics of Difference." In *Feminism/Postmodernism*, edited by Linda J. Nicholson. New York: Routledge, 1990.

Zaleski, Carol. "Foreword." In *German Mystical Writers*, by Karen J. Campbell. New York: Continuum, 1991

# Index of Biblical Passages

# General Index

250